Was wäre, wenn wir heute hinterfragen, w
könnten?

Unsere Gesellschaft bewegt sich in Konstrukten aus Normen und Grenzen, die unser Denken und Handeln bestimmen. Diese Gebilde kann man als Systeme von Wahrheiten bezeichnen; sie sind machtvolle Apparate, die unser Zusammenleben organisieren und uns vorgeben, was wir gut und was wir schlecht finden sollen. Architektur besteht, als Teil unserer Gesellschaft, auch aus solchen Wahrheitssystemen: Regelwerke, wie Baugesetze, Konstruktion oder Stil, koordinieren, was und wie wir entwerfen. Kritik ist ein Werkzeug, um sich der unterschiedlichen Machtformen und -effekte dieser Systeme bewusst zu werden und sie in Frage zu stellen. Dies ist notwendigerweise mit Perspektivwechseln verbunden: Einem Phänomen kritisch auf den Grund zu gehen erfordert, es von verschiedenen Seiten aus zu beleuchten. Auf diese Weise wird zugleich die eigene Position in Frage gestellt. Kritisieren heisst damit auch, Sicherheit aufs Spiel zu setzen.

In den Entwurfsprojekten der Studierenden am Departement Architektur wird gegenwärtig wenig riskiert. Themen, Konzepte und Darstellungsformen gehen konform mit den vermeintlichen Leitlinien der Entwurfslehrstühle. Der Studierende ist dadurch in vielen Projekten praktisch unsichtbar. Es scheint, die Angst, für die eigene Idee einstehen zu müssen, überwiegt.

Warum tun wir Dinge, von denen wir möglicherweise nicht einmal überzeugt sind, nur weil wir glauben, dass es der korrekte Weg ist? Was sind tatsächliche hierarchische oder disziplinäre Zwänge, denen wir uns beugen müssen? Und welche Beschränkungen haben wir uns selbst auferlegt? Wenn wir nicht von aussen bestimmt werden wollen, sollten wir uns fragen, was wir gut finden! Wir müssen Haltung beziehen, auch auf das Risiko hin, angreifbar zu sein – nur so kann Diskussion um Neues entstehen.

Auch wir von der trans Redaktion stellen uns die Frage: Welchen vermeintlichen Wahrheiten vertrauen wir? Welche Freiheiten haben wir tatsächlich? Was finden wir gut? Das Gefühl, einer fiktiven ‹trans-Maschine› gefolgt zu sein, hat uns eingeholt. Denn:

Inhaltlich sind wir unabhängig. Wir können und wollen unsere Meinung äussern.

Das Departement befindet sich im Wandel. Eine grosse Zahl neu besetzter Professorinnenstellen, der Dekanwechsel und politische Aktivitäten wie die der Parity Group sind Zeichen, dass bestehende Systeme nun auch von institutioneller Seite überdacht werden. Die Frage danach, was die Schule sein möchte, stellt sich neu. trans ist Teil der Schule und ihrer Stimme. Wir wollen daher in dieser und den kommenden Ausgaben vermehrt den Blick auf das richten, was an der Schule entsteht.

Produktion und Gestaltung des Magazins haben wir neu ausgerichtet: Das Format ist kleiner, das Papier leichter, das Layout dichter. Dies mit der Vision, eine handliche Architekturzeitschrift zu produzieren, die geknickt, gerollt und unterwegs gelesen werden kann!

trans 31 wird an alle Studierenden des Departements Architektur gratis verschickt. Als Aktion getarnt, ist es ein Aufruf an alle Studierenden, trans in der Zukunft verstärkt als Plattform zu nutzen: Am Departement entstandene Arbeiten und kursierende Themen sollen den Kern des Heftes bilden, angereichert durch Beiträge von ausserhalb der Institution.

Kritik ist projektiv, wenn sie Aktivitäten anregt, Alternativen vorschlägt und Handeln vorausbestimmt. Dieser Wunsch nach Veränderung macht aus ihr eine produktive Kritik. trans 31 verstehen wir als Beginn dieser Veränderung.

Ruben Bernegger, Saida Brückner,
Dorothee Hahn, Adrien Meuwly

What if we were to challenge today who we could be tomorrow?

Our society is set within a structured network of norms and borders which determine our thoughts and actions. They can be seen as systems of truths; they are powerful mechanisms that organise our social structures and predefine what we should approve and disapprove of. Architecture with its important societal function, also consists of such systems of truths: building laws, construction and architectural styles are regulations, they direct what and how we design. Critique is a tool for us to become conscious of the systems' different forms of power and gives us the permission to challenge them. This calls for a change of perspective: the critical conception of a phenomenon requires its examination from diverse angles. Necessarily the personal position will be questioned. Critique is therefore intrinsically linked to the compromise of our own safety.

Today students at our architecture department tend to take few risks in their design projects. Topics, concepts and graphic representations are usually conforming with the directives and policies of the design chairs. In many projects the student remains thus practically invisible. It seems that the fear of having to defend own ideas prevails.

Why do we do something of which we are not convinced, just because we think it is the appropriate thing to do? What are the real hierarchical and disciplinary constraints to which we have to succumb? And what kind of restrictions did we impose on ourselves? If we do not want to be dictated from the outside, we need to ask ourselves what we believe is good! We have to take a stand, even at the risk of becoming vulnerable—this is the only way a constructive discussion can arise.

We, as editors of trans, also ask ourselves: which accepted truths do we trust? Which liberties do we really have? What do we think is good? We were caught up by the feeling of having followed a fictional ‹trans-machine›. For we are independent of content restrictions. We can and want to express our opinion.

The department is evolving. The new chairs of architectural design, the change of dean and political activities, such as the

Parity Group, are indications that existing systems are now also being reassessed by the institution. The question of what the school wants to be is being revised. trans is part of the school and its voice. We therefore want to focus the forthcoming issues more on what is being developed at the school.

The production and design of the magazine has been redefined: a smaller size, lighter paper, a denser layout carry the vision of a handier architecture journal, one that can be folded, rolled and read en route.

trans 31 will be sent to all students of the Department of Achitecture. Disguised as an initiative, it should be understood as an appeal to all students to use trans as a critical platform: works that were produced at the department and circulating topics will be the essence of the magazine, supported and complemented by contributions from outside the institution.

Critique is projective, if it stimulates activities, proposes alternatives and demands action. This desire for change makes it a productive critique. trans 31 hopes to mark the beginning of this change.

Ruben Bernegger, Saida Brückner,
Dorothee Hahn, Adrien Meuwly

Der Kritiker
Die trans Redaktion im Gespräch mit Niklas Maak und Roman Hollenstein

Der Kritiker soll objektiver Vermittler sein. Er muss von aussen betrachten was im Inneren geschieht. Und gleichzeitig ist sein Werkzeug, die Kritik, von Subjektivität bestimmt. Zwei analoge Interviews beleuchten die unterschiedlichen Positionen zweier Architekturkritiker.

Interview mit Niklas Maak

TR Sie sind Architekturkritiker einer grossen deutschen Tageszeitung, der ‹Frankfurter Allgemeinen Zeitung› (FAZ). Was verstehen Sie unter dem Begriff ‹Kritik›?

NM Es wird ja immer wieder nach einer neuen Form von Kunstrichtertum gerufen, nach Streit, Lärm, Urteilsfreude, und das ist auch wichtig. Doch viel zu selten wird eine Diskussion über die Axiomatik der Architekturkritik geführt: Aufgrund welcher Überzeugungen, Einschätzungen, Erkenntnisse, Vorstellungen von Stadt, Gesellschaft, Gemeinschaft, Intimität, Öffentlichkeit, Privatheit beurteilen wir einen Raum, einen Bau so oder so? Das ist ein Problem: Denn wenn ich nicht begründen kann, was die Axiome meines Urteilens sind, bleibt es bei blossen Meinungen und mehr oder weniger unterhaltsamen Geschmacksäusserungen. Ich würde gern von Kritikerinnen und Kritikern genauer wissen, was ihre Vorstellung von Baukunst, Stadt, Urbanismus, vom Menschen prägt und was sie oder er in einer Stadt, von einem Bau will, worauf das fusst, wie es sich ändert. Wenn Kritiker das genauer benennen könnten, wären ihre Kritiken auch schärfer, klarer und nachvollziehbarer.

TR Der Architekturkritiker in einer Tageszeitung wird oft als Vermittler zwischen dem internen Diskurs einer Disziplin und der Öffentlichkeit betrachtet. Inwiefern sehen Sie sich in dieser Rolle? Wie definieren Sie für sich die Aufgabe des Kritikers?

NM Natürlich sollte Kritik diese Vermittlung leisten, sie sollte nicht nur das Sichtbare, etwa den Bau, beurteilen, sondern auch die unsichtbaren Kräfte aufdecken, die dazu führen, dass ein Bau, die Stadt, so aussehen, wie sie aussehen. Die Kritikerin oder der Kritiker muss auch die politische Ökonomie des

Interview mit Roman Hollenstein

TR Bis zu Ihrem Rücktritt Ende Juni 2017 waren Sie Redaktor für Architektur und Design sowie Kritiker einer grossen Schweizer Tageszeitung, der ‹Neuen Zürcher Zeitung› (NZZ). Was verstehen Sie unter dem Begriff ‹Kritik›?

RH Unter Architekturkritik verstehe ich die professionelle Auseinandersetzung mit Architektur auf theoretischer und ästhetischer Ebene. Es geht dabei weniger um das Bemängeln von Fehlleistungen als vielmehr um das aufbauende Begleiten von architektonischen Zuständen und Entwicklungen in Praxis und Theorie.

TR Der Architekturkritiker in einer Tageszeitung wird oft als Vermittler zwischen dem internen Diskurs einer Disziplin und der Öffentlichkeit betrachtet. Inwiefern sehen Sie sich in dieser Rolle? Wie definieren Sie für sich die Aufgabe des Kritikers?

RH Das Vermitteln von Architektur ist eine wichtige Aufgabe der Tageszeitungen. Dabei geht es aber nicht in erster Linie um das Vermitteln zwischen dem internen architektonischen Diskurs und der Öffentlichkeit. Denn ausser bei speziellen Entwicklungen wie der Postmoderne, dem Schweizer Minimalismus oder dem Dekonstruktivismus interessiert sich – meiner Erfahrung nach – das Publikum kaum für architekturinterne Diskussionen und Debatten. Dies gilt ganz besonders heute, da die Szene durch verschiedene, für Aussenstehende nicht immer klar erkenntliche Strömungen bestimmt wird. Umso wichtiger ist es, dass qualitätsvolle Bauten gewürdigt werden. Dies gilt ganz besonders in der Schweiz, wo die Stimmbürger immer wieder über Architekturprojekte wie Schulhäuser, Stadien, Kongressgebäude, Museen und andere kulturelle Bauten an der Urne zu befinden haben. Im Gegensatz zur Leserschaft der

Bauens aufdecken: Was ist etwa der Einfluss von Baustofflobbies, politischen und ökonomischen Interessen, Investoren etc, die zu einer Form führen oder sie verhindern?
Ich glaube aber ausserdem, dass Kritik – im Sinne einer Auseinandersetzung mit dem Vorhandenen angesichts des Denkbaren – sich nicht darauf beschränken sollte, bloss reaktiv das, was andere an Formen und Räumen herstellen, in Texten zu beurteilen. Ich unterrichte neben meiner Tätigkeit für die FAZ an der Graduate School of Design in Harvard und baue gerade mit meinen Studierenden einen Prototyp für eine neue Form von Bauwerk, in dem Geflüchtete und Berliner anders zusammenleben können als bisher, verteilt über die ganze Stadt in kleineren Einheiten, nicht in Massenunterkünften wie den MUFs [modulare Unterkünfte für Flüchtende, Anm. d. R.]. Der Prototyp wird im kommenden Jahr in Berlin errichtet, dank der Hilfe der Bundeskulturstiftung; er verbindet Wohneinheiten, Gemeinschaftsorte mit einem Markt, Räumen für Bildung und Begegnung mit Wohnzonen auf eine neue und hoffentlich interessante, weiterführende Weise. Auch das, der spekulative Prototyp, ist Kritik, wie ich sie verstehe.

TR   In einem Beitrag wird der ehemalige ‹New York Times›-Kritiker Paul Goldberger zitiert: «An architecture critic has a lot of authority but not much real power. […] I don't think architecture critics have the power. It used to be said that ‹The New York Times› critic can close a Broadway show. Well, that's power. But nobody tears down a building if an architecture critic doesn't like it.» [siehe S. 119] Wie sehen Sie Ihre Einflussmöglichkeiten auf den Diskurs und die Praxis? Welchen Einfluss haben Sie auf die öffentliche Meinung?

NM   Da hat der verehrte Paul Goldberger so nicht recht, das ist zu depressiv. Nehmen sie ein Beispiel: Gottfried Knapp schrieb im Jahr 2000 in der ‹Süddeutschen Zeitung›, wie unmöglich die geplante Verschandelung des Olympiastadions durch das Büro Behnisch wäre – und schon war der geplante Bau vom Tisch. Keine Kritikerin, kein Kritiker entscheidet allein über einen Bau – aber auch kein Politiker und kein Unternehmer. Bauten entstehen (oder, siehe Palast der Republik in Berlin oder Rem Koolhaas' Den Haager Theater, verschwinden) als Ergebnis einer gemeinsamen Auseinandersetzung. Kritik ist immer ein Teil davon.

TR   Beeinflusst Ihre räumliche und zeitliche Verortung (Ihre Subjektivität) zum Objekt der Kritik die Kritik selbst? Jane Rendell beispielsweise vertritt die Haltung, dass eine Kritik immer durch die Position des Autors Fachzeitschriften handelt es sich bei den meisten Leserinnen und Lesern von Architekturtexten in Tageszeitungen um Laien. Ihnen muss das komplexe Gebiet der Architektur mittels einer leicht verständlichen Sprache nähergebracht werden. Dabei ist es wichtiger, Begeisterung für gute, wegweisende Architektur zu wecken, als an mediokren oder gar schlechten Bauten herumzunörgeln. Bei noch nicht realisierten problematischen Projekten hingegen muss der Kritiker wenn immer möglich warnend seine Stimme erheben. Da in den Tageszeitungen nur wenig Platz für Architektur zur Verfügung steht, ist die Auswahl eines zu besprechenden Projektes oder Gebäudes schon ein wesentlicher Akt der Kritik. Man entscheidet sich meistens für bedeutende Gebäude, die dann auch ihre Schwächen haben können, wie ein Blick auf den Erweiterungsbau des Landesmuseums in Zürich von Christ & Gantenbein oder das Swiss-Re-Gebäude am Zürcher Mythenquai von Diener & Diener zeigt.

TR   In einem Beitrag wird der ehemalige ‹New York Times›-Kritiker Paul Goldberger zitiert: «An architecture critic has a lot of authority but not much real power. […] I don't think architecture critics have the power. It used to be said that ‹The New York Times› critic can close a Broadway show. Well, that's power. But nobody tears down a building if an architecture critic doesn't like it.» [siehe S. 119] Wie sehen Sie Ihre Einflussmöglichkeiten auf den Diskurs und die Praxis? Welchen Einfluss haben Sie auf die öffentliche Meinung?

RH   Ich kann die Aussage von Paul Goldberger nur unterstützen. Man geniesst als Architekturkritiker eine gewisse Autorität. Das habe ich gemerkt, als mir nach der Bekanntmachung meines Rücktritts viele Leserinnen und Leser schrieben und befürchteten, dass sich nun niemand mehr für eine unabhängige Architekturberichterstattung in der NZZ einsetzen werde. Aber auch Architekten schätzen meine Meinung, oft sogar, wenn ich kritisch über sie schreibe. So hat mich beispielsweise Jacques Herzog schon mehrmals kontaktiert, nachdem ich ein Gebäude von Herzog & de Meuron kritisiert hatte. Daraus entstanden interessante Dialoge und – im Zusammenhang mit dem Olympiastadion von Peking – ein vielgelesenes Interview über die Problematik des Bauens in autoritär regierten Staaten. Einfluss auf den Diskurs kann der Kritiker vielleicht mitunter nehmen, auf die Praxis aber kaum. Gerade Bauherrschaften, die man mit Artikeln in der Tagespresse ja gerne zum guten Bauen hinführen möchte, lassen sich kaum beeinflussen.

zum Objekt der Kritik bestimmt ist. In ihrem Text ‹To Miss the Desert› nimmt sie als Autorin bewusst verschiedene Positionen ein, um ein komplexes, kritisches Bild zu erzeugen. [siehe S. 109] Wie wichtig ist eine bewusste Distanz zwischen Kritiker und Objekt?

NM Jeder Kritiker hat seine eigene Geschichte, ist in Räumen aufgewachsen, hat gute oder schlechte Erinnerungen, die sich an Räumen festmachen. Jemand, der eine glückliche Kindheit in einem Flachdachbungalow verbrachte, aber unter seiner düsteren Jahrhundertwende-Schule litt, wird Gründerzeit und Nachkriegsmoderne anders erleben und bewerten als jemand, bei dem es andersherum war. Es gibt Menschen, die langweilen sich auf einer italienischen Piazza zu Tode und wollen lieber im Flimmern einer Strasse von Tokio sitzen.

Die eigene Geschichte spielt noch in die scheinbar objektivste Kritik hinein: Schreibe ich über bestimmte Kunst anders, weil ich Philosophie und Architektur studiert habe? Mag ich abstrakte, architektonische Kunst mehr als Kollegen, die, wie Werner Spies und Eduard Beaucamp, aus der Literatur kommen und anderes Interesse an gegenständlicher Narration haben? Und schreibt jemand, der Musik studiert hat, wieder anders über Kunst? Und: Kann man so einfach «verschiedene Perspektiven» einnehmen? Ich glaube nicht. Man kann versuchen, andere denkbare Haltungen als die eigene zu verstehen und verständlich zu machen, was zu einer lauteren Kritik, die nicht nur Polemik ist, dazu gehört. Aber mehr ist schwer möglich. Sich klarzumachen, ob und warum das so ist und wie es das eigene Schreiben beeinflusst, ist aber fundamental und auch sehr spannend im Sinne einer Autoanalyse, deswegen «ja» zur Frage:

TR Ist Selbstkritik Teil einer kritischen Auseinandersetzung?

TR Wenn Sie im Namen der FAZ arbeiten, wer entscheidet welche Projekte und Architekten kritisiert werden sollen und inwiefern redigiert die Zeitung die Kritiken?

NM Ich entscheide allein, was wie besprochen wird. Natürlich erwarten die Zeitung und der Leser einen Text, wenn etwa die Elbphilharmonie eröffnet wird, die kann man, da sie ein Objekt öffentlichen Interesses ist, nicht weglassen, nur weil man sie vielleicht nicht überzeugend findet. Jenseits dieser Informationspflicht gibt es aber keine Einschränkungen oder inhaltliche Eingriffe durch Redaktion und Kollegen – ausser kritischer Lektüre und Diskussion des Geschriebenen durch sie, die jeden Text besser und schärfer macht. Nur: Man hätte immer gern mehr Platz und Zeit, zumal jetzt, wo es so viel spannende, inte-

Im Fall des vorhin erwähnten Swiss-Re-Gebäudes hat meine kritische Analyse offensichtlich – wie man mir mitteilte – dazu geführt, dass das Unternehmen Inserate in der NZZ gestrichen hat. Man wollte keine Kritik hören.

TR Beeinflusst Ihre räumliche und zeitliche Verortung (Ihre Subjektivität) zum Objekt der Kritik die Kritik selbst? Jane Rendell beispielsweise vertritt die Haltung, dass eine Kritik immer durch die Position des Autors zum Objekt der Kritik bestimmt ist. In ihrem Text ‹To Miss the Desert› nimmt sie als Autorin bewusst verschiedene Positionen ein, um ein komplexes, kritisches Bild zu erzeugen. [siehe S. 109] Wie wichtig ist eine bewusste Distanz zwischen Kritiker und Objekt?

RH Die räumliche und zeitliche Verortung des Kritikers spielt sicher immer eine Rolle. Der Kritiker ist ein Mensch und somit auch abhängig von all den uns Menschen bestimmenden Faktoren. Dessen muss man sich dort besonders bewusst sein, wo persönliche Zuneigungen oder Ablehnungen mit im Spiel sind. Ich versuche immer, ein Gebäude oder einen architektonischen Kontext auch von der anderen Seite – also aus der Optik des Architekten, des Bauherren oder der gesetzlichen Bedingungen – zu sehen. Das Vorgehen von Jane Rendell mag ein interessantes Experiment für sie als Kritikerin sein, ob Jane Rendell aber den Leserinnen und Lesern ihrer Kritiken damit einen Dienst erweist, möchte ich bezweifeln. Denn letztlich möchte man als Leser einer Kritik ja auch eine möglichst klare und eindeutige Position vermittelt bekommen. Eine Position, der man zustimmen oder die man entschieden ablehnen kann.

TR Ist Selbstkritik Teil einer kritischen Auseinandersetzung?

RH Selbstkritik nur in der Form, dass ich meine Texte am Schluss durch die Augen derjenigen zu sehen versuche, die mich oder meine Arbeit nicht mögen. Das hilft mir bei der exakten Formulierung meiner Texte.

TR Wenn Sie im Namen der NZZ arbeiten, wer entscheidet, welche Projekte und Architekten kritisiert werden sollen, und inwiefern redigiert die Zeitung die Kritiken?

RH So lange ich als Redaktor für Architektur und Design im Feuilleton der NZZ tätig war, bestimmte ich, welche Bauten und Projekte besprochen und welche Architekten vorgestellt wurden. Die Texte von freien Mitarbeiterinnen und Mitarbeitern wurden von mir redigiert, denn der Fachredaktor ist bei der NZZ für die publizierten Texte verantwortlich. Es gibt keinen anonymen «Mister NZZ», der alle Texte auf einen zeitungskonformen Inhalt hin prüft und bearbeitet. Künftig wird

ressante, diskussionswürdige Architektur gibt wie schon lang nicht mehr.

TR Armen Avanessian, zeitgenössischer Philosoph und Theoretiker, hinterfragt die Relevanz von Kritik für die Gegenwart vor dem Hintergrund eines Zeitenwechsels. Die Zeit komme heute nicht mehr aus der Vergangenheit, sondern aus der Zukunft; Entscheidungen in der Gegenwart basieren nicht mehr auf Erfahrungswerten, sondern Prognosen und Wahrscheinlichkeitsrechnungen. In Anbetracht dessen können Reflektion und Kritik, deren Gegenstand die Gegenwart oder Vergangenes ist, nicht mehr als Werkzeuge für die Architekturpraxis herangezogen werden. Stattdessen schlägt Avanessian Spekulation, Rekursion und Kontingenz vor [siehe S. 71]. Kann Kritik in Ihren Augen heute noch produktiv sein und Neues hervorbringen?

NM Ich teile Armens Ansicht, dass Kritik als rein reaktives Werkzeug ausgedient hat in einer Zeit, in der – das meint ja die poetische Wendung der Attacke aus der Zukunft – Algorithmen von Google, Facebook etc unser Handeln vorausberechnen und uns mit Annahmen über unser zukünftiges Ich konfrontieren, wenn etwa ein Google-Algorithmus aus allen Suchanfragen der Vergangenheit herausrechnet, wo wir bald essen gehen, schlafen, hinreisen, einkaufen wollen könnten. Daher meine Idee einer spekulativen Kritikalität, die Prototpyen als Vorwegnahme kommender Formen herstellt, bevor diese von anderen berechnet und manipuliert werden können. Das ist mehr als ein Text, der einen vorhandenen Bau begeht. Wir müssen weiter ausgreifen, mehr spekulieren, horizontal und vertikal, als Algorithmen das können. Das ist die einzige Chance, sie zu kritisieren, und Neues jenseits der Vorausberechenbarkeit zu schaffen.

TR Wir verstehen den Begriff Kritik meist im Zusammenhang mit dem Aufruf zu einer Diskussion. Erhalten Sie auf Ihre Rezensionen und Kritiken Reaktionen?

NM Ja, viele Briefe, E-Mails, zustimmend, ablehnend, konstruktiv, polemisch, scharf, wirr; alles grossartig, weil es zeigt, dass Texte erregen, euphorisieren, erbosen, die Schärfung des eigenen Denkens anstacheln können.

TR Wie kann der Kritiker zu einer dynamischen Debatte anregen und eine differenzierten Anschauung ermöglichen?

NM Indem er – oder sie, es gibt doch auch Kritikerinnen! – Dinge, Machtverhältnisse, Absprachen, Lobbyismus, Ideologie sichtbar macht – all das Unsichtbare, aber Bauentscheidende, das hinter jedem Bau steckt: Indem er die Fassade wegreisst. Vielleicht wird kein Haus sofort abgerissen, nur weil ein meine Nachfolgerin, deren Namen in den nächsten Tagen publik werden sollte, darüber entscheiden, was im Feuilleton der NZZ besprochen werden soll. Wenn ich als freier Architekturkritiker weiter für das NZZ-Feuilleton schreiben möchte, werde ich ihr meine Vorschläge unterbreiten. Meinen soeben erschienenen und bereits als freier Mitarbeiter verfassten Beitrag über den neuen Palacinema von Locarno habe ich mit dem Feuilletonchef, René Scheu, abgesprochen, wobei ich inhaltlich frei schreiben konnte.

TR Armen Avanessian, zeitgenössischer Philosoph und Theoretiker, hinterfragt die Relevanz von Kritik für die Gegenwart vor dem Hintergrund eines Zeitenwechsels. Die Zeit komme heute nicht mehr aus der Vergangenheit, sondern aus der Zukunft; Entscheidungen in der Gegenwart basieren nicht mehr auf Erfahrungswerten, sondern Prognosen und Wahrscheinlichkeitsrechnungen. In Anbetracht dessen können Reflektion und Kritik, deren Gegenstand die Gegenwart oder Vergangenes ist, nicht mehr als Werkzeuge für die Architekturpraxis herangezogen werden. Stattdessen schlägt Avanessian Spekulation, Rekursion und Kontingenz vor. [siehe S. 71] Kann Kritik in Ihren Augen heute noch produktiv sein und Neues hervorbringen?

RH Muss Kritik produktiv sein und Neues hervorbringen? Ich zweifle daran. Wichtiger ist, dass sie die Leute dazu bringt, über Architektur nachzudenken. Neue baukünstlerische Entwicklungen wurden nie von Kritikern initiiert, sondern immer von praktisch tätigen Architekten. Das galt schon in der Antike, und es gilt wieder seit der Renaissance. Aber auch die Stilentwicklung im Mittelalter hin zur Romanik und dann zur Gotik ging von den Baumeistern und nicht von den Auftraggebern – Klerus, Politiker, reiche Bürger – aus. Und schon gar nicht von schreibenden Kritikern. Die gab es ja damals noch nicht. Armen Avanessians Haltung ist für mich ein philosophisches Glasperlenspiel. Ohne die Vergangenheit zu kennen, können wir auch nicht die Gegenwart beurteilen und schon gar nicht Zukunft erahnen. Eine geschichtslose Gesellschaft, die für mich ein Albtraum wäre, würde mit dem Untergang der Kultur einhergehen. Auch der architektonischen Kultur. Zudem hat die Zukunftsforschung in den letzten 100 Jahren immer wieder gezeigt, wie falsch ihre Prognosen waren. Wer hätte einst gedacht, dass der Computer in der Architektur zum wichtigsten Entwurfswerkzeug würde? Und wer weiss, ob es in einigen Generationen die Welt, wie wir sie kennen und lieben, überhaupt noch geben wird? Die geschichtsblinde Weltsicht entspricht nicht

Kritiker es nicht mag, aber das immerhin, die Fassade für einen Moment entfernen, hindurchschauen und das Auge der Öffentlichkeit hineinlassen: Das kann er.

Dieses Interview wurde im August 2017 per E-Mail geführt.

der europäischen Tradition. Sogar jüngere Architekten interessieren sich für Vergangenes, das zeigt etwa das breite Interesse der mittleren Generation an der Mailänder Nachkriegsarchitektur oder die Begeisterung, mit der man derzeit die grosse Armando-Ronca-Ausstellung im Kunsthaus Meran erwartet. Sie wird zeigen, wie überlegen die italienische Architektur der 1950er und 1960er Jahre baukünstlerisch und städtebaulich gegenüber der heutigen war.

TR Wir verstehen den Begriff Kritik meist im Zusammenhang mit dem Aufruf zu einer Diskussion. Erhalten Sie auf Ihre Rezensionen und Kritiken Reaktionen?

RH Ja, ich erhalte viele Reaktionen auf meine Kritiken und Rezensionen. Solche werden – sofern sie sich eignen – als Leserbriefe veröffentlicht. Für Diskussionen oder gar Debatten im Anschluss an eine Architekturbesprechung gab und gibt leider im Feuilleton der NZZ (und in den Feuilletons anderer Zeitungen) keinen Platz.

TM Wie kann der Kritiker zu einer dynamischen Debatte anregen und eine differenzierten Anschauung ermöglichen?

LC Man kann durch extreme Positionen oder polemische Formulierungen die Leute aus der Reserve locken und sie zu einer Debatte bewegen. Ich habe das vor einem Jahr mit meinem Lob des umstrittenen Swiss Mill Tower in Zürich versucht, auf den es aus Architektenkreisen viel Zustimmung, von Laien aber viel Unverständnis, ja sogar Ablehnung gab. Am Schluss blieben wohl alle bei ihrer vorgefassten Meinung. Ob solch zugespitzte Texte letztlich der Kritik nützen, darf man bezweifeln. Es handelt sich bei solchen Übungen eher um ‹l'art pour l'art›.

Dieses Interview wurde im August 2017 per E-Mail geführt.

Das Hotel, die jungen Architekten und die Leute

Abb. 1

Das Hotel, die jungen Architekten und die Leute
Rabea Kalbermatten

Kritik von Nicht-Architekten gehört zu unserem Alltag. Die Bandbreite reicht dabei von ungefragten (Verbesserungs-)Vorschlägen über Unverständnis zu Ablehnung und kollektiver Anfeindung unseres Berufsstands. Doch ist nur gut, was gefällt? Und ist ein Projekt gescheitert, wenn es nicht verstanden wurde?

«Ich verstehe zwar nicht viel von Kunst, aber das ist für mich definitiv ein Baugerüst und keine Kunst. Einheimische sowie Touristen fragen sich, was hier gebaut wird. Falls dies mit unseren Steuergeldern bezahlt wird, finde ich es fast schon eine Frechheit.»

David Heinzmann, Brig-Glis, Onlineumfrage, www.1815.ch

Im Sommer 2015 lobte die Kulturkommission der Gemeinde Brig-Glis einen öffentlichen Wettbewerb aus.

«Temporäre Objekte sollen als ‹Stadtmöbel› Plätze und Orte im Siedlungsgebiet beleben und aufwerten und können sowohl artifizielle als auch funktionale Gegenstände des alltäglichen Gebrauchs sein, z.B. zum Verweilen, Nachdenken, Spielen, oder zum Erfüllen von fiktiven oder erfundenen Tätigkeiten dienen, mit dem Ziel, das Leben der Stadt katalysatorisch und gestalterisch während dem Sommer 2016 aufzuwerten.»[1]

Unser ‹Grandhotel› war eines von sieben Projekten, die aus diesem Wettbewerb hervorgingen. Die Idee für dieses Projekt, das wir im Juni 2016 mit Hilfe von Freunden, der Unterstützung von Experten und dem Beitrag von 5000 CHF der Kulturkommission realisierten, beruht auf einer Postkarte, die uns zufällig in die Hände fiel. Sie zeigt den so vertrauten Briger Sebastiansplatz, die Sebastianskapelle, den Brunnen vor dem Restaurant ‹Commerce›, das Gliserhorn im Hintergrund, die Szenerie überragend. Eine Schwarzweiss-Fotografie, nachträglich koloriert. (Abb. 1)

Dominiert wird das Bild von einem Gebäude, das uns völlig unbekannt war, dem ‹Grandhotel Couronne et Poste›, wie wir später erfahren sollten. Der kulturelle Mittelpunkt der Alpenstadt, in dem einst die Königshäuser Europas abstiegen, Sänger und Schauspieler logierten und Cäsar Ritz seine Laufbahn im Hotelfach begonnen haben soll, bevor er in die Welt zog, um sein Hotelimperium aufzubauen. Ehe man sich im Morgengrauen aufmachte, um den Simplonpass zu bezwingen, nächtigte man im ‹Couronne›. Abends hielten demnach öfter Pferdekutschen vor dem Grandhotel, Musik versprühte das Flair einer italienischen Piazza und die Sonnenterrasse war bis auf den letzten Platz besetzt.

1840 erstmals in einem Reiseführer erwähnt, wurde das ‹Couronne› in seiner Geschichte wiederholt Anpassungen an die jeweils herrschende Epoche unterworfen. 1800 unterzog man das Gebäude einer Umwandlung hin zum Klassizismus, die Mittelachse wurde westwärts weg vom Turm verschoben und mit einem

Giebel versehen, der Turm selbst verblieb im barocken Stil (Abb. 2). Hundert Jahre später wurde der Bau mit einem Dachgeschoss und zahlreichen Fenstergauben ergänzt, der Giebel wurde entfernt, der Turm nach dem Vorbild der französischen Renaissance mit einem helmartigen Aufbau bekrönt, der barocke und klassizischte Stil wurde gänzlich abgelegt (Abb. 3). 1935 liess der damalige Besitzer den Ostflügel abreissen, es kam zu einer teilweisen Öffnung zugunsten des Strassenverkehrs. Der überhöhte Mittelrisalit wurde zum Eckturm (Abb. 4).

Als das ‹Grandhotel› am 21. Dezember 1951 einem Brand zum Opfer fällt und man die aus Naters herbeieilende Feuerwehr an einem Löscheinsatz hindert – wie böse Zungen behaupten – passiert, was früher oder später sowieso passiert wäre: der Strasse, die bisher mit einer 9 m breiten Durchfahrt Vorlieb nehmen musste, wird mehr Platz eingeräumt, Gemeinde und Kanton fordern eine Korrektur der Fahrbahn zulasten des «unschönen Hotelkastens»[2]. «Anstelle des ‹hässlichen› historistischen Hotels sollten nun die bisher ‹verdeckten hübschen Häuser, die bei aller Bescheidenheit schön rhythmisiert sind›, als neue Südfassade in den erweiterten Platz einbezogen werden.»[3] Gebaut wurde ein giebelständiges Haus, leicht vorversetzt im Verhältnis zur Kapelle (Abb. 5). Die Repetition des Giebels war weder der Alleinstellung der Kapelle noch einem städtischen Haus in diesem Kontext zuträglich. Dass sich der Neubau quasi nahtlos an die Kapelle anreihte und auf der anderen Seite offen blieb für jede Ergänzug, veränderte die Wahrnehmung des Sebastiansplatzes nachhaltig: Aus dem Platz war nun ein Schlauch geworden. Heute lässt sich der Fussabdruck des Prunkbaus lediglich als Treppenpodest erspüren, im Dezember erstrahlt auf dem obersten Treppenabsatz ein grosser, geschmückter Weihnachtsbaum, im Sommer setzt man sich auf die Treppenstufen, um ein Eis aus der Gelateria nebenan zu geniessen.

Für uns stand der Wandel, dem der Platz unterworfen war, im Zentrum des Interesses. Das Hotel mochte barock, klassizistisch oder historisch sein, immer bildete es die Kulisse für einen wunderbaren Platz im Kern der kleinen Alpenstadt. Diesen Platz als städtischen Raum, als Zimmer ohne Dach, vergass man unter den Bemühungen, dem verstärkt aufkommenden Verkehr mehr Raum zu geben. Doch muss man sich mit den Fehlern der Vergangenheit abfinden? Oder besitzen städtebauliche Entscheidungen nicht eher eine zeitlich begrenzte Gültigkeit? Ist nicht jeder Städtebau auch Ausdruck seiner Zeit?

Während unseres Studiums an der ETH wurden wir immer wieder mit der Fragestellung konfrontiert, inwieweit historische Städte fertiggebaut sind oder offen bleiben sollten für Veränderung. Die europäische Stadt war in ihrer Geschichte unzähligen Transformationen ausgesetzt. Sie wurde abgerissen, neu-, um- und abgebaut und dabei immer wieder mit neuen Bedürfnissen und architektonischen Auffassungen konfrontiert. Man kann sie sich vorstellen als Crèmeschnitte: Die einzelnen Schichten machen sie zu dem, was sie ist. Unter diesem Gesichtspunkt scheint

Abb. 2–5

> «Es handelt sich hierbei ganz klar um eine Behinderung für alle Passanten... Schon erstaunlich, wie und für was die Steuergelder in Brig-Glis... verlocht werden.»
>
> Peter, Onlinekommentar, www.1815.ch

> «Man könnte z. B. neben dem Gerüst ein grosses Plakat hinstellen mit dem Worten: Das soll ein Kunstwerk sein!»
>
> Charles Stünzi, Brig-Glis, Leserbrief Walliser Bote

es mir unbestreitbar, dass die Diskussion über die Entwicklung von Brigs Stadtzentrum wieder eröffnet werden sollte – vor allem seit die Stadtmitte nach der Überschwemmung im Jahr 1993 vom Verkehr befreit wurde.

Mit unserem Projekt, das wir 2016 realisierten, wollten wir diese Diskussion anstossen und den Umgang mit der historischen Innenstadt thematisieren, die zunehmend lebloser wird. Für einen Sommer lang sollte die kollektive Erinnerung an das Grandhotel wieder zum Leben erweckt werden.

Es ging uns dabei nicht um eine historische Rekonstruktion sondern vielmehr um eine freie Neuinterpretation, nicht als eindimensionale Schaufassade sondern als raumhaltige, erlebbare Installation. Ähnlich wie im Bühnenbild zu ‹Dogville› von Lars von Trier (Abb. 6) werden die raumbildenden Elemente lediglich bruchstückhaft angedeutet. In von Triers Film besteht eine Kleinstadt nur aus Fragmenten. Ein loses Stück Fassade mit einigen Fenstern steht für ein Wohnhaus, die Kirche besteht aus ein einzelnen Bankreihen und einem Glockenturm, der von der Decke schwebt. Den Rest muss man sich denken.

Unser Werkstoff war das Baugerüst, normiert und normalerweise lediglich Geburtshelfer für Werdendes, sollte es für einmal selbst die Hauptrolle spielen. Die Gerüststangen umreissen die Kubatur, zeichnen Erker, Turm und Dächer nach und spannen Netze auf, die einen Empfangsraum und ein Vordach zum Platz bilden. Ein Spiegel steht schräggestellt hoch oben im Gerüst und lässt den Passanten den Ausblick aus dem Hotelzimmer nachvollziehen. In der Nacht werden einzelne Stäbe mit Bauleuchten nachgezeichnet, an der Platzecke wird die ‹American Bar› lesbar, die namensgebende Krone (‹couronne›) tritt hervor und der Eingang wird des Nachts bereits von der Bahnhofstrasse her erkennbar.

Unsere Installation war ein weiterer, temporärer Zustand ein und desselben Gebäudes. Wie alle anderen Kleider, in die dieser Bau bereits geschlüpft war – das barocke, das klassizistische und das historistische – bediente sich auch dieser Zustand an Zeichen. Anders als die ‹Grandhotels› der Geschichte, die sich als einer bestimmten Epoche zugehörig deklarierten, sollte unser Kleid, unsere Installation die kollektive Erinnerung an vergangene Zeiten wecken (Abb. 7).

Das Konzept von Kunst im öffentlichen Raum geht auf die Bewegung der 68er zurück: Die Kunst sollte die Museen verlassen, zum Volk kommen, vermitteln und erziehen. Kunst im öffentlichen Raum definiert sich nicht nur über ihren Standort, sie ist also mehr als Kunst unter freiem Himmel, im besten Fall tritt sie in eine Wechselbeziehung zum Ort, indem sie sich beispielsweise auf historische oder aktuelle Aspekte bezieht, sie lenkt die Aufmerksamkeit auf Themen, denen ein Platz im kollektiven Bewusstsein zusteht. Kunst lässt sich dabei nicht auf Ästhetik reduzieren, bestenfalls interagiert sie mit dem Betrachter, wirft Fragen auf, erzeugt Reibungen, entfacht Diskussionen und regt an, kritisch zu sein. Mit unserem Grandhotel weckten wir die Brigerinnen und Briger auf, wir riefen ihnen zu: Wollt ihr es hinnehmen, dass sich städtebauliche Entscheidungen, die vor vielen Jahren unter anderen Bedingungen getroffen wurden, manifestieren? Stört es euch nicht, dass die Innenstadt zunehmend lebloser wird? Sehnt ihr euch nicht – wie wir – nach einem pulsierenden Zentrum? Werdet städtebaulich mündig!

Die Diskussion stagnierte dann jedoch auf einem weitaus profaneren Niveau, als wir uns das gewünscht hatten: Im Zentrum des Interesses standen nicht die Gedankenspiele, zu denen wir mit unserer Installation anregen wollten, niemand fragte, inwiefern unser Grandhotel im Sinne der ursprünglichen Idee funktionierte. Die Ablehnung, die unserer Installation entgegengebracht wurde, gründete nicht darauf, dass man das Projekt in seiner Absicht als gescheitert betrachtete, man lehnte vielmehr die profanen Umstände ab. Der Unmut entlud sich auf allen Kanälen, über Leserbriefe, Onlinekommentare, Karikaturen in der Fasnachtszeitung, ja sogar ein Wagen des Karnevalsumzugs wurde dem Thema gewidmet. Der Fokus lag auf der Frage nach der Finanzierung, auf der Sorge, dass sich jemand beim Beklettern der Installation verletzen könnte, auf den Bedenken, dass «das Gerüst» Touristen abschrecken würde. Der Preis des Grandhotels erschien den Brigerinnen und Brigern besonders hoch in Anbetracht der Tatsache, dass man keinen Mehrwert zu erwarten hatte, im Gegenteil, in den Augen der Öffentlichkeit kam es nur zu Einschränkungen: Die Installation versperrte einem nicht nur die Sicht, sie stand im Weg.

Doch «wer bildet die Öffentlichkeit der Architektur? Die Architekten selbst? Oder doch die Leute – und zwar alle – die Architektur gebrauchen?»[4] Frisch aus dem Studium kommend und den Diskurs mit unseren Assistenten und Professoren gewohnt, unterschied sich ‹unsere Öffentlichkeit› wesentlich von ‹der Öffentlichkeit›. Unsere Mitstudenten und Arbeitskollegen kennen dieselben Referenzen wie wir, sprechen in den gleichen Termini, oftmals genügt eine Andeutung, um einen ganzen Assoziationsraum zu öffnen. Nun hatten wir die Brigerinnen und Briger unvermittelt mit unserer Installation konfrontiert. Und damit zum ersten Mal einem Nutzer ausgesetzt. Dass uns nicht bewusst war, inwieweit der Abstraktionsgrad unserer Installation nach Erklärungen verlangte und wir den Diskurs mit der Bevölkerung sträflich vernachlässigten, geht auf unsere Rechnung.

Es fehlte uns nicht nur eine gemeinsame Sprache mit der Briger Stadtbevölkerung, auch das Vokabular war schwer zu finden. Denn wenn immer man über Architektur spricht, spricht man über Räume. Man beschreibt Dimension, Materialität und Proportion. Man diskutiert, inwieweit ein Raum angemessen, wohlproportioniert, gut belichtet, funktional oder auch einfach nur schön ist. In Brig mussten wir ohne unser stärkstes Argument auskommen: Die Installation vermittelte lediglich einen Hauch von Raum und war deswegen schwer fassbar. Während das Grandhotel für uns immer mehr zu einem städtebaulichen Substitut wurde, zu einem abstrakten Bedeutungsträger,

Abb. 6

«Nach meiner Meinung hätte man... das Projekt abbrechen sollen. Das hätte ich auch getan, läge es in meiner Verantwortung.»

Louis Ursprung, Stadtpräsident von Brig-Glis, Onlineumfrage, www.1815.ch

«Endlich hat jemand den Mut gefunden, ‹Kunst in der Stadt› zu kritisieren. Bis heute habe ich noch keine Person angetroffen, die positiv über diese sogenannte Kunst gesprochen hat. Muss das irrsinnige Gerüst auf dem Sebastiansplatz wirklich den ganzen Sommer da stehen? Ich frage mich, was kostet die ganze Angelegenheit?»

Peter R. Kalbermatten, Brig-Glis, Leserbrief Walliser Bote

wünschten sich viele Passanten, mit denen wir ins Gespräch kamen, das Gerüst lediglich als Tragwerk einer Abbildung der Originalfassade und damit eine konkrete Anlehnung am wirklichen Bauwerk.

Es fiel uns schwer, interpretierend über unser Grandhotel zu sprechen, wir erwarteten von der Bevölkerung eine grosse Bereitschaft für die Auseinandersetzung mit unserem Werk und eilten nicht mit erklärender Unterstützung zu Hilfe. Die Briger Stadtbevölkerung erfasste die Installation nicht in unserem Sinne und liess sich nicht auf die von uns antizipierten Gedankenspiele ein.

Dass das Projekt provozieren würde, war uns klar. Dass man es beinahe einstimmig ablehnen wird und dass der Unmut bis heute anhält, hat uns hingegen überrascht. Woran lag es? War die Installation zu minimalistisch, zu abstrakt? Gelang es uns nicht, den Assoziationsraum der geschichtlichen Erinnerung zu öffnen und wieder zu beleben? Oder ist uns der Blick der Bewohner auf ihre Stadt, auf ihren Platz völlig entgangen?

Dass die Installation in der Öffentlichkeit wahrgenommen wurde, dass man vom Grandhotel sprach, sich fragte, weswegen es für einen Sommer lang einen prominenten Platz in der Stadt einnahm, war trotz alledem ein Erfolg. Das Grandhotel bewegte die Leute dazu, kurz stehen zu bleiben, das Gespräch zu suchen, sich zu informieren und eine Meinung zu bilden. Es regte an, sich Gedanken über die eigene Stadt zu machen und warf Fragen auf.

Wir freuten uns, als der Wirt der Gartenwirtschaft am Sebastiansplatz seine Bestuhlung bis unter das Vordach des Grandhotels erweiterte und an warmen Sommerabenden Touristen und Einheimische vor der Installation anstiessen. Als an einem Abend im Oktober Tanzkünstler aus der ganzen Schweiz angereist kamen, mit Seilen gesichert immer weiter hoch ins Gerüst kletterten und Hotelgäste verkörpernd der Installation akrobatisch Leben einhauchten, erlebten wir, wie sich die Briger Stadtbevölkerung auf unser Anliegen einliess: Das Grandhotel nahm dem Stadtraum nicht nur etwas weg, es öffnete den Raum für Möglichkeiten. Auch wenn unsere Installation diesen Leerraum nicht nach den Vorstellungen der Bevölkerung zu füllen vermochte, merkten die Brigerinnen und Briger, wie gut es tut, kollektive Erinnerungen wachzuhalten, Gedankenspiele zu betreiben, zu diskutieren und Stellung zu beziehen.

1 Auszug aus dem Wettbewerbsprogramm der Stadt Brig-Glis.
2 Walter Ruppen, ‹Hotel Couronne et Poste in Brig, abgebrochen 1953 – Nostalgie am Platz!›, in: ‹Unsere Kunstdenkmäler: Mitteilungsblatt für die Mitglieder der Gesellschaft für Schweizerische Kunstgeschichte›, Ausgabe 29, 1978, S. 414.
3 Ebd.
4 Giancarlo De Carlo: ‹Die Öffentlichkeit der Architektur›, in: Susanne Hauser, Christa Kamleithner, Roland Meyer (Hg.), ‹Architekturwissen. Grundlagentexte aus den Kulturwissenschaften. Zur Logistik des sozialen Raumes›, Bielefeld 2013, S.412.

Abb. 1 – 5: Walter Ruppen, ‹Hotel Couronne et Poste in Brig, abgebrochen 1953 – Nostalgie am Platz!›, in: ‹Unsere Kunstdenkmäler: Mitteilungsblatt für die Mitglieder der Gesellschaft für Schweizerische Kunstgeschichte›, Ausgabe 29, 1978.
Abb. 6: https://theredlist.com/wiki-2-17-513-863-1311-1318-view-underground-indie-5-profile-2003-bdogville-b.html. Retrieved: 28.08.2017.

Namibia Flores Rodriguez, ‹Namibia›, 2016

Open to Criticism
Jack Self

To be critical is never to simply indulge in criticism. No matter how much you critique and criticise a condition, in the end—as architects—we must always make a proposal and a proposition. That is the essence of the ‹project›, without which there would be no architecture.

The Roman emperor Marcus Aurelius once wrote that your beliefs are your weapons and you should be with them like the boxer, not the gladiator. This is because a gladiator picks up his sword only to put it down again when he doesn't need to perform, while a boxer needs only to close his fists. In other words, you should defend what you believe actively and permanently, not simply parade. Otherwise you run the risk of becoming a hypocrite. But inasmuch as it is very important to be vocal about your ideas and to be dedicated to your practice, something Aurelius doesn't cover is how to deal with design criticism.

Certainly when I was studying, and still now when I visit architecture schools, I cringe to see a student take criticism personally. They might cry, get angry, become arrogant or defensive. In every case, they become too attached to their design as a representation and agent of their own ego. In fact, it is very important to have some critical distance from one's own work, and to understand that just because you have produced a bad design (which is easy to do) this does not mean you are a bad person. And when a teacher tells you your work is no good, they are not necessarily saying you have failed. It is very hard to do a good design and it takes a very long time.

Students who feel themselves overly sensitive about their work will sometimes create a defense by disowning the work, as if it was somehow totally external to themselves. This is almost as bad as being overly attached. Critical distance is not the same thing as simply being distant and divorced from your process: you must always assume responsibility for your work and ideas, including their consequences, and truly own them. Design is a highly personal activity. It is a process that involves introspection and personal reflection, labour and then standing back from the results to judge them with fresh eyes. This means that while working it must be all consuming, and when finished it must be assessed as if it was by a stranger.

The importance of understanding how to accept criticism, and to be critical of one's own work, is vital in many fields of practice. If you work in your own firm alone, then you have no peer or mentor to offer advice. All of the job of a jury must take place in your own mind. And if you work with others, then collaborating to solve a design issue is not possible if one person is always trying to claim the idea as their own. In a sense, this description of criticism is one that concerns how to form judgements and make design decisions. It is the formation of a methodology that you can apply to a given problematic—for example, as you develop your own way of understanding context and interpreting a site, you also develop a critical approach.

This is somewhat different from what could be called ‹the critical eye›, which is used in fields like writing, editing and cinema. Here criticism means the application of an ideological framework rather than a direct methodology. For example, the semiotics of photographs (as developed by Roland Barthes) is a conceptual device for interpreting the meaning of what we experience and see. The editor or writer is mainly involved in the act of analysis and comprehension; the architect is mainly involved in the act of interpretation and proposal. The writer improves or changes their vision of the world; the designer puts forward a vision of the world.

The most important aspect of all types of criticism is to always use it as a means to expand the horizon and scope of your self-awareness and awareness of the world. Whenever you think you have understood a work, ask what exists beyond the limits, or what invisible assumptions you have made to draw your conclusions. Without questioning the act of questioning, we tend to think we must be correct—because we incorrectly think we have understood the big picture and grasped the extent of knowledge.

To avoid this, it is vital to be always open to criticism.

«What does critique mean to you?»
Vincent Bianchi, Yann Salzmann

When we read about the theme of this issue at the beginning of the semester, we asked ourselves: is critique present in the architecture design courses? Studying at both ETH Zurich and EPF Lausanne, we are experiencing that students mainly understand critique as a dry commentary, highlighting the shortcomings of their design project. In this negative understanding, critique is downgraded to a simple tool to judge something as good or bad.

‹Tischkritik› is followed by ‹Zwischenkritik› is followed by ‹Schlusskritik›: Even though critique is omnipresent in our pedagogical process, we sometimes forget its real potential: a generator of new ideas! We deeply believe in this proactive definition of critique, one that does not simply dismantle an idea, but can be expressed projectively to help construct new perspectives. As students, do we care enough about our own critical thinking? How do our professors try to introduce us to critical thinking? How much space is allocated for critique in the framework of studios, apart from judgemental discussions?

Throughout this issue, you will encounter different interviews with teachers from ETHZ and EPFL. In these conversations we talked about their understanding of critical thought, and the role it plays in their teaching pedagogy. The choice of the seven professors was a subjective one: we selected them because we were curious to have their opinions on the topic. We hope that our choice will represent a panorama of positions.

We initially expected that blending these opinions would form a debate on the value of critical thought within the pedagogy. However, a general attitude was prevailing, which could, simplified, be summed up as: «yes, students should be critical». Maybe our question was rhetorical?

We would like to express our gratitude to Dieter Dietz, Tom Emerson, Anette Gigon, Christian Kerez, Alex Lehnerer, Oliver Lütjens, Thomas Padmanabhan, Luca Ortelli, Peter Swinnen, Daniel Zamarbide for the discussions we had that were instrumental in the making of this paper. We would also like to thank Nina Guyot and Vincent Hauser for their time to discuss this piece of research.

The Critical Architect
Jonathan Hill

While a prospect of the future is implicit in many histories and novels, it is explicit in a design, which is always imagined before it is built. The architect is a ‹physical novelist› as well as a ‹physical historian›. We expect a history or a novel to be written in words, but they can also be delineated in drawing, cast in concrete or seeded in soil.

Associated with words not drawings or buildings, and the writer not the designer, architectural criticism is widely known and understood. But it is assumed that few architects are critical. This assumption is open to criticism however. First, because it relies on a limited understanding of what is architectural. Second, because it caricatures who and what is critical. To consider both issues, the history of the architect is a useful point of departure.

Drawing Forth

Before the fifteenth century the status of the architect was low due to the association with manual labour and dispersed authorship. Of little importance to building, the drawing was understood to be no more than a flat surface and the shapes upon it were but tokens of three-dimensional objects. The Italian Renaissance introduced a fundamental change in perception, establishing the principle that the drawing truthfully depicts the three-dimensional world, and is a window to that world, which places the viewer outside and in command of the view. For the first time, the drawing became essential to architectural practice.

The command of drawing unlocked the status of the architect. Interdependent, the drawing and the architect affirm the same idea: architecture results not from the accumulated knowledge of a team of anonymous craftsman working together on a construction site but the artistic creation of an individual architect in command of drawing who designs a building as a whole at a remove from construction. Thus, the architectural drawing depends on two related but distinct concepts. One indicates that drawing is an intellectual, artistic activity distant from the grubby materiality of building. The other claims that the drawing is the truthful representation of the building, indicating the mastery of architects over building production.

The histories of the architect and the drawing are interwoven with that of design. The term design comes from the Italian disegno, meaning drawing, and suggesting both the drawing of a line on paper and the drawing forth of an idea. Dependent on the assumption that ideas are superior to matter and, thus, that intellectual labour is superior to manual labour, disegno enabled architecture, painting and sculpture—the three visual arts—to be identified as liberal arts concerned with ideas, a position they had rarely been accorded previously.[1] Disegno is concerned with the idea of architecture not the matter of building. Leon Battista Alberti notably states that «It is quite possible to project whole forms in the mind without recourse to the material.»[2]

Alongside the traditional practice of building, architects acquired new means to practice architecture: drawing and writing. To affirm their status as exponents of intellectual and artistic labour, architects began increasingly to theorise architecture in images and books. Sebastiano Serlio and Andrea Palladio are notable early exponents of this tradition, Le Corbusier and Rem Koolhaas more recent ones.[3]

Often a design does not get built and an architect must be persuasive to see that it does. Sometimes a building is not the best way to explore an architectural idea. Consequently, architects, especially influential ones, tend to talk, write and draw a lot as well as build. The relations between the drawing, text and building are multi-directional. Drawing may lead to building. But writing may also lead to drawing, or building to writing and drawing, for example. If everyone reading this text listed all the architectural works that influence them, some would be drawings, some would be texts, and others would be buildings either visited or described in drawings and texts. Studying the history of architecture since the Italian Renaissance, it is evident that researching, testing and questioning the limits of architecture occurs through drawing and writing as well as building. As drawings, books and buildings are architectural, they are potential sites for critical architecture, independently or together.

Ideas and Appliances

The history of design from the fifteenth-century to the twenty-first is not seamless however, and a significant departure occurred in the eighteenth century when the meaning of a design and an idea changed significantly. Opposed to utility, the classification of the fine arts — notably poetry, music, painting, sculpture and architecture—is primarily an invention of that century. Associated with utility, the design disciplines that proliferated due to industrialization, such as product design, are defined as applied arts at best. In the Renaissance a form was synonymous with an idea. But, especially since industrialisation and the codification of type, a form may be less about an idea and more about a product. Painters and sculptors discarded design once it became associated with collective authorship and industrial production. Among the fine arts, which include the three original visual arts, only in architecture is the term design regularly referred to today. Many people associate design with the newer design disciplines, which informs how architectural design is understood. But in the discourse of architects, the older meaning of design—drawing ideas—and the newer meaning of design—drawing appliances—are both in evidence. The architectural profession is more compatible with the newer concept of design, and is a significant hindrance to critical architecture. Since the nineteenth-century, architects and non-architects alike assume that it is natural for the architect to be a professional and that there is no alternative. To the apparent benefit of practitioners, consumers and the state, the professions reflect the desire to manage capitalism's excesses and reduce the threat of economic and social disorder. Professionals are neither expected nor paid to generate ideas, whether critical or not. Focusing on technical competence and acquiescence to commercial and regulatory forces, the architectural profession wants neither architecture nor architects to be critical. To be critical, the architect must be critical of the profession.

Designs on History and Fiction

The eighteenth century was pivotal in other ways. Countering the Platonist philosophical tradition in which knowledge is acquired by the mind alone, and the subsequent distrust of the senses in Renaissance theory, empiricism emphasised that experience is key to understanding, which develops through an evolving dialogue between the environment, senses and mind. Associating the natural world with subjective experience and drawing attention to the conditions that inform self-understanding, the eighteenth century fundamentally transformed the visual arts, its objects, authors and viewers. The architect associated with disegno was in its infancy when another type of architect appeared alongside it, exemplifying a new form of design and a new way of designing that valued the ideas and emotions evoked through experience and acknowledged the creative influences of the user and the weather. The first example of such a design practice occurred in gardens and garden buildings because they were closer to nature and more subject to seasonal and yearly change. Rather than refer to universal ideas, forms and proportions, design can draw forth an idea that is provisional and dependent on experience at conception, production and reception.

The empirical method stimulated innvoations in literature as well as landscape. In the sixteenth century, history's purpose was to offer useful lessons and accuracy was not necessary. In subsequent centuries, empiricism's emphasis on the distinction between fact and fiction transformed historical analysis. Rather than focus on individual achievements, the historian began to characterise changing cultural, social and economic processes in which the deeds of specific protagonists were contextualised. But this transition was slow and most eighteenth-century histories inherited some of the rhetorical approach of earlier histories.

In valuing direct experience, precise description, and a sceptical approach to ‹facts›, which needed to be repeatedly questioned, the empirical method created a fruitful climate in which the everyday realism of a new literary genre—the novel—could prosper as ‹factual fiction›.[4] The uncertainties and dilemmas of personal fortune and identity in a vibrant, secular society were ripe for narrative account. Notably, Daniel Defoe's Robinson Crusoe, 1719, which is often described as the first English novel, is a fictional autobiography.[5] Defoe describes another novel, Roxana, 1724, as ‹laid in Truth of Fact› and thus ‹not a Story, but a History›, a claim echoed by other novelists throughout the eighteenth century.[6] History's uncertain and evolving status supported authors' claims that the first novels were in fact histories. Even Jonathan Swift's Gulliver's Travels, 1726, is presented as true. The frontispiece depicts Lemuel Gulliver, a ship's surgeon and captain, who claims to verify his story in a number of ways, including by reference to the stingers of three gigantic wasps, which he teasingly claims to have donated to the first home of the Royal Society. Swift gently mocks empiricism while using its method.[7]

Focusing on the fate of individuals, the early novels—fictional autobiographies—developed in parallel with the early diaries—autobiographical fictions. People have written about themselves for millennia but the formation of modern identity in the seventeenth and eighteenth centuries is associated with a new emphasis on diary writing that Michel Foucault describes as a ‹technology of the self›, the process of self-examination by which moral character and behaviour are constructed and maintained in conjunction with other social forces.[8]

Objectivity may be an aspiration but no diary is entirely truthful and the diarist cannot fail to edit and reinvent life while reflecting upon it, altering the past as well influencing the future. Equivalent to a visual and spatial diary, the process of design—from one drawing to the next iteration and from one project to another—is itself an autobiographical ‹technology of the self›, formulating a design ethos for an individual or a studio. An architectural drawing can be autobiographical, as well as a means of negotiation between an architect and others, and thus subject to a more complex authorship. A building or landscape can also be an autobiography of its principal author, even if many people are involved in its design, construction and use. Equally, a building or a landscape can be the combined autobiographies of its many protagonists, with some getting more attention than others.

The early eighteenth century stimulated the simultaneous and interdependent emergence of new art forms, each of them a creative and questioning response to empiricism's detailed investigation of subjective experience and the natural world, namely the picturesque landscape, analytical history and English novel. The picturesque landscape is equivalent to a history, formulating an interpretation of the past in the present through classical reconstructions, antique sculptures and imported trees. Equally, the picturesque landscape is equivalent to a fiction, triggering fractured narratives, unexpected digressions, and reflections on identity and society. The conjunction of new art forms instigated a new design practice and lyrical environmentalism that profoundly influenced subsequent centuries.

The Physical Historian and the Physical Novelist

To design, the architect must decide what to remember and what to forget. In 1969 Vincent Scully concluded that the architect will «always be dealing with historical problems—with the past and, a function of the past, with the future. So the architect should be regarded as a kind of physical historian … the architect builds visible history»[9]. Like a history, a design is a reinterpretation of the past that is meaningful to the present. Whether implicit or explicit, a critique of the present and a prospect of the future are evident in a history and a design, which is always imagined before it is built. Architects have used history in different ways, whether to indicate their continuity with the past or departure from it. From the Renaissance to the twentieth century, the architect was a historian in the sense that a treatise combined design and history, and a building was expected to manifest the character of the time and knowingly critique earlier historical eras. Modernism ruptured this system in principle if not always in practice, but it returned in the second half of the twentieth century as modernism's previously dismissive reaction to social norms and cultural memories was itself anachronistic. The architect is a historian twice over: as a designer and as a writer.

Histories and novels each display a concern for the past, present and future. The historian acknowledges that the past is not the same as the present, while the novelist inserts the reader in a place and time that feels very present even if it is not. Histories and novels both need to be convincing but in different ways. Although no history is completely objective, to have any validity it must appear truthful to the past. A novel may be believable but not true, convincing the ‹reader› to suspend disbelief. While a prospect of the future is implicit in many histories and novels, it is explicit in a design, which is always imagined before it is built. The architect is a ‹physical novelist› as well as a ‹physical historian›. We expect a history or a novel to be written in words, but they can also be delineated in drawing, cast in concrete or seeded in soil.

Creative and critical architects have often looked to the past to imagine the future, studying an earlier architecture not simply to replicate it but to understand it as unfinished and open to further development. Twenty-first century architects need to appreciate the shock of the old as well as the shock of the new.

Postscript: The Critical User

Architecture is usually experienced habitually, when it is rarely the focus of attention. But, as empiricism made evident, habit is not passive. Instead, it is a questioning intelligence acquired through experience and subject to continuing re-evaluation. Rather than necessarily a deviation from habit, a critical and creative use can instead establish, affirm or develop a habit that is itself unexpected and evolving. In contrast to a singular focused activity such as reading, use is a particular type of awareness in which a person performs, sometimes all at once, a series of complex activities, some habitual, others not, that move in and out of conscious attention. Just as the reader makes a book anew through reading, the user makes a building anew through using, either by a physical transformation, using it in ways not previously imagined, or in conceiving it anew.[10] Architects do not have a monopoly over architecture. And neither do they have a monopoly over critical architecture.

1 Plato, Timaeus, Critias, Cleitophon, Menexenus, Epistles, trans. R. G. Bury, Cambridge MA: Harvard University Press, 1929, p. 121.
2 Leon Battista Alberti, On the Art of Building in Ten Books, trans. Joseph Rykwert, Neil Leach and Robert Tavernor, Cambridge MA and London: MIT Press, 1988, p. 7. Written in 1452 and first published in 1485 as De re aedificatoria (Ten Books on Architecture).
3 Sebastiano Serlio, Sebastiano Serlio on Architecture, vol. 1, books I-V of Tutte l'opere d' architettura et prospectiva, 1537–51, trans. Vaughan Hart and Peter Hicks, New Haven and London: Yale University Press, 1996. Andrea Palladio, The Four Books on Architecture, trans. Robert Tavernor and Richard Schofield, Cambridge MA: MIT Press, 1997; first published as I quattro libri dell' architettura in 1570. Le Corbusier, Towards a New Architecture, trans. Frederick Etchells, London: Rodker, 1927; first published as Vers une architecture in 1923. Rem Koolhaas, Delirious New York: A Retroactive Manifesto for Manhattan, Rotterdam: 010, 1994; first published in 1978.
4 Lennard J. Davis, Factual Fictions: The Origins of the English Novel, Philadelphia: University of Pennsylvania Press, 1996, p. 213. First published in 1983.
5 Daniel Defoe, Robinson Crusoe, Oxford: Oxford University Press, 2007.
6 Daniel Defoe, Roxana, or the Fortunate Mistress, ed. P.N. Furbank, London: Pickering and Chatto, 2009, p. 21.
7 Jonathan Swift, Gulliver's Travels, London: Penguin, 2001.
8 Michel Foucault, ‹On the Genealogy of Ethics: An Overview of Work in Progress›, in The Foucault Reader, ed. Paul Rabinow, London: Penguin, 1984, p. 369; Michel Foucault, ‹Technologies of the Self›, in Luther H. Martin, Hugh.
9 Gutman and Patrick H. Hutton, eds, Technologies of the Self: A Seminar with Michel Foucault, London: Tavistock, 1988, pp. 18-19.
10 Vincent Scully, American Architecture and Urbanism, London: Thames & Hudson, 1969, p. 257. Roland Barthes, ‹The Death of the Author›, in Image-Music-Text, trans. Stephen Heath, London: Flamingo, 1977, pp. 142–48.

«Comment développer l'esprit critique des étudiants, M. Swinnen?»

«Il est important de fournir deux pistes parallèles à l'étudiant. D'une part une liberté, une générosité de pouvoir connaître l'histoire lointaine et récente de l'architecture (la matérialité, la tectonique, …) afin de pouvoir expérimenter. Le problème est que cela reste souvent le seul niveau de l'éducation. D'autre part, il y a une pratique politique de l'architecture. Je considère celle-ci comme une profession libérale pour l'intérêt commun. J'ai un dégoût de l'architecture pour l'architecture. Malgré tout l'argent et l'énergie investis afin de préparer des générations d'architectes, la valeur critique de l'architecture dans la société, aujourd'hui, est presque nulle.»

«Que pensez-vous du rôle de l'architecture dans la société aujourd'hui?»

«Je crois qu'en tant qu'architectes on a la capacité d'ouvrir des perspectives sur des questions sociales que d'autres experts n'envisageraient pas ou alors différemment. Chaque défi économique, écologique ou social se matérialise immanquablement dans l'espace sociétal. À ce titre, il faut reconnaître que les preneurs de décisions politiques ne sont pas suffisamment conscients de l'impact que l'architecture puisse apporter aux politiques futures. La démarche éthique et sociale de la discipline vis-à-vis de la politique contemporaine demeure sous-exposée et sous-explorée, tant dans la pratique que dans la théorie, l'académie et l'éducation.

Le ‹political agenda setting› est pour moi une volonté. Mais pour cela, il faut enseigner aux étudiants comment s'infiltrer de façon proactive, le plus en amont possible, dans des mécanismes sociopolitiques où, tôt ou tard, il y aura de l'architecture. Pouvoir, tout en gardant l'intérêt commun comme cadre de référence, activer un moment de surprise dans un processus architectural en disant: ‹j'ai proactivement détecté un besoin, une urgence et vous pouvez m'aider, en tant qu'investisseur ou que politicien›, ça a une vraie valeur sociétale. Parce l'architecture ne peut devenir une pratique politique que si elle dépasse la simple réponse réactive à un cahier des charges pour devenir réellement pro-active. Je crois qu'il y a une demande pour une telle stratégie d'architecture mais qu'il n'y a pour l'instant pas de vrai marché pour cela. On peut le co-créer en préparant des étudiants à défendre des positions critiques dans la société en utilisant l'architecture comme outil critique et non pas comme fin esthétique en soi.

L'architecture comme lobby culturel possède, certes, une valeur. Mais en restant uniquement dans un contexte ‹artistique›, elle tourne en rond. D'autant plus que le cadre académique se protège trop du monde. Il est souvent hors du champ de la société. La réalité de la profession architecturale, elle, est tant violente que directe. Il ne suffit pas de se pencher sur l'architecture elle-même. C'est avant tout aussi une tâche politique et un modèle économique. Même si je suis persuadé que la culture est aujourd'hui extrêmement urgente, nous vivons une époque où elle n'est pas au sommet de l'agenda politique.»

«Comment cela se matérialise dans votre enseignement?»

«Dans l'atelier, nous essayons d'avoir des partenaires de l'extérieur, d'aller frapper à des portes sans être sollicités pour demander: ‹avez-vous besoin d'architecture?› Comment peut-on apprendre à détecter des clients qui ne se rendent pas encore compte qu'ils peuvent l'être? Comment peut-on créer sa propre demande sociétale? Non pas individuellement en tant qu'architecte, mais en tant que discipline qui, en co-définissant l'agenda social, possède vraie valeur sociétale. Je crois peu dans un modèle où, en tant que praticien, on travaille de façon réactive à un concours. À travers ceux-ci, l'architecture ne parvient que rarement à assumer un rôle proactif. Économiquement, ils ne sont également plus défendables. Le marché a découvert qu'il suffit de payer un pécule pour que les architectes déballent toute leur intelligence d'un seul coup. Je ne connais aucune autre profession qui fasse cela.»

«Comment aidez-vous l'étudiant à développer son regard critique en tant que tel, de manière à ce qu'il se forge sa propre opinion?»

«Dans le studio, on donne beaucoup d'ouverture aux étudiants pour aller à l'encontre de ce qui est proposé. Malgré tout, peu en tirent vraiment parti. Certes, j'essaie toujours de pousser un étudiant dans une direction, mais s'il essaye de m'entendre d'une façon précise, il découvre rapidement la possibilité de se positionner personnellement. Il y a, à l'ETH plus qu'ailleurs, une sorte de réticence à le faire. J'aime être contredit, ça me fait réfléchir, c'est une remise en question personnelle.

Il est très important pour nous de nourrir les étudiants avec beaucoup de références. Elles donnent l'opportunité d'être extrêmement critique, parce qu'elles sont très concrètes. Pourquoi ne pas copier un projet, tout en conservant une démarche critique? Lorsque j'étais étudiant, un collègue avait pris un projet de Steven Holl, qu'il avait placé dans un autre contexte avant de faire son autocritique. J'avais trouvé ça génial. On ne peut être critique qu'en connaissant aussi bien l'histoire que l'actualité. Tout cela doit être infiltré un maximum dans l'enseignement. Ce qui implique de mobiliser tout le ‹build-up› historique disponible. Utiliser une référence, j'ai toujours l'impression que les étudiants trouvent ça sale. Comme si nous étions des maîtres géniaux. Pourquoi cette idée fantasque et improductive d'être génial? Ce sont de faux génies.»

Ce texte est extrait d'un interview de Peter Swinnen le 13 juin 2017, à l'ETH Zurich, par Vincent Bianchi et Yann Salzmann.

Gegenwind
Elena Pibernik

Unsere Schule für Tüftler und Freidenker bekannt,
wissenschaftliche Fachrichtungen gibt es allerhand.
Voller Neugier werden Herausforderungen vernommen,
hierfür ist das fundierte technische Wissen willkommen.
Vor nichts Unbekanntem wird zurückgeschreckt,
viel Zeit in die Forschung hineingesteckt.
So werden stets neue Erkenntnisse gewonnen,
unterschiedliche Fakten der Welt zusammengesponnen.

Diese Werte liegen auch im Departement Architektur zu Grunde,
hat man ein breites Spektrum wählbarer Professuren im Bunde.
Die Möglichkeit unterschiedliche Ansätze und Haltungen zu testen,
sind an der ETH fern von eiskalter Marktlage die Besten.
So lasst uns nicht in den vorgegebenen Aufgaben versteifen,
sondern die einmalige Chance zur Eigeninitiative ergreifen.
Professoren mit Diskurse konfrontieren,
mit grosser Vielfalt beim Diplom brillieren!

Wagemutig Ungewohntes durchdenken,
Gewohntem kritische Tiefe schenken.

Von Ästhetik und Dimension einiger Pläne und Modelle geblendet,
wird schnell viel Zeit in gedankenlose Produktion verschwendet.
Stattdessen sollen wir den gegebenen Kontext präzise erhellen,
Zusammenhänge zwischen Kultur, Geschichte und Theorie herstellen.
So habt dabei Mut zu mehr hässlichen Arbeitsproben,
denn die lassen unsere Experimentierfreude toben.
Anschliessende kritische Auseinandersetzung
folgt dem Konzept immanenter Umsetzung!

Wagemutig Ungewohntes durchdenken,
Gewohntem kritische Tiefe schenken.

Schnell zieht das eigene Projekt einen in den Bann,
Mangel neuer Inspiration und Überrezeption fängt an.
Zweifellos wurde Mies' Barcelona Chair zum Allrounder erkoren,
geht auch mit René Magrittes Mann die Spezifik verloren.
So lasst uns öfters durch Natur und gebaute Architektur flanieren,
gemeinsam mehr über vielfältige Lektüren präzise sinnieren.
Alle unsere Sinne sollen erklingen,
denn nur so kann Architektur gelingen!

Wagemutig Ungewohntes durchdenken,
Gewohntem kritische Tiefe schenken.

So sei dies ein Appell für mehr kritisches Reflektieren,
eine Kritik am unüberlegten Produzieren.
Das Studium als einmalige Chance zu verstehen,
mit Herzblut das Risiko des Versagens eingehen.
Vor keiner möglichen Inspiration Halt machen,
dabei feurige Diskussionen zu entfachen.
Um eine persönliche Architekturhaltung zu entdecken,
unsere Räume, Städte und Landschaften zum Leben zu erwecken!

Document 1, n.d.: Poster for ‹Parity Talks›, designed by Ursina Völlm and Martina Walthert

Architects Who Make a Fuss[1]
Torsten Lange and Charlotte Malterre-Barthes
for the Parity Group

A speculative investigation into the archive of a grassroots initiative for gender parity at the department of architecture ETH Zurich, 2014–2017.

Prologue

Nikolai Zagrekov, ‹Girl with the t-square›, (portrait of Ursula Nachtlicht, daughter of the Jewish architect Leo Nachtlicht), cover image for ‹Die Jugend›, no. 44, 1929

In 2014, following yet another final critique in a design studio with an all-male panel of guest critics, a group of teaching assistants and students gathered in a café on Hönggerberg to give vent to their anger about the persistent gender inequality within the department. This marked the beginning of the Parity Group, an informal grassroots initiative whose goal was to establish greater balance between men and women, especially in leadership positions. Over the course of the past three years, Parity Group members have not only intervened in the department's institutional structures, but they also organized two symposia and workshops with the participation of experts who work at the intersection of gender and architecture (and the design professions more generally). By doing so, the group became part of an international network of similar activist organizations. Through the expertise of these external partners and thanks to the active participation of members from all levels of the department, the Parity Group developed a set of measures, the so-called ‹9 Points for Parity›, aimed at improving gender equity. In May 2017, the Professors' Conference voted unanimously to adopt and implement a Gender Action Plan for the department. This decision included a commitment to institutionalize the work of the Parity Group, so far carried out on an informal and purely voluntary basis, by creating a Parity Board tasked with the delivery of this plan. The task ahead is to formulate and implement a series of concrete measures as part of the department's obligation—as set out by the ETH Zurich Executive Board—to develop such a plan in line with its own specific needs.

This article formulates a situated critique of the department and its structures, as well as of our critical engagement with, and interventions into, these structures in a wider context of gender-based activism within and beyond the architectural discipline. It adopts the form of a ‹site-writing›, an engaged and spatialized mode of writing first developed by feminist architectural historian and theorist Jane Rendell.[2] Drawing on psychoanalysis and autobiography, and by referring to «spaces as they are remembered, dreamed and imagined, as well as observed», site-writing combines «different genres and modes of writing […] whose critical ‹voices› are objective and subjective, distant and intimate», in order to put forth «alternative understandings of subjectivity and positionality».[3] In what follows, we seek to reconstruct the site of our involvement in attempting to transform the department into a more dynamic, diverse, and democratic space. The text proceeds as a conversation between distinct voices that cut across time (past, present, and future), real and imagined spaces, and visual and textual registers. Fictitious journal entries by a scholar who visits ETH Zurich for a week in March in 2024 as part of her research on women in architecture are juxtaposed with actual archival documents from the Parity Group, as she discovers them, and with a description of the group's work and its intellectual and institutional contexts.

I. Taking place, claiming space

Monday, March 4, 2024. Day one in the archive. 10 am. Meeting with the archivist on Hönggerberg. She's a woman, possibly in her late forties. Everything has been perfectly arranged. On the desk are a couple of boxes with the inscription ‹ETH/D-ARCH Parity Group, 2014–2017›, a drawing tube that has the words ‹posters and prints› written on it, a lever-arch file full of ‹correspondence›, and a hard disk whose label reads ‹original data/audio and video recordings›. She says: «All that's left is here, but feel free to ask if you'd like to know more». She had been a PhD candidate back then. Few of those who were involved in the group's activities stayed in the institution. And almost all of the women who, at the time, held Chairs in the department are either Professors emeriti by now, or have left the school once their appointments as Guest Professors ended. Who took their places?

Like any act of design, architecture is at its most basic about imagining a desirable future. How is it that today—almost a century after the adoption of the female vote in most European countries—it still is mainly men who plan this future? What's more, it seems to be a very small and homogenous group of men: predominantly white and middle-class. As we've become increasingly aware that ever more people are affected by design decisions, the faction of those who make those decisions continues to expand at an exceedingly slow pace. Architecture thus, by and large, remains a bastion of male exclusivity. Men continue to dominate not only the profession, but also architectural education. Even though there is now near gender parity among students, women's career opportunities in the field of architecture continue to look dire.[4] For instance, at the end of 2013, 44.5% of the student body in our department were female, while only 11.8% of the professorships were held by women.[5] In addition to the shockingly low representation of women among the professors, lecture series and panel discussions with only male speakers are still the norm, and female architects in the curriculum are largely unheard of. Thus, for about half of the student body, role models are lacking.

Document 2, dated March 8, 2016: ‹Parity Talks› photos

Amidst the recent international resurgence of feminist thinking, calling out persistent injustices as well as pushing back against both new and reemerging sexism, misogyny, and other forms of gender-based discrimination, the Parity Group formed out of a loose network of people who were frustrated about the grossly ‹unbalanced› state of affairs in their immediate day-to-day environment at our department. With the retirement, among others, of Uta Hassler in 2015, the department embarked on a generation change that would see the appointment of nearly ten professors over the course of a four-year period. We seized this opportunity to address this situation of inequity and demand steps towards equal representation of men and women.

Document 3, dated March 8, 2017: ‹Parity Talks II› phot

We were, of course, aware of the particularly conservative Swiss social context, where women were granted the right to vote in 1971 and gender equality legislation did not come into effect until 1996. But only through our gradual engagement in this process, we understood just how slow the pace of change had really been: It took 130 years from the foundation of the Federal Polytechnic and 114 years from the enrolment of the first female student, Nadezhda Smeckaja, that, in 1985, with the appointment of the architect Flora Ruchat-Roncati the first woman became a professor at ETH.[6]

But one does not have to go that far back in history to get a sense that progress moves at a snail's pace. Research by Parity Group member Sarah Nichols revealed that more than a third (40 of 108) of all doctoral dissertations at the Institute for the History and Theory of Architecture (gta)—one of four research institutes—were written by women.[7] Ever since the first thesis was submitted by a female scholar in 1986, this number has steadily grown. A success, one might think at first. Yet, since its foundation in 1967, no woman ever held a Chair in the Institute. Hence not a

single one of these PhD theses had been produced under a female supervisor. While some of the former doctoral students seem to have literally disappeared after earning their degree, a handful have ended up in positions far below their level of qualification. Many others have pursued careers outside ETH Zurich, whether in Swiss Universities of Applied Sciences or abroad.[8] It seems to be instances like these, in which the otherwise deceptively abstract phrase of the ‹leaky pipeline›, takes on a personal dimension.

Further to the lack of female professors, women architects—both Swiss and foreign—remain conspicuously absent from the curriculum. Compared to their male counterparts, pioneering figures such as Lux Guyer, Flora Steiger-Crawford, or Beate Schnitter are rarely discussed in design studios, lectures and seminars. The same is true for prominent international modernists as Eileen Gray, Charlotte Perriand, or Lilly Reich, to name but a few. In a conversation, a student once reported that Lina Bo Bardi was, in fact, the only female architect whose work was explicitly mentioned. How is one to know one's future, without knowing one's past?

Such collective amnesia is by no means unique to our department. Instead, it points to a wider absence of women from mainstream histories of the discipline, not to say their willful erasure from such histories. Regardless of the requirement to «integrate gender-specific aspects in research and teaching»[9] there remain significant reservations and misconceptions, even anxieties, among faculty members as to the introduction of gender into the curriculum. In a recent interview, the outgoing Dean, Professor Annette Spiro, rejected the need for gender scholarship in architecture. For, in her opinion, there is no «female or male architecture».[10] «I must admit», she adds, «that I am simply not interested in questions of gender. Important are oeuvre and perception, no matter if the author is a man or a woman». Yet does this understanding not precisely overlook the inherent gender bias of such categories as oeuvre and authorship, which have effectively served to suppress within historiography the role and contribution of women in the production of the built environment?

To claim space in favor of increasing diversity in our discipline—both in the act of rewriting its history as well as in its present and future making—means more than just inserting women into an established canon. It requires a wholesale reconstruction of the conceptual and methodological frameworks that underpin this canon—the consequent and sustained undoing of ‹master› narratives.

II. Institutional critique

Tuesday, March 5, 2024. Received a message from supervisor who asks about progress. It was her who recommended coming here in the first place. «ETH Zurich—a very peculiar case», she had warned. A young Associate Professor at the time, she was part of an expanding network of critical architects and intellectuals, who realized that improving social justice and diversity in architectural education—and the wider discipline—required a sustained critique of the academic and professional institutions, as well as their underlying structures and modus operandi. Went through plenty of material in just two days. From the distance, the situation seems surreal. Surprisingly little awareness and great reluctance to take action by the department. One can notice the frustration among students and staff. Yet, there also seem to be a sense of urgency and grassroots activism, rigor, creativity, and humor.

In their combination, architecture and academia seem to form an impenetrable substance. Like an ultra-hard block of cement, architectural education is exceptionally resistant to cracks and changes. And more often than not, in trying to secure its disciplinary integrity, the internal power structures of this monolith appear to be working against women. Of course, one can always blame some distant outside—an abstract social, political, or economic context that first has to change in order for academia to follow suit. But this would mean overlooking the inherent contradictions and struggles inside the institution itself.

In our Parity Group meetings, above all the two Parity Talks symposia and workshops in 2016 and 2017, there have often been heated discussions as to what might be the possible structural causes for the often unconscious gender bias. From the way in which job profiles are written to the hard and fast criteria for excellence, there appears to be little awareness about the ways in which the system of the architectural academia is pitted against women. Too often, then, these systemic features are viewed as natural givens that must remain unchallenged if the integrity of good and rigorous scholarship is to be preserved. The fact that the size of an oeuvre is typically understood as an indicator of excellence in the architecture school automatically puts women at a disadvantage, as the former, for different reasons, tend to realize buildings later and at a slower pace than their male colleagues.

Add to this the recent obsession with young age and the ongoing excellence-focused and output-oriented restructuring of academia, and you'll have an especially toxic mix. As philosophers Isabelle Stengers and Vinciane Despret have warned:

«[c]ompetition and the will to excel […] are today officially on the agenda as unavoidable imperatives. […] Knowledge worthy of this name must not fear evaluation, they say to us, and this evaluation must be objective: how many articles, published in which journals? How many contracts? How many collaborations with other prestigious institutions, thus contributing to the «positioning» of the university in the European or global market?»[11]

However, numerous studies have exposed how evaluation procedures frequently reproduce, rather than remove, existing gender biases, and thus may, in fact, contribute to sustaining sexism and gender-based discrimination in the academy.[12] For instance, male lecturers are frequently ranked higher by their students than women for no obvious professional reasons.[13] In architecture, such an underlying bias may indeed be further amplified by socially constructed and historically cultivated notions of ‹mastery› or ‹creative genius›.

III. Networking and public campaigning

Wednesday, March 6, 2024. Invitation from one of the Chairs in Architecture and Design to give an impromptu studio talk about my research on ‹women in architecture›. «As required by the curriculum…», the message started. Where to begin? What to tell them? Last night, the archivist took me out for a drink in the city. Met one of her friends, who has been running an office with two other female ETH graduates for nearly a decade. «We were either in the middle of, or just about to, start our Master's projects when that whole Parity Group stuff started», they said. «Only one of us went back to teach as an Assistant for a while.» Decided to take the entire class to their office to see first-hand a ‹female practice›. Impressive work!

During one of the roundtable discussions at the first Parity Talks, Karin Sander highlighted how important solidarity and cooperation had been in the early stages of her career as an artist. In many ways, the Parity Group was motivated by a similar ethics of self-help and collaboration. In this spirit, and tired of the lazy excuse that there aren't enough talented women out there, two group members—Charlotte Malterre-Barthes and Harald R. Stühlinger—set out on an urgent and immediately practical task: to establish a Swiss database of women in architecture, aimed at all those involved in inviting guest speakers, programming lecture series, setting up search committees for the appointment of Chairs, and drawing up lists of suitable candidates for professorships. This database was then published as a special issue of ‹Archithese› in June 2016.[14]

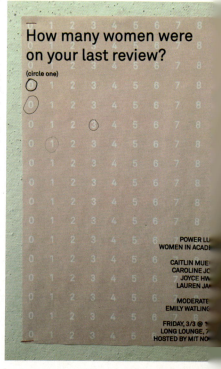

Document 4, dated March 3, 2017: NOMAS power lunch ‹Women in Academia› at MIT

Document 5, dated June 8, 2016: special issue of Archithese ‹Architektur, die [fem.], Baukultur ist auch weiblich!›, no. 2 (2016)

Lacking institutional support as well as discipline-specific knowledge and expertise on gender, we turned to the many like-minded international groups on architecture and gender that had come to flourish over the last few years, eager to learn from them. Their work has been a constant source of inspiration and empowerment. Of those connections, which included links to the Australian association ‹Parlour—Women, Equity, Architecture›[15], and to Justine Clark in particular, or the ‹Feminist Art and Architecture Collaborative (FAAC)›[16], a group of young scholars based at different North American universities, the one to KTH Stockholm became the most lasting. There, in the Technical University's architecture department under Malin Åberg Wennerholm as Director of Studies, an ambitious gender-based curriculum had been launched. Feminist thinking became integral not only to architectural design, but also in history and theory through the work, among others, of Hélène Frichot. Following her invitation, Parity Group members Torsten Lange and Emily Eliza Scott chaired a roundtable about architecture and feminist pedagogies at the ‹Architecture and Feminisms› themed annual conference of the Architectural Humanities Research Association (AHRA).[17]

Finally, the research team consisting of Eliana Perotti, Katrin Albrecht, Helene Bihlmaier, Irina Davidovici, and Katia Frey, all engaged in the activities of the Parity Group, that investigates the life and work of Flora Ruchat-Roncati within the framework of a major SNF-funded project, will reestablish a hidden network of connections between actors in Switzerland and abroad.[18]

IV. Policy design and development

Thursday, March 7, 2024. Day four. The tedious side of research: filing an interim research report to my school. Doing this research trip on a grant for emerging female scholars in architecture. Recall how my supervisor recently told me that access to scholarships from this fund helped launch her career. But, the levels of bureaucracy… Must finish this quickly! Only one day left and still got hours of video and audio recordings of the parity workshops to go through. Why on Earth would anyone create such long and complex online forms to fill in? Those useless heaps of data…

Information is power. Knowledge and data are key to providing arguments for policies. However, what is recorded, and how, is not neutral. Devising plans and formulating goals constitute political activities by default. They need to be publicly debated with those most directly affected by those plans. For, it is they who are the true experts.

Right from the start, our work focused on designing concrete measures to improve gender parity at all levels of the department, but especially in the appointment procedure of professors.[19] As early as June 2015, through a collaborative process among assistants, we identified five key measures. One of them was the production of a directory of female practitioners and scholars, now available as a resource. The others included a double award system for Master and PhD theses as well as doubling guest professorships to ensure parity, a travel fund for incoming and outgoing female assistants, and gathering more precise data about gender in the department beyond the basic monitoring by ETH Equal every two years.[20] For instance, the latter should also include figures about female representation in studio critiques, public talks, and panel discussions, all of which are vital for increasing the visibility of women and their perception by aspiring students as role models.

Those aspects, among others, were then taken up in the so-called ‹9 Points for Parity›, the major outcome of the first Parity Talks in 2016. The ‹9 Points› represent a comprehensive set of measures, in line with the general principles of the ETH Zurich Gender Action Plan of 2014 as well as in response to the specific needs of our department acknowledging that there exist several distinctively architectural obstacles that need to be

9 POINTS FOR PARITY

1. BILDUNG EINES PARITY BOARD BESTEHEND AUS JE EINER VERTRETUNG ALLER INSTITUTE DES D-ARCH, DER PROFESSORENSCHAFT, DES FACHVEREINS DER ASSISTENTINNEN UND ASSISTENTEN DES D-ARCH (AAA), DES FACHVEREINS DER ARCHITEKTURSTUDIERENDEN AN DER ETH ZÜRICH (ARCHITEKTURA), DER PARITY GROUP SOWIE EINER EXTERNEN FACHPERSON. DAS PARITY BOARD IST DAFÜR VERANTWORTLICH, DIE GENANNTEN MASSNAHMEN FÜR EINE GESCHLECHTER-PARITÄT, IHRE GRADUELLE UMSETZUNG SOWIE IHRE ENTSPRECHENDE FINANZIERUNG IN ANGRIFF ZU NEHMEN UND WEITERE ÖFFENTLICHE VERANSTALTUNGEN WIE DIE JÄHRLICHEN PARITY TALKS ZU ORGANISIEREN.

2. JÄHRLICHES INTERNES WIE EXTERNES MONITORING UND VERÖFFENTLICHUNG DER BISHER ERREICHTEN ERGEBNISSE DER GLEICHSTELLUNG.

3. GESCHLECHTER-PARITÄT BEI PROFESSUREN, DOZENTUREN, OBERASSISTENZEN, GASTVORTRÄGEN UND GASTKRITIKEN.

4. GESCHLECHTER-PARITÄT INNERHALB DER BERUFUNGSKOMMISSIONEN AM D-ARCH SOWIE UNTER DEN EINGELADENEN KANDIDATINNEN UND KANDIDATEN, DIE IN DIESEN KOMMISSIONEN VORSTELLIG WERDEN SOLLEN.

5. INTEGRATION UMFASSENDER GENDER-RELEVANTER THEMEN UND VERMITTLUNG GESCHLECHTSSPEZIFISCHER KOMPETENZEN IN DAS CURRICULUM DER AUSBILDUNG AM D-ARCH DURCH WAHLFÄCHER, SEMINARE SOWIE VORTRAGSREIHEN IM BACHELOR-, MASTER- UND IM POSTGRADUALEN STUDIUM SOWIE DURCH EINE BEWUSSTE UNTERRICHTSMETHODIK. EINE MÖGLICHE SOFORTMASSNAHME WÄRE DIE AUFSTELLUNG EINER GESONDERTEN FINANZIERUNG EINES SOLCHEN KURSES AM D-ARCH, DER JEDES SEMESTER VON EINEM ANDEREN LEHRSTUHL VERANSTALTET WERDEN WÜRDE.

6. BILDUNG EINES ADVANCED-AWARD-PROGRAMMS, DAS STIPENDIEN AN WISSENSCHAFTLERINNEN VERGIBT, DIE SICH DADURCH GANZ AUF IHRE FORSCHUNG UND LEHRE KONZENTRIEREN KÖNNEN. DIESES STIPENDIUM SOLL IN ERSTER LINIE IN EINER ÜBERGANGSZEIT ZWISCHEN EINZELNEN STUFEN IM AKADEMISCHEN CURRICULUM (DOKTORAT, HABILITATION UND PROFESSUR) VERGEBEN WERDEN, BIS EINE ANGEMESSENE GESCHLECHTER-PARITÄT ERREICHT WIRD.

7. BILDUNG EINES FONDS ZUR FINANZIERUNG VON GASTVORTRÄGEN EXTERNER REFERENTINNEN UND ZUR BEZUSCHUSSUNG DER REISEKOSTEN VON WISSENSCHAFTLERINNEN DES D-ARCH BEI EXTERNEN VORTRÄGEN, TAGUNGSBESUCHEN ETC. DIESER FONDS SOLL IN ERSTER LINIE IN EINER ÜBERGANGSZEIT DIE WAHRNEHMUNG VON AKADEMIKERINNEN UND ARCHITEKTINNEN ERHÖHEN, BIS EINE ANGEMESSENE GESCHLECHTER-PARITÄT ERREICHT WIRD.

8. EINFÜHRUNG EINES STIPENDIUMS FÜR WEIBLICHE UND MÄNNLICHE DOKTORIERENDE, DIE SICH IN IHRER ARBEIT MIT EINER GENDER-THEMATIK IN ARCHITEKTUR ODER STÄDTEBAU BESCHÄFTIGEN.

9. GESCHLECHTER-PARITÄT BEI AUSZEICHNUNGEN AN STUDIERENDE FÜR HERAUSRAGENDE MASTER- UND DOKTORARBEITEN DURCH DIE BEREITSTELLUNG VON JEWEILS ZWEI RESPEKTIVE GERADZAHLIGEN PREISEN. EINE SOLCHE PARITÄTISCHE AUSZEICHNUNG WÜRDE DIE VORBILDLICHE PRAXIS DER AUFNAHME JEWEILS EINER STIPENDIATIN UND EINES STIPENDIATEN PRO JAHR IN DEN LAUFENDEN DOKTORATSPROGRAMMEN AM D-ARCH AUFGREIFEN.

---

1. Creation of a Parity Board consisting of representatives from each institute of the D-ARCH, a representative of the professorship, a delegate from the Association of Teaching Assistants at the D-ARCH (AAA), one representative from the architectural students association at the ETH Zurich (architektura), the representatives of the Parity Group and one external expert. The Parity Board would be responsible for instigating the measures by which gender parity is achieved, their gradual implementation, the connected fundraising tasks, and the organisation of future public events such as the annual Parity Talks.

2. Annual internal and external monitoring and publication of the achieved parity-related results.

3. Gender parity for professorships, lectureships, senior research and teaching positions, guest lectures, and guest critics.

4. Gender parity within the appointment committees of the department, and of invited candidates that come before such search committees.

5. Integration of broader gender issues or gender-related skills into the educational curriculum of the D-ARCH through elective courses, seminars, lecture series in graduate and post-graduate studies, and explicit teaching tools. This could be immediately achieved for example through dedicated funding for one such course each semester by different chairs within the D-ARCH.

6. Creation of an Advanced Award Program, comprising research and teaching grants for female scholars pursuing an academic career. This award is specifically aimed at bridging the gap (the leaky pipeline) in the academic curriculum (doctorate, habilitation, professorship) until reasonable parity is achieved.

7. Creation of a travel fund devoted to inviting female scholars for lectures from outside and to support female scholars of D-ARCH to travel for lectures, congresses, etc. This fund is specifically aimed at bridging the gap in academic and professional visibility until reasonable parity is achieved.

8. Creation of a fellowship for female and male doctoral students devoting their thesis to gender-related issues in architecture and town planning.

9. Creation of a fellowship for female and male doctoral students devoting their thesis to gender-related issues in architecture and town planning.

Document 6, dated April 20, 2016: ‹9 Points for Parity›

overcome. Those ‹9 Points› were published in ‹Hochparterre›, along with a response by Annette Spiro.²¹ Yet, internally a bizarre silence prevailed. Over the course of the year, none of our proposed measures were adopted. No doubt, the department was going through a challenging and difficult phase, as many appointment procedures ran in parallel. But gender parity —which we had argued was fundamental to those appointments—seemed to have slipped down the agenda. «We have too few female applicants», was the Dean's rather matter-of-fact response. At the time, some of us were active in search committees for new Chairs, and so were able to gain insights into the appointment process and its underlying gender bias, from shortlisting and invitation criteria of candidates and committee members alike through to applicant evaluation, and incidents of mansplaining.

As the year drew to a close and it became clearer that none of the ‹9 Points› would see implementation, the nomination of Parity Delegates from all three faculty groups, students, assistants, and professors the only exception, we decided to organize a second Parity Talks symposium and workshop in March 2017. Again, the department supported this event from the start. The goal was to facilitate an open discussion of our proposed measures, first and foremost with all members from our department and with external experts on gender and diversity. We were eager to hear from both these groups how viable and effective they thought our suggestions would be, and to gather further support for our initiative. In four parallel roundtable discussions, each of them covering two to three measures, the ‹9 Points› were developed in more detail. The resulting annotated list of measures should now become the basis for the final set of measures that will make it in the department's Gender Action Plan.

V. «Staying with the trouble»

Friday, March 8, 2024. Last day on Hönggerberg. Morning coffee with the archivist. Rumors have been spreading, she tells me, that the Executive Board overturned the department's recommendation for a young woman to be appointed as successor of one of the outgoing female design professors. Apparently, it's been decided—another man with a busy practice is going to fill her position. There's a spontaneous walk-out from classes and studios. A leaflet by the staff and student associations is passed around the crowd that has gathered on the square in front of the building. «17% in 170 years—half a millennium to reach 50%? Parity now! Openness, Transparency, Accountability», it reads. Someone had pinned up ‹Miss Mies› and her sisters, the old Parity Talks posters. «Here we are, again», the archivist says, «standing together on International Women's Day, talking about the same thing. Denial is no longer an option.»

It would be futile to add up the countless hours, lunch meetings, and late nights spent on Parity Group work. Being critical of our institution, for most of us, was a call of duty. It meant caring for its past, present, and future. However, there were several situations in which we experienced what we affectionately came to call ‹parity fatigue›. Moments when we simply wanted to give up. Making trouble is not much fun. Especially if one's career hangs on a thin thread, employment is precarious and non-permanent, and the pressure to stay focused on one's career as a researcher and teacher, and to fulfil ever-increasing performance and output targets, keeps mounting.

Why even bother? Shouldn't we just «stop that c[rap]», as one angered male student had advised us in an email? In Trump-style capitals, he argued that «WE DON'T HAVE A GENDER PROBLEM», so «stop making problems where there is [sic] none». Yet, we knew, as many others did, that there were problems; that, contrary to the student's assertion, not «every individual, male or female, has the same opportunities to become a professor at ETH». Like many others whom we personally invited to engage in the discussion, the student chose not to participate in any of our events.

True, we did receive messages of support and expressions of sympathy, too. But were we being coopted? Had we become, without noticing it, a shining example for how well bottom up initiatives function, a fig-leaf merely covering the lack of institutional structures and the absence of decisive and sustained action from above? In an institution like our department that is itself inherently transitory, where fresh cohorts of students and assistants (typically) come and go in six-year cycles, how can one fulfil the concomitant tasks to «make trouble, to stir up potent responses […] as well as to settle troubled waters and rebuild quiet places»[22] without losing energy, momentum, knowledge, and expertise—without starting from scratch each time?

This is why, on May 3, 2017, we asked the Professor's Conference and the department's Conference the following week to vote on a proposal to introduce a Gender Action Plan in our department, and to create a Parity Board supported by the Board of Deans and department's administrative staff, whose task will be the development and implementation of this plan. Since then, it has been in their hands.

Epilogue

Isn't it surprising that urgent questions of gender and diversity at ETH Zurich have been left to individual initiatives to be addressed? How come so little was done on these matters prior to our engagement? Is institutional inertia inherent to big institutions? And what will happen now? While «making a fuss» here at the department, one can't help but think about Audre Lorde's famous phrase: «The master's tools will never dismantle the master's house.»[23] But the cynicism of that terrifying sentence must not be taken as a shutdown. It is true that many aspects in Swiss society still have to change until women will be able to take their seats at the table, starting with the way family and childcare are understood. The work undertaken by the Parity Group cannot fix that. But a discussion has been launched and there is no turning back now; change must happen.

Many signs are pointing in the right direction. Of the three fixed-term Visiting Lectureships recently awarded to young Swiss architectural firms, two include women. Moreover, a couple of open Professorships were split into four positions, allowing the appointment of An Fonteyne and Momoyo Kaijima alongside Arno Brandlhuber and Jan De Vylder. And with Anne Lacaton another internationally outstanding female architect has now become Professor for Architecture and Design, thus doubling within one year the number of Chairs held by women in the school.

1   This article (and our work more broadly) takes inspiration, among others, from Belgian philosophers Isabelle Stengers and Vinciane Despret, who – as part of a collective of female scholars – call on their colleagues to actively confront persistent injustices within and beyond academic institutions, question their careers, and examine their roles and responsibilities as women intellectuals. See: Isabelle Stengers, Vinciane Despret, ‹Women Who Make a Fuss: The Unfaithful Daughters of Virginia Woolf›, Minneapolis 2014.
2   Jane Rendell, ‹Site-writing: the architecture of art criticism›, London 2010.
3   Ibid., p. 18.
4   On the women in the professional association SIA see: Beatrice Aebi, ‹Frauen in die Kommissionen!›, in: Tec 21, no. 42 (2016), p. 24.
5   Prof. Dr. Renate Schubert and Honorata Kaczykowski-Patermann, ‹Gender Monitoring 2013/14: Departementsbericht Architektur›, https://www.ethz.ch/content/dam/ethz/associates/services/Anstellung-Arbeiten/chancengleichheit/Strategie_und_Zahlen/Monitoring%20und%20Studien/1314/1314_Gender_Monitoring_DE. Retrieved: 01.07.2017.
6   See: ‹History of women at ETH›, https://www.ethz.ch/services/en/employment-and-work/working-environment/equal-opportunities/strategie-und-zahlen/frauen-an-der-eth/geschichte-der-frauen-an-der-eth.html. Retrieved: 01.07.2017.
7   This subject will also be explored in a small contribution curated by Sarah Nichols to the main 50th anniversary exhibition ‹gta 50›, which is due to open on September 28, 2017 at ETH Zurich, Hönggerberg.
8   For the profiles of those three female professors at D-ARCH (out of sixteen at ETH during the

Beschlussvorlage Gender Action Plan des Departement Architektur

In Einklang mit den im Gender Action Plan (GAP) der ETH Zürich von Februar 2014 definierten Verantwortlichkeiten, verpflichtet sich das Departement Architektur (D-ARCH) einen GAP zu entwickeln, diesen zu präsentieren und eine jährliche interne Fortschrittskontrolle durchzuführen. Um dieser Pflicht nachzukommen, wird das D-ARCH zum Herbstsemester 2017 einen eigenen, an die spezifischen Anforderungen des Departements (»9 Punkte für die Gleichstellung«) angepassten GAP implementieren.

Zur praktischen Umsetzung dieses Beschlusses verpflichtet sich das D-ARCH:
- Zur Einrichtung eines »Parity Board«, bestehend aus Vertretern der Studierenden, Assistierenden sowie Professorinnen und Professoren. Es formuliert konkrete Zielvorgaben, Massnahmen und Mechanismen zur Verbesserung der Gleichstellung von Mann und Frau im Rahmen des GAP an unserem Departement.
- Zur jährlichen Fortschrittskontrolle, für welche die Parity Talks als bereits bestehendes Gefäss verwendet werden sollten.

In line with the responsibilities set out in the Gender Action Plan (GAP) ETH Zurich, dated February 2014, the Department of Architecture (D-ARCH) undertakes to develop and present a GAP, and to put into place appropriate mechanisms for annual progress tracking. To this end, the D-ARCH will implement a GAP that reflects the specific needs and requirements of the Department (»9 Points for Parity«) by fall semester 2017.

To facilitate practical implementation of this decision, the D-ARCH commits to:
- *The creation of a »Parity Board«, consisting of representatives of the student, assistant, and professorial body. It formulates concrete goals, measures, and monitoring mechanisms to improve the gender balance within the framework of the GAP at our Department.*
- *An annual mechanism for measuring progress, and to continuing Parity Talks as a suitable means for doing so.*

Document 7, dated May 3, 2017: ‹Proposal for the implementation of the Gender Action Plan at D-ARCH›, as voted by the Professors' Conference

mid-1990s), see: Stelle für Chancengleichheit von Mann und Frau an der ETH Zürich (ed.), ‹Wege in die Wissenschaft. Professorinnen an der ETH Zürich – 16 Portraits›, Zürich 1997. For example, Bettina Köhler, who spent a considerable amount of time at the Institute gta (however, without obtaining her PhD there), first as a Research Assistant, then as an Assistant Professor for History and Theory of Architecture then moved to a professorship at FHNW Muttenz. Maia Engeli, former Assistant Professor for Architecture and CAAD holds a professorship in Canada. Their career paths (for reasons that would require further investigation) led away from the school in the early-2000s, when Flora Ruchat-Roncati retired from her Professorship in Architecture and Design.

9 See: ‹ETH Zürich, Gender Action Plan, 2014›, https://www.ethz.ch/services/en/employment-and-work/working-environment/equal-opportunities/strategie-und-zahlen/gender-action-plan.html. Retrieved: 01.07.2017.
10 Rahel Marti, ‹«Wir haben zu wenig Bewerberinnen»›, in: Hochparterre no. 9 (2016).
11 Stengers and Despret, ‹Women Who Make A Fuss›, pp. 15–16.
12 ‹Gender Bias in Academe: An Annotated Bibliography of Important Recent Studies›, January 26, 2015, https://www.hastac.org/blogs/superadmin/2015/01/26/gender-bias-academe-annotated-bibliography-important-recent-studies. Retrieved: 01.07.2017.
13 Jules Holroyd and Jennifer Saul, ‹Will the Teaching Excellence Framework be sexist?›, in: The Guardian, April 4, 2016, https://www.theguardian.com/higher-education-network/2016/apr/04/will-the-teaching-excellence-framework-be-sexist. Retrieved: 01.07.2017.
14 ‹Architektur, die [fem.], Baukultur ist auch weiblich!›, special complementary issue with Archithese, no. 2 (2016) ‹Bildungslandschaften›.
15 http://archiparlour.org. Retrieved: 01.07.2017.
16 FAAC was founded by Ana María Léon, Tessa Paneth-Pollak, Martina Tanga, and Olga Touloumi. https://www.facebook.com/faacollaborative/. Retrieved: 01.07.2017.
17 Torsten Lange and Emily Eliza Scott, ‹Making Trouble to Stay With: Architecture and Feminist Pedagogies›, in: Field (2017) forthcoming.
18 See their research blog for further information: http://www.flora-ruchat-roncati-snf.ch. Retrieved: 01.07.2017.
19 Michael Kuratli, ‹Falsch gebaute Karriereleiter›, in: ZS – Zürcher Studierendenzeitung, 14. September 2015, http://zs-online.ch/falsch-gebaute-karriereleiter/. Retrieved: 01.07.2017.
20 ETH Equal is the organ in charge of «equal opportunities» within the ETH Zurich. However, the structure is underequipped to face the challenges ahead. With 3 part-time staff members and little budget of its own, ETH Equal appears a mere alibi. While giving the impression that gender and diversity are priorities for the institution, the structure simply does not have the means to do much more then basic monitoring and career counseling. ETH female staffs have even criticized the latter, because it appears Equal's efforts are concentrated on prepping women for job interviews rather than tackling structural discrimination and institutional core issues. For instance, Equal leaves it up to the deans of each department to implement the Gender Action Plan it drafted. It also relies extensively on private initiatives and individuals' forces within departments to push the gender and diversity agenda, partially explaining why so little progress has been achieved since its creation in 1991 (as Frauenanlaufstelle).
21 Marti, 2016.
22 Ibid.
23 Audre Lorde, ‹The Master's Tools Will Never Dismantle the Master's House›, in: Cherríe Moraga, Gloria Anzaldúa (eds.), This Bridge Called My Back: Writings by Radical Women of Color, New York 1983, pp. 94–101.

Involuntary Critique
GruppoTorto

Scrutiny over urban transformation is no longer restricted to authorities, artistic or intellectual production but can be triggered by a large group of people. It can be considered a historical change in which the crowd gains major importance.

The artists Lucie de Barbuat and Simon Brodbeck present throughout ‹Silent World›[1] (fig.a) a series of images of extreme emptiness and surreal reverie. Each image is created from cutting apart multiple stills from digital videos of the world's busiest intersections, avoiding the pixels that contain fragments of people. By draining the images from all traces of human life, Lucie & Simon drained the depicted public spaces from their most intrinsic component—the people themselves. By doing so, the artists conceived contemplative cityscapes, which are by no means mere urban utopias, but rather accurate depictions of a threatening future scenario. The concentration of people can determine the success or failure of a public space. Seeing usually crowded places in such empty conditions leaves us with a feeling of alienation up to the point that we can barely recognise them. It is therefore not surprising that representations of future urban interventions are commonly crowded with people.

The described alienating feeling can be linked in various ways to the increasing impact of the digital realm on our lives and our behaviour. Certainly, «cultures, places and spaces, are much more resistant, and (...) are thus not so easily abolished».[2] On the other hand, there are a significant number of activities (e.g. social integration, political debate[3]) which are shifting away from the physical public space to the digital realm. Even if tourist migrations might partially hide this imminent process of decline, citizens retreat more and more from public life. Are we facing a crisis of the public space due to collective renunciation?

In order to get to the heart of the matter, it is important to reconsider how the term of ‹public space› could be defined in the first place: its definition depends very much on which of its constituents (‹public› or ‹space›) we focus on. It is either the ‹public› part which implies the social sphere (as to say without society there is no public space) or the ‹space› part which presumes physical definition with buildings, objects, landscape etc. (without architecture there is no public space). Public space can be defined as the main conceptual component of the city, the most complex habitat of a species, as well as the most visible representation of material culture. Both described notions (‹public› and ‹space›) are heavily shaken by the new trends of technology and need to be reassessed.

Revolution without revolutionaries

As technology starts to embrace every aspect of our daily life, also the relationship between the citizen and the city changes radically. While only a few decades ago it was very difficult to collect useful information concerning the city (number of inhabitants, the quality of life, the social issues of particular neighbourhoods), nowadays, the same kind of information can be gathered in a few seconds and even be live-broadcasted by the citizens themselves.[4]

The technologies we are surrounded by are only a glimpse into an endless series of inventions and innovations: we are standing on the shoulders of giants such as the development of telecommunications, transportation and computers which started a long time ago. Among the more recent innovations we can identify the internet of things, artificial intelligence and the ascent of digital networks (clouds etc.). Though these are still too new to derive reliable predictions, it is, however, possible to trace two different tendencies that could dominate the future of our cities. The first follows the mentioned shift, whereby communication, exchange of goods, political manifestation, and other forms of exchange largely move into the virtual. Internet becomes «the public space of the 21st century»[5]. The second assumes a turning point in which public space retains its main functions and is enriched (punctually or area-wide) by digital technology via ‹smart› objects. The digital realm turns into a superimposed layer on top of the existing. In this way public space becomes ‹accessible› again, thanks to new gateways, which are based on the exchange of information. In contrast to former systems appearing physically in our environment (fig. b), the new gateways are completely invisible. The borders between the physical and digital worlds become increasingly blurred and ‹smart cities›

fig.a: Brodbeck & De Barbuat, ‹Madison square› from the series ‹Silent World›, Baryta print, 160x210cm, 2009

fig.b: ‹Stockholm Telephone Tower›, 1913, Courtesy Tekniska Museet

witness the genesis of ‹smart citizens›[6]. The two described tendencies would lead to completely different outcomes regarding the role of the planer: the first which assumes the retreat of activities from public space would lead to the entire loss of an important field of activity. The second, i.e. the superimposing of a new layer, would bring on the contrary new challenges as well as new tasks. As a result, we are confronted with a radical crossroads in the planning field that can turn out to be existential. In this way we can assert that the public space can only persist with the implementation of the digital.

One of the most striking aspects of the second scenario is that scrutiny over urban transformation is no longer restricted to authorities, artistic or intellectual production but can be triggered by a large group of people. It can be considered a historical change in which the crowd gains major importance. By disclosing our behaviour, we voice critique by the simplest actions and choices: choosing one parking lot instead of another, sitting on a bench, riding the bike to work, etc. By choosing and reacting to the environment, the act of living turns itself into an involuntary critique of the city. Surely there has always been a certain degree of such critique. The main difference is that the critique is nowadays accessible throughout endless dataflow.

In order to understand the meaning of the expression ‹involuntary critique›, it is crucial to have a closer look at the term ‹critique› itself. Coming from Ancient Greek word ‹krino›, it stands for ‹to sort›, or ‹to separate›, also translated as ‹to decide›[7]. In this way ‹critique› can be related to a judgement succeeded by an act of decision. It can be argued that the act of such ‹decision› is the manifestation of ‹critique› itself and as such it does not require a precise receiver or a particular system of evaluation. The reception of such ‹critique› by the possibilities of digital networks allows for an increase in power on behalf of citizens and thus induces a slow transformation of the city. Surely, on one hand, the process of evaluation is necessary to sort out inaccuracies and false assumptions, as well as to devise concrete strategies and develop political agendas. On the other hand, the evaluation process is unable to constitute ‹critique› per se, but relies on acting performers.

Users or consumers?

At this point of time the amount of collected data is immense and keeps growing constantly. Therefore it is not only the question of who is willing to interpret ‹big data›, but who is actually able to deal with them. In the last decade large media firms managed to develop a dominant position in data evaluation and started to develop commercial schemes: whilst smartphones have already become a notorious, widespread tool of data collection, Google released an innovative product in

fig.c: Banksy, ‹One Nation Under CCTV›, Graffiti, London 2008

2012[8], called ‹Google Glass›. The use of the new product offers a good example of the mechanisms that lead to commercial application of involuntary critique. The concept behind this wearable device is quite simple: you no longer need a screen to access the digital world. The reality becomes the screen: right when you turn on your Google Glass, the digital world is directly imposed on your visual field and you can interact with it, both in a digital and a physical way. Throughout different apps you can access cloud services such as photos, calendar, contacts, maps, emails, text messaging—just to name a few. By the provided camera and audio input, calls can be turned into so called ‹hangouts›, which use screen sharing and geo-localisation.[9] Subsequently, an algorithm searches for recurring patterns and preferences. On this base, users will receive commercial suggestions on all their cloud connected devices and data are turned into a profitable source for advertising business.

The sheer amount of information coming from the most private sphere of the performing individual is so extensive that The Telegraph described Google Glass as «Orwellian surveillance with fluffier branding», specifying that, «You don't own the data, you don't control the data and you definitely don't know what happens to the data. Put another way—what would you say if instead of it being Google Glass, it was Government Glass?»[10] The described controversy about privacy (fig. c) took on a whole new dynamic in which users of Glass were insulted as ‹Glassholes›[11] and threatened in broad daylight. It seems, indeed, that facing public life with a camera on eye level has exceeded the limits of acceptance. Indeed, in the beginning of 2015, only after a couple of years, sale was shut down for end-users.[12] The comeback in the professional market is deliberately avoiding to interference with public spaces and is currently in progress.

Functions like gathering and socializing are associated increasingly with commercial features. It is not surprising if London's first ‹Smart street›[13] was conceived in order to improve shopping experience and not the quality of their public space. Indeed people who walk on the energy-generating pavement are not rewarded with a real improvement in the quality of the space, but mostly with discounts at the stores they are just walking past. The mentioned examples show how companies mainly pursue commercial aims; due to economic and technical reasons it can be stated that involuntary critique is therefore mostly registered and used for financial purposes.

To build with bits and bytes

The question that arises is whether there are other, non-commercial ways to deal with involuntary critique. How could urbanism and architecture benefit from its potential? Whilst most of the data is processed by big private companies, there are more and more

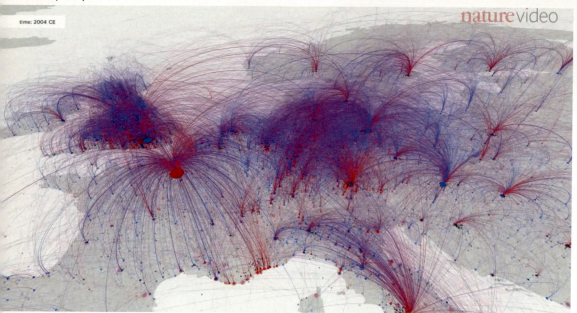

fig.d: Maximilian Schich, Mauro Martino with Nature Video, ‹Birth and Death›, Screenshot from ‹Charting Culture›, 2014

disciplines that gather involuntary critique following ‹public aims› and collective interest, among them town planning and welfare services.

One of the emerging applications is the creation of ‹Data Urbanism›[14] which is a new tool that is based on the visualisation of scientific data enriched by dynamic, user-emitted information. This approach allows, according to leading online platforms like ‹morphocode›[15], a «critical evaluation of active policies and city services by transforming otherwise hidden patterns into visual arguments». «Data we generate on a daily basis, either directly or as a by-product of our social activities» is taken as opportunity due to the fact that it «is often associated with contextual meta-information about location, usage and people». This underlines the potential of the link between people's choices taken as valuable critique. The way out of the difficult implications of privacy issues is hereby to turn individual data into anonymous group patterns. To achieve representative results, data urbanists clearly opt in favour of «making data visible, accessible and actionable».[16] With only a few parameters provided by user data, it is possible to come to intriguing conclusions about main urban factors. As such there is the work of Schich (et al.)[17] which points out the growth and decline of urban areas simply by tracing the birth and death date of ‹recorded people›[18]. Their results reflect the idea that the people's decision where to live is already a significant critique on the opportunities they aspire for. Throughout their written report and a video project (fig. d) entitled ‹Charting Culture›[19], Schich (et al.) have turned simple data into a «sociologists' and anthropologists' study [about] the growth and evolution of human culture.»[20]

Another relevant example of Data Urbanism as a tool to benefit from involuntary critique is the project of the Danish architect Jan Gehl who in 1993 began to assess the quality of public space and public life in Melbourne.[21] The study was reassessed in 2005 and another decade later, in 2015. Throughout this long period of time his team was able to point out the success of urban strategies in Melbourne which aimed at «long-term commitment to increasing the levels of pedestrian accessibility.»[22] The more data is available from acting individuals in the city, the more precise is the evaluation. Data Urbanism represents in general a valuable example which fosters the public aim and can devise a chance for urban planning guidelines.

From ‹act› to ‹enact›

Dealing with possible applications of involuntary critique leads inevitably to the question whether ‹critique› needs consciousness and intention in order to become an effective tool for urban transformation. What would happen if involuntary critique was turned into deliberate choice—shifting from the notion of ‹act› to ‹enact›?

The consequence would generally be that citizens would feel more responsible for their environment[23] i.e. they are more aware of issues around them and they start thinking about pros and cons of top-down decisions. Throughout the possibility of expressing critique without big effort, citizens could give voice to their needs and desires. Engagement hereby plays an important role since «meeting the desires of communities can only happen when citizens are engaged in the shaping of their cities.»[24] The idea to implement participatory mechanisms in the city is surely not new. Architects and urban planners from the 60s and 70s (fig. e) put this topic at the top of their agenda and pushed the idea to its theoretical limits. The novelty about it is

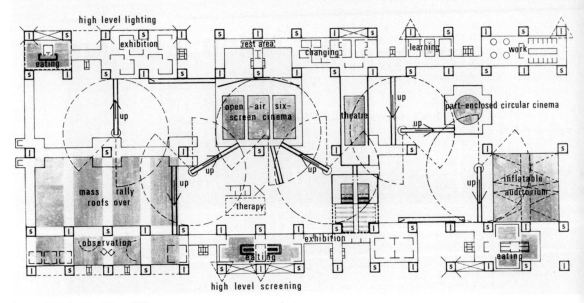

fig.e: Cedric Price, ‹Fun Palace›, 1961

the possibility of individuals to interact via modern mobile devices in broader digital networks. The ultimate step would be hereby the idea to translate critique into architectural and urban programmes. The question is how is it possible to achieve this with the new means of the digital age?

At this point we set foot on unknown territory where we need to pursue more speculative concepts. Generally we can see a potential for the emergence of voluntary critique in the combination of the two tendencies: ‹Big Data Collection› and ‹Participatory Planning›. Both exist but do not work together. The aim would be to take the immediacy and efficiency of the first and bring it together with the commitment and engagement of the second.

The described combination could arise from reinforcing awareness on the side of the performing individual and from developing suitable evaluation tools. To move from involuntary to voluntary critique, people's consciousness is needed. Only people with a sharpened awareness could be regarded as actively engaged. The evaluation of the critique is by far the biggest part of the challenge. There is the technical part in which appropriate systems need to be available for processing the Big Data. Moreover, there must be a meta-process, a sort of ‹evaluation of the evaluation› which ensures the right framework. The reason for granting a critical instance is that behaviour patterns cannot be considered a ‹volonté generale›[25].

In the not too distant future the ‹Internet of Things› will be just a reminiscence of the past. The ‹Internet of Living Things›[26] will have gained far more importance. Individuals deliberately choose to record their daily acts within automatic feedback-recognising systems (e.g. voice, eye-movement recognition). In this way the above mentioned act of choosing one particular parking lot instead of another, is turned into a ‹judgemental statement›. The collected and processed information could be further shared and discussed in common platforms. Planners enter into the digital discussion and can benefit from the processed information. In consequence, the IoLT starts having not only digital but physical impact on streets, squares and parks. Public space would thus regain a collective value newly accessed by digital means, eventually being enriched by them.

As planners we witness a striking impact of the digital not only in our lives but also in our field of profession: public space, as we are used to perceive it, is radically changing. This can be regarded as an important opportunity rather than a setback: apart from commercial endeavours which suggest an impoverishment of the public space, we can see a big opportunity to work with involuntary critique of citizens through digital networks. The potential lies on the one hand in the pursuit of public interest and on the other hand in the application to urbanism. The design and management of public space itself ends up gaining further value. We believe that this value is reinforced in the moment when performing individuals become more conscious of their involuntary critique turning into a deliberate, collaborative choice. These considerations lead us to think about new ways of interaction for citizens via digital tools. It must be carefully handled in order not to fall into ‹demagogic› use of people's opinions. What makes a participatory design valuable, besides the planning results, is probably the effect of the process itself, that is, citizens' interest, engagement and action. It can be argued, therefore, that digital means could trigger a behavioural change which redefines public space both in its social as well as territorial dimension.

In Saint-Exupéry's ‹The Little Prince› we learn an important lesson about responsibility which applies also to the involvement of citizens in public space: As the fox said to the Little Prince «People have forgotten this truth. But you mustn't forget it. You become responsible forever for what you've tamed. You're responsible for your rose.» That is to say, that involvement has to be bound to effort and dedication which goes beyond mere expression of opinion.

   The digital world has plunged public space into an existential crisis but it could also be the key for its survival.

1 Brodbeck & De Barbuat, ‹Silent World›, 2009-2010, available at: http://www.brodbeckdebarbuat.com, Retrieved: 21 July 2017.
2 Manuel Castells, ‹Public space in the information society›, 1994, in: ‹Ciutat real, ciutat ideal: significat i funció a l'espai urbà modern›, 1994, Centre de Cultura Contemporània de Barcelona (Ed.).
3 Toloudi Zenovia, ‹Are We in the Midst of a Public Space Crisis?›, in: ‹The Conversation›, 7 June 2016, available at: www.theconversation.com/are-we-in-the-midst-of-a-public-space-crisis-56124.
4 A number of these advanced systems of collecting data can be found in the work of the Senseable City Lab at MIT, guided by Carlo Ratti.
5 Hillary Clinton, Speech in Washington, 15 February 2011, available at: http://www.kuna.net.kw/ArticlePrintPage.aspx?id=2145484&language=en, Retrieved: 20 July 2017
6 Carlo Ratti and Maria Grazia Mattei, ‹Smart City, Smart Citizen›, Milano, EGEA, 2014.
7 Alain Badiou, ‹The Critique of Critique: Critical Theory as a New Access to the Real›, Transcription of Lecture made by Duane Rousselle, 2014.
8 Post on Google Plus, 2012, available at: https://plus.google.com/+-GoogleGlass/posts/aKymsANgWBD, Retrieved: 19.7.2017.
9 Evan Dashevsky and Mark Hachman, ‹16 Cool Things You Can Do With Google Glass›, in: ‹PCMAG›, 15 April 2014.
10 Nick Pickles, ‹Google Glass: Orwellian surveillance with fluffier branding›, 19 March 2013, available at: http://www.telegraph.co.uk/technology/google/9939933/Google-Glass-Orwellian-surveillance-with-fluffier-branding.html.
11 Matthias Huber, ‹Google fürchtet Glassholes›, in: ‹Süddeutsche Zeitung›, 19 February 2014, available at: http://www.sueddeutsche.de/digital/datenbrille-google-fuerchtet-glassholes-1.1892992.
12 Roland Lindner, ‹Datenbrille: Google Glass Versucht Comeback›, 19 July 2017, in: ‹Frankfurt Allgemeine Zeitung›, available at: www.faz.net/aktuell/wirtschaft/datenbrille-google-glass-versucht-comeback-15113228.html.
13 Barbara Eldredge, Barbara, ‹World›s First ‹Smart Street› Turns Footsteps into Energy›, in: ‹Curbed›, 5 July 2017, available at: www.curbed.com/2017/7/5/15921382/smart-street-london-bird-street-pavegen.
14 Morphocode, https://morphocode.com/blog, Retrieved: 22.7.2017.
15 Idem.
16 Idem
17 Maximilian Schich, Caoming Song, Yong-Yeol Ahn u.a., ‹A Network Framework of Cultural History›, in: ‹Science›, American Association for the Advancement of Science (Ed.), 1 August 2014, available at: www.science.sciencemag.org/content/345/6196/558.
18 Based on datasets from freebase.com, Shutdown August 2016.
19 Maximilian Schich, Caoming Song, Yong-Yeol Ahn u.a., ‹Charting Cultures›, https://www.youtube.com/watch?v=4gIhRkCcD4U&feature=youtu.be, Retrieved: 22 July 2017.
20 Description of Report, in: ‹Science›, available at: http://science.sciencemag.org/content/345/6196/558.
21 Jan Gehl Architects, ‹Melbourne Miracle›, available at: http://gehlpeople.com/cases/melbourne-australia.
22 Morphocode, https://morphocode.com/blog, Retrieved: 22.7.2017.
23 Chris Walker and Stacey Rapp, ‹Local Initiatives Support Corporation›, available at: www.lisc.org.
24 Participatory Urbanism 2017, available at: http://urbanite.people-friendly-cities.eu/about/, Retrieved: 20.7.2017.
25 Iring Fetscher, ‹Historisches Wörterbuch der Philosophie›, Basel: Schwabe (Ed.), 1971-2007, Bd. 11, Sp. 1141 ff.
26 Term coined by Anthropologist Genevieve Bell, Vice President and Fellow at Intel, Corporate Sensing & Insights group.

L'Ensemble et l'Unité: a tale of two apartments
Philippe Nathan and Mélissa Vrolixs

The double height attracts us. Like an impressionist painting, the windows frame Marseille's ‹quartier nord› slabs, brightly lit by the evening sun. They sit peacefully between a sea of trees, the hilly backdrop and a dark-blue sky. A picturesque scene dissimulating the violence of social instability and unrest, in which the role of architecture is still a topic of debate.

fig. a

L'Ensemble de La Tourette[1] and the Unité d'Habitation[2] were simultaneously erected in Marseille as part of the post-war program of the ‹Reconstruction›. During a visit of those seemingly antagonistic architectures, curiosity arose after an unexpected reaction by students. What triggered their enthusiasm for the barely acknowledged over the canon? Did History bypass a major figure of architecture? This essay aims at a suspension of criticism in favor of a tale. Two women, non-initiated in architecture but experts in the art of living it, opened their doors and proposed a different lens to look at those masterpieces. A diptych of two dwellings reveals the relativity of architectural critique and its consequences on architectural education.

«L'âme d'un appartement, c'est la femme.»[3]

Moment & Situation (fig. a)

There it was. That view, onto the Mediterranean Sea and the ferries that link Marseille to Algiers, slowly entering or leaving the harbor. That round table, dressed in a faded napkin, on which Monique had carefully placed 5 fruits in a centered porcelain bowl, next to spectacles indicating a possibility of different perspectives for those willing to confront an insisting setting sun.

Yet we came to realize that it was more than the combination of an impressive view and well-positioned furniture, more than the dialectics of eternal landscape and ‹nature morte› that affected us. All these elements conspired together to form a moment, a situation, that had moved us three months ago during our first seminar week visit[4], and we came to understand how architecture, in its humblest expressions, made such experiences possible.

Hatch (fig. b)

As we rush up the steps clad in broken Cassis stone leftovers, the temperature of the southwest-facing staircase raises one floor at a time. Monique took the elevator, and we don't want to let her wait. Arriving on the 4th floor, she decides to take us up one more flight of stairs. There, on an intermediate ‹palier›, she nostalgically indicates the waste disposal system, which was previously shared by 4 apartments but had been abandoned for hygiene reasons. She doubts that claim. The archaic system, a cast-iron hatch linked to a large pipe, enabled to directly clear domestic garbage from every split-level, at close range of 4 apartments, without needing to walk all the way to the bin, and back. It represented a commodity that simplified daily life, especially for elderly people. Monique leads us back down.

Handle (fig. c)

Against all expectations, and in contrast to the staircase, the apartment we enter is fresh. Monique turns left to the kitchen. «I didn't clean the windows.» Yet the awe-inspiring scene just seems to gain in strength. Facing southwest, a vertical window frames the distant horizon drawn by the Mediterranean. Perret by the book. The glass is indeed fogged by the salt and the wooden framework discloses scars of its battles against the harsh mistral. Monique's apartment is located in one of the 5 buildings composing Pouillon's La Tourette Ensemble. This particular building, a 150 meter long, 9 floors high slab, had been drawn and built to protect the ensemble from the rough winds. Judging from Monique's kitchen windows, the building must do its job. Yet it all boils down to the handle.

The urban genius has no effect if local domestic demands are not met. In Marseille, this means amongst others, being able to ventilate. In order to handle the various scales of stakes, Pouillon first drew traversing apartments, opening as much to the sea on the southwest as to the city on the northeast. Secondly, he designed a lever that allows keeping both wings of the window in a fixed position, opening a split that spreads from floor to ceiling. This mere 10cm vertical slit, when reproduced on both sides of the building, enables the best possible aeration while resisting the brute force of the Mistral.

Loggia—laundry, gentrification sacrifice (fig. d)

Behind the kitchen sink, a door gives access to the laundry. According to Monique, each apartment was originally equipped with such a ‹buanderie› facing the sea, recessed in a loggia. This layout made it possible for clothes to dry quickly, but above all to manage these household tasks in the most generous of conditions. Yet it ultimately led many (new) owners to use the space differently, and drastically change the layout of the apartments. The sacrifices of gentrification.

Opposite to the kitchen door, a second door gives access to one of the three bedrooms. The loggia can thus act as a second circulation, parallel to the night hall. A disposition that enables additional usage scenarios of the apartment.

Distributing flyers for Macron (fig. e)

At first Monique was reluctant to meet us, and skeptical about an article on her or her apartment, claiming that she had become rather busy, and rather political recently. She sees herself obliged to prevent Mélanchon from coming to more power. Apart from the radicalism of his positions, she asserts that the ideas have been tested, and failed, and that now we have to move on. And so tomorrow, she plans to distribute flyers for Macron, at a nearby school. A pile of blue «La République En Marche» handouts are waiting patiently next to the entrance door.

Quite coherently, Monique's apartment is no manifesto, no experimental attempt at revolutionizing housing, but its dimensions, its layout, materials and pragmatic details make it a 60-year-old contemporary adaptive tool for living, for life. With capacities, and constraints. Pouillon's architecture does not seem to impose positions, habits, or predefine usages. Rather, in a stiff system primarily

fig. c

fig. b

fig. d

fig. e

fig. f

designed and streamlined to fit the logics of construction and economy, the architecture appears to facilitate different lifestyles. Thus, the apartment stands as a liberal take on organizing one's dwelling and household, one's family or post-family life. Could we understand Monique's apartment as the spatial application of what the blue flyers we stumbled upon, claim? An implicit politics of dwelling? The architecture is at once conventional, generic, qualitative and robust enough to permit a continuous flexibility, matching the evolutions inherent to life, and adapting to the ever-changing existences of its inhabitants.

With its three bedrooms, a couple might live in an overly generous luxury, yet a luxury that will not be troubled by the presence of one or two children or visiting friends. The same counts for co-housing, multi-generational living or renting out rooms to strangers, i.e. Airbnb, as in Monique's case. The apartment acts as a host to conditions of financial wealth, demographic growth and contemporary small-scale businesses. According to Monique, space becomes the true luxury in a non-luxurious dwelling.

Everything feels square (fig. f)

This capacity is made possible as much by the size of the dwelling, as by the dimensions, proportions and organization of the different spaces. Just as on the urban scale of the ensemble, upon entry in the apartment one first penetrates an open space articulating between kitchen on the left, living room on the right, sleeping rooms and night corridor in the front. All these functions interlock on the entrance sequence, which can be split from the kitchen by concealed sliding doors, and from the living room by an accordion door, making it a perfect buffer zone in-between functions, or an entrance and circulation hall of the ‹über-traditional› French apartment with split functions in separate rooms. The generous traversing space with its qualities of natural lighting and its capacity of full ventilation might be lost, but is in fact traded for the additional potential of co-habitation between people and lifestyles. The simultaneity of uses is only made possible by the dimensions and proportions of the different spaces. «Everything feels square» notes Monique, who explains that the spaces do not impose a sense of direction and/or use, but rather open up a field of possibilities on how to furnish, inhabit and use the rooms.

And so the architecture withstands not only the harsh climate conditions of mistral winds, salty rains and violent sun, but also and foremost private evolutions and societal shifts, from family to uberisation.

Prophecies and Proficiencies (fig. g)

fig. g

All this comes at the expense of a plan that looks at first sight less clean, less rigorous, less radical, less exciting. But for Pouillon, the plan is merely a medium carrying a message of construction, not an artifact of seduction at first sight. At La Tourette, squares glide and intersect, liberate loggias or create potential corridors and ‹antichambres›. He who did not draw for the pilot but for the pedestrian, seems to have considered the domestic sequence as much as the urban structure. The sensitive reading of domestic practices and the humble architectural interpretation of those diverse applications and behavior patterns, makes Monique's Pouillon apartment an inspiring example of a kind of sustainability. The architect chose not to project a model lifestyle. Pouillon's proficiency lies in not venturing into prophecy. His system—the structural grid, the building depths, the spaces' dimensions and proportions along with its materialization, consisting amongst others of load-bearing facades built in concrete cast in natural stone formwork, concrete bloc interior walls, cement-tiles and massive wooden window-frames—limits all superfluous application and use of easily degrading materials. Pouillon's systematical approach to architecture answered to quicker, cheaper, better. Yet his investments and investigations in cost calculations, stone cutting techniques, concrete formworks or contractor negotiations, have a hard time making their way into our textbooks. Nevertheless, the market value of his production proves him right. Post-mortem.

Monique witnesses how the population at La Tourette slowly changes. She voices how younger, wealthier residents replace the original inhabitants, most of whom traded their desolate houses, that were to be demolished, for dwellings at La Tourette.

The ensemble: living together, apart. (fig. h)

fig. h

In accordance with Monique's current socio-political convictions, neither the ensemble nor the apartment imposes a collective lifestyle. The La Tourette ensemble is conceived as a piece and a part of the city. For its individual residents, it works with its surrounding context and functions and does not attempt to create an autonomous urban entity. Yet is also illustrates the limitations of such an attitude: the critical mass of apartments relies on an certain number of circulation systems, distributing merely 2 apartments per floor, and increasing both building and maintenance costs. Furthermore, the distribution of apartments into a multitude of single blocs, even if part of a larger urban whole, splits the rather considerable ensemble population into small fractions of individuals, who will not benefit of additional, shared services or commodities.

The architect, who was briefly a member of the communist party, before pulling back in a violent way, appears to dodge all form of doctrine, of political dogma. What counted for him was to build a critical mass of dwellings, fast, cheap, better. The lack of ideological concept for collective and community, other than the spatial quality of the ensemble, might indicate an opportunistic stance to make the project politically feasible. But as it came to existence, this lack still marks the project, La Tourette as a place, a home, appealing to the broadest range of citizens, as political animals, able to afford it. As such, with regard to the individual versus the collective, Pouillon's La Tourette seems to adhere to Ayn Rand's definition of freedom: «To ask nothing. To expect nothing. To depend on nothing.»[5]

High heels & expectations (fig. i)

The mistral is blowing hard this late afternoon. We are waiting on the deck of the renowned restaurant «Le Ventre de l'Architecte». The sea far off and the trees beneath us seem to dance under the afternoon sun. Dominique arrives: high heels and red leather jacket. Her glasses remind us of something; she wears the brown model Lucie 131 of Caroline Abram, same as Monique. Two women, two owners, both passionate about the architecture they inhabit, wear the same glasses. Pure coincidence?

She just came back from a weekend in Syracuse, where she was shocked by the negligence by which people deal with historic monuments. «When I see how people are harassing me here for a double-glazed instead of a simple-glazed window!» Dominique is the owner of the Hotel Le Corbusier as well as an apartment on the second floor. She arrived 14 years ago, without any knowledge or interest for Le Corbusier. Now she is one of his greatest admirers and advocates.

L'Ensemble et l'Unité: a tale of two apartments

fig. 1

fig. k

fig. l

Strange familiarity, architecture and emancipation (fig. j)

«Why is it working so well? Because the human being was his core concern. Beyond housing, he proposed a lifestyle. He liberated the women! The soul of an apartment is the woman. It is the family. He freed the woman from domestic slavery and conceived this Unité d'habitation for the workingwoman, the modern wife. With the help of Charlotte Perriand, he transformed the emancipation of women into something real.» It's difficult to keep pace. Following both her walk and her words is ambitious. Dominique rushes out of the restaurant over to the letterboxes to the lifts. Out of the lift, into the dark and low corridor. 45 steps, we stop at an orange door. She lets us in, natural light at last. We're in a stranger's home, feeling strangely familiar. Like bumping into a famous person.

The double height attracts us. Like an impressionist painting, the windows frame Marseille's ‹quartier nord› slabs, brightly lit by the evening sun. They sit peacefully between a sea of trees, the hilly backdrop and a dark-blue sky. A picturesque scene dissimulating the violence of social instability and unrest, in which the role of architecture is still a topic of debate.

Making a case (fig. k)

Dominique gets right down to business: during the visit of her apartment, she will demonstrate all the domestic wonders built for the family and according to her, especially the women. «Everything is done to relieve the woman in her daily gestures.» The apartment is dissected down to its smallest details. Exhibits of evidence: the ice and groceries box at the entrance, the door which opens left in order to veil a part of the kitchen to the entering guests, the piece of furniture between the kitchen and the living room high enough to hide the working surface but low enough to let the housewife participate in the discussion, the stairs easy to walk up and down without having to watch one's steps, the fixed changing table with drawers one can close with the knees, the children's shower with the switch on the exterior ensuring control of the length of time for the shower…

The central hall on the first floor, where the stairs land and give access to all rooms, this space, which sits in the middle of the very deep and narrow unit, without any natural light, feels surprisingly comfortable. Boarded by simple but smart built-in furniture and the kids' shower under the shape of a plug-in cell, it demonstrates what architecture of scale jumps can fulfil. From the urban right down to the furniture, and we come to discover the latter in all its latitude. The case is made, evidence provided.

An architect's choreography (fig. l)

«If you want to be a great architect, think first of the happiness of people living in your apartments. Le Corbusier wanted the people to take care of themselves. Proposing separate private bathrooms for parents and children at this time… it is extraordinary! I stem from a working-class environment, I still had to groom in the kitchen. This Unité d'Habitation really reflects the adage: a healthy soul in a healthy body.» Dominique tries to balance the architect's fascist reputation with his hygienist ambitions and achievements. She levels his megalomaniac attitude with the ergonomics and the attention to practical detail. A trained choreography: Dominique dances the Modulor. She spreads and lifts her arms, sits, leans, points out. No luxury but a real quality of the space and its fittings; Dominique keeps repeating: «Tout ce qu'il faut, mais rien que ce qu'il faut !» According to her, those flats are like an ‹haute couture› dress; so successful and

fig. j

perfectly cut it doesn't need laces or flounces. To understand and feel it, one must live in it. That's why despite the constant advice to turn her hotel into a luxury boutique, she resists: «I want this place to remain accessible to everybody. To experience Le Corbusier's spaces shouldn't be a luxury, it is a necessary experience for so many young architects. You cannot imagine my joy when I see a Japanese student going into raptures when he discovers his cellule!»

She demonstrates the sliding door between her guest-room and her son's bedroom. We notice the hearts drawn with chalk on the door as she pulls it open. «They called the Unité ‹la maison du fada›, and this is why: Corbusier wanted children to draw on the walls of their dwelling. Unimaginable in pre '68 France!»

Mutiny on the Unité (fig. m)

Much to her great disappointment, more and more Airbnb are opening into the Unité. According to her, it is in total contradiction to the spirit of the place: there's no exchange with the visitors, sometimes they even find the key in the box outside the flat and don't meet the owner. «Airbnb is making tax fraud official! People renting their flat do not pay any social security contributions and kill the life of the place: by buying a flat without living in it, one does not participate in the communitarian life of the Unité. Don't misunderstand me, I am right-wing politically orientated, I run this hotel also to earn my living. But everything here is made to live in harmony together. Today, the Unité has found a good balance between individualism and the community. The fact that people are owners ensures a good care of the building, because they feel invested.»

fig. m

L'unité sits in the landscape as a ship, barely touching the ground. Listening to Dominique, one can sense a suggestion of treason, or mutiny. A fragile equilibrium. Contemporary societal shifts affect the project, which aimed beyond pure architecture. The prophesized domestic dematerialization might make the original apartment layouts more contemporary and coherent to daily life again, while the current ‹uberisation› clashes with the collective and several of the implemented functions.

Social condenser (fig. n)

fig. n

Inside an apartment community life is facilitated too; children and parents both have their territories. Her son, preparing his baccalaureate upstairs, bursts into the living room, provoking a couple of questions: «Are you working or listening to music? Did you order something? I found this in the mailbox. Is it shoes again?» The latter goes to the concierge, on the ground floor, to retrieve the parcel. This post service is only one among many commodities offered to the residents[6]. On the flat roof, the spirit of Lilette Ripert, first headmistress of the nursery school, is still present. «Can you imagine how incredibly comfortable it must have been for the mothers at that time to simply bring their children to the nursery school by taking the elevator? Le Corbusier was really a visionary.»

These different commodities and added services are only possible because of the critical mass of inhabitants in the Cité Radieuse. On a daily basis, all must cross a similar long dark corridor, the same hall and use the same elevators or stairs, and all can benefit from the rooftop terrace, concierge and postal service, amongst others. It raises questions on the balance between program and the standards of spatial quality. Something clearly had to give in order to provide additional experiences or services. L'Unité stands quietly as an argument against our frenzy of norms and standards. A political whisper to investigate, to dare the specific, to deal with the costs.

L'Ensemble et l'Unité: a tale of two apartments

Dominique speculates that the architect designed the rooms that form her hotel today as a set of additional rooms to be shared between residents, according to specific, punctual needs. «Le Corbusier understood well that having a guest room is a tremendous loss of space. It is empty most of the time and ends up with everything we don't want to see in the apartment. With the hotel, our visitors can have their independence and a good quality service. It is just more simple and comfortable for everybody.» A visionary takes on contemporary questions of property and the benefits of sharing. We're halfway out of the apartment. Dominique gets a call from the hotel and rushes back to her fridge to check if she has some spare cheese to bring up to the kitchen. We try to keep the cat in. Anecdotic detail: the doormat is recessed in the hardwood floor. The cat doesn't care. We leave.

«Look, one more wonder. The dark atmosphere produced by the soft lighting of the corridor makes people speak very quietly. Like this, one doesn't disturb the neighbours. It is also an excellent tranquilizer after a long day of work before reaching the family cell. A moment of procession in the calm… living at the Unité is definitely on the edge of living a mystical experience.» Back in the lift, chats with other inhabitants and visitors arise: «Oh, you are also attending the yoga class on the roof? Yes, this teacher is so great. I am attending his class on Saturday morning… With this wind I hope you won't fly away!»

Seminal Architecture (fig. o)

Somewhere between the anecdotic small talk and the mystical, between exposed concrete facades and cardboard interior walls, somewhere between ‹pilotis› and rooftop terrace, between bright double heights and dark corridors. An architecture that may have become seminal, not only through the obsessive propaganda of its author, but through its consideration and understanding of life as ‹in-between›. An ‹in-between› that can never be better grasped than by looking through the eyes of the inhabitant.

1 Fernand Pouillon (1912-1986).
2 Le Corbusier (1887-1965).
3 Dominique Girardin during the visit of her apartment in Marseille on the 06.06.2017.
4 « Pouillonism », Marseille and Aix-en-Provence, 20-24.03.2017 by Studio Swinnen.
5 Rand Ayn, ‹The Fountainhead›, United States 1943.
6 Restaurant, hotel, collective services, workshops, offices, service staff accommodation, …

Figures a-n: Philippe Nathan, Marseille 2017.
Figure o: Mélissa Vrolixs, 2017.

fig. o

RHINOCEROS: I believe that the moment is at hand when by a paranoid advance of the mind it will be possible to systematize confusion and completely disregard reality.[7]

Neunzehn Tage ohne Denken
Metaxia Markaki

Characters:
Narrator,
Delirious,
New York,
Rhinoceros,
The Logician*

ACT ONE

NARRATOR: «I want to talk to you about something that you never heard. I will narrate a story about something that you haven't yet seen. I want to stand here, in front of you, and claim something that maybe you don't see; in a language that maybe you don't understand.

And you cannot but listen and at the end … believe me.»

ACT TWO

On 20 May 1515, an Indian rhinoceros arrived at the port of Lisbon. The rhinoceros, that an Indian sultan sent as gift to the King of Portugal, was the first living example of the species seen in Europe since Roman times.

Few people saw the tropical beast and witnessed its mythical existence, before it would be packed up again in a ship and get lost chained in a shipwreck off the coast of Italy.

At around the same time of its arrival, a letter of unknown authorship reached Nuremberg. The writer described the figure of the animal, enclosing a sketch by an unknown artist. Albrecht Dürer, acquainted with the Portuguese feitoria, never saw the actual rhinoceros; he read the letter, though. Based on the verbal description he reconstructed the figure of the mythical beast, in two pen and ink drawings and a woodcut.

The inscription at the woodcut with historical accuracy and nominological, encyclopedic precision described:

«On the first of May in the year 1513 AD, the powerful King of Portugal, Manuel of Lisbon, brought such a living animal from India, called the rhinoceros. This is an accurate representation. It is the colour of a speckled tortoise, and is almost entirely covered with thick scales. It is the size of an elephant but has shorter legs and is almost invulnerable. It has a strong pointed horn on the tip of its nose, which it sharpens on stones. It is the mortal enemy of the elephant … It is said that the rhinoceros is fast, impetuous and cunning.»[1]

The woodcut circulated in Europe and spread the imagery that was maintained for centuries as the main impression of a rhinoceros, even after a real, but different, Indian rhinoceros was witnessed.

DELIRIOUS: He fabricated…
NEW YORK: What?
DELIRIOUS: The evidence…
RHINOCEROS: I was a fact.
DELIRIOUS: He never saw that you were real.

ACT THREE

[Paranoia, {para+nous, parallel to thinking} a thought process believed to be heavily influenced by anxiety or fear, often to the point of irrationality and delusion. Paranoid thinking typically includes persecutory beliefs, or conspiracy beliefs, which are absolutely justified through the linkage of a series of unrelated facts by the believer.][2]

However the delirium, the paranoid state of thinking, follows a *clear logic*.

THE LOGICIAN*: Here is an exemplary syllogism. All the cats are mortal. Socrates is mortal. So Socrates is a cat.[3]

Interpretations, although very subjective, are methodically articulated into a systematic structure. This aspect of paranoia reveals the critical ability of the brain to perceive links between elements, which are not rationally connected.

It mainly implies the possibility of fabricating a well-documented construction of reality outside the frame of rationale.

Deriving from this observation, *paranoiac-critical thinking* was invented as an instrument for

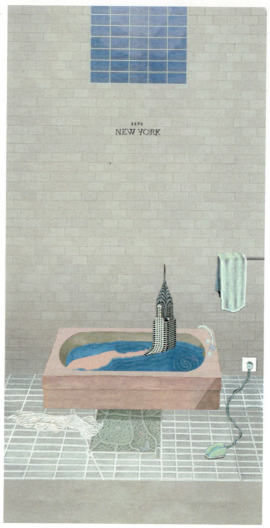

NEW YORK: Give me a smoke…

the surrealists[4]. It was defined as «a spontaneous method of irrational knowledge based on the critical and systematic objectivity of the associations and interpretations of delirious phenomena»[5].

(Delirious steps in the front and pronounces clearly and loud with an emphasis of a declaration. The Logician*, propped up against the wall, with a little grey moustache, eyeglass and a straw hat[3] performs a parallel monologue)

DELIRIOUS: With the meticulous care of a collector and the precision of a scientist, he collects…
THE LOGICIAN*: Allow me to introduce myself.[3]
DELIRIOUS: …images, events, facts. The real world is his protagonist.
THE LOGICIAN*: I am a professional logician.[3]
DELIRIOUS: The most precise the medium of evidence, the most convincing his conjecture.
THE LOGICIAN*: Here is my card.
DELIRIOUS: As a thief, he robs reality…
THE LOGICIAN*: Let me explain the method of a syllogism.[3]
DELIRIOUS: …but his whole art lays in the fabrication;
THE LOGICIAN*: It consists of a main proposition…[3]
DELIRIOUS: …in the methodical engineering of evidences; the critical interpretation of stolen elements from the real world to support his own conjecture.

(Rhinoceros crosses the stage murmuring)
RHINOCEROS: Physics of paranoia; mathematics of a paranoid system…
(pause)
NARRATOR: … It has been claimed that the above method was used for the construction of important manifestos of the 20th century.
NEW YORK: Give me a smoke…

ACT FOUR

«How to write a manifesto—on a form of urbanism for what remains of the 20th century—in an age disgusted with them? The fatal weakness of manifestos is their inherent lack of evidence. Manhattan's problem is the opposite: it is a mountain range of evidence without a manifesto.»[6]

(New York naked, in a pink bath-tab, while taking a shower)
NEW YORK: (singing) du bi du bi du…
DELIRIOUS: If you were not who you are, then who you would be?
NEW YORK: It has been claimed that the father of Modernism discovered the anti-city here; the existing ancestor to kill, before he re-invents his own theory of modernism.
DELIRIOUS: If the frantic delirium of a paranoiac's mind could re-figure everything from scratch…?
NEW YORK: It has been claimed that the father of Surrealism, found the evidences to re-invent the post-modern city here. Du bi du bi du…
DELIRIOUS: If 1978 was 1609…?
NEW YORK: It has been boldly claimed that Manhattan existed even before Manhattanism projects its delirious theory on the blocks of the Grid.
DELIRIOUS: And if the city was a Globe…?
VOICE FROM THE RADIO: «Movie stars who have led adventure-packed lives are often too egocentric to discover patterns, too inarticulate to express intentions, too restless to record or remember events. Ghostwriters do it for them. In the same way I was Manhattan's ghostwriter.»[6]
DELIRIOUS: He fabricated…
NEW YORK: What?
(pause. Rhinoceros crosses the stage murmuring)
RHINOCEROS: I believe that the moment is at hand when by a paranoid advance of the mind it will be possible to systematize confusion and completely disregard reality.[7]

ACT FIVE

(All sitting around a poker table)
DELIRIOUS: Split.
NEW YORK: Cut.
RHINOCEROS: Bad hand of cards.
DELIRIOUS: Re-shuffle…
(lights off)
NARRATOR: «I want to stand here in front of you and tell a story, not well-told; a story that you know, because it has for years been re-told. And then I want to speak again; meticulously decompose and precisely re-order; word by word, the syllables, the letters; until up is down and right is left;

And you cannot but listen and at the end … believe me»

1 Clarke, Tim H., The Rhinoceros from Dürer to Stubbs, 1515-1799, (London: Philip Wilson for Sotheby's Publications, 1986).
2 Collins English Dictionary—10th Edition, (Glasgow: William Collins Sons & Co. Ltd, 2009).
3 Eugène Ionesco, ‹Rhinoceros›, (Paris: 1959). Abstracts. THE LOGICIAN* is a character from the play.
4 Salvador Dalí, ‹Conquest of the Irrational›, (New York: Julien Levy, 1935).
5 Salvador Dalí qtd. in Breton, André (1934), What is surrealism, lecture in Brussels.
6 Rem Koolhaas, Delirious New York, (New York: The Monacelli Press, 1994).
7 Salvador Dalí, «The Stinking Ass» in La Femme Visible (Paris: Éditions Surréalistes , 1930).

fig.1 based on Albrecht Dürer, Rhinocerus, 1515 (woodcut, National Gallery of Art, Washington). Potlatch Architecture, 2016
fig.2 based on Madelon Vriesendorp, Illustrations for Delirious New York, (New York: The Monacelli Press, 1994).

«What about critique at an institution, Mr. Emerson?»

«The department at ETH is very large with many different positions and pedagogical methods. At ETH, like many continental school, there is a strong hierarchy between professor, student and assistant. When I was studying at Cambridge, I would never call my professor: ‹professor›. It's almost unthinkable. What you call a professor is not so important but it does make authority and power visible which runs all the way through teaching to evaluation.

One of the sacred parts of the academic structure in Cambridge is that a teacher is never allowed to grade his or her own students (this is done by a committee of examiners from other studios). Students can therefore have a very lively relationship with their professor; one that is full of conflicts, of stimulation and agreement but it can never be carried to the assessment (which does not necessarily produce better work). The evaluation and the strong hierarchy at ETH is a factor in the maintaining of a certain status quo. It can be more difficult for a student at ETH to disagree than it would for a student in Cambridge. I would not say that Cambridge or the AA are better schools. I believe that ETH provides one of the best educations in architecture in the world. But there is space for more critical discourse. The AA has more cross-studio forums within which the work is debated. This means that it's not just the work of the students which is discussed but it's also the position of the studio. The people leading the studio, whether they're professors or not, are accountable within the school. At ETH, the structure is almost like separate studio/ professorship silos. Each one is untouched by another. Maybe the students do not see us debating enough amongst ourselves.

The ETH is such a big school that it has a lot of inertia. It's difficult to change a culture that is deeply rooted in the institution, in the structure, in the building. But we are witnessing an interesting time in the department. There are and will be many new professors within a very short period of time. It will be interesting to see how that evolves. I'm excited but I wouldn't expect radical changes overnight. It is more likely that there will be a progressive evolution. Institutions like the ETH shouldn't change too fast, they would lose a lot of the depth that is in the department. It's not just the chairs which are powerful, it's also the collective knowledge and traditions. Where power comes from and how it's exercised is not that well understood or transparent in the department. If it was more visible, we could squeeze, push and twist more critically. I try to create an environment in which criticism is encouraged. I'm not easily offended and if somebody disagrees with me it's fine. It requires a certain amount of maturity, confidence and mutual respect on both sides to accept significant differences and allow them to be under the same roof. It's also about the pedagogical methodology. To what extent are you instructing, or do you know the correct solution before you started? If this inquiry is open ended, there's more space for students to be involved, critical and forming the agenda as well as responding to it. Finding the balance between developing a precise position and offering enough freedom to be critically active is one of the most important journeys students and teachers need to search for.»

«Do you think that it is your job to provide this confidence to students?»

«Yes, that is most certainly part of my job and their job. I hope that I allow students to talk about what they think and what they feel in an honest and candid way. I have to try and channel their comments critically and productively. At the same time, I wonder how easy it is to feel safe in your protest in a group a 60-65 students? One voice in 65 is a very small minority. In the UK, we have 12 or 14 students in a studio. One voice rings louder.

I think this also has to do with the broader cultural and political situations that are pretty much defining our times. It is not only in architecture that critical debate could be stronger, it is also in political engagement. I wish that students would be more politically assertive, that I would be more often challenged by different positions. The way in which your generation exercises its opinion, its power, its feelings, is very different to previous generations. The media, means, and processes are fundamentally different. ‹Where am I supposed to find a sense of identity and the confidence to be critical?›. It's fascinating. Macron, Trump are they both the product of the same system, a new type of popular, highly individual rejection of established positions and institutions? Is there going to be a revolution at ETH next year? I don't know. You know it better.»

«And maybe, as a final question, how would you relate criticality with the pavilions that you have so often done?»

«There are various theoretical and thematic ideas in these projects but there are also social ones. It has to do with getting students to know one another, to trust each other, to realize what they can get from one another, as well as from their teachers. Creatively and critically it is an interesting process to go through. When do you stand up and say: ‹no› and when do you just participate and help push the whole thing along? It does not mean being endlessly individualistic. Being critical is knowing when there is a bigger purpose that's worth working for. It's about the confrontation of the idea with individual authorship and responsibility towards one's own work, and one's responsibility towards what is fundamentally collective and shared. Architects need to know the difference and how to behave accordingly.»

This text is taken from the skype interview with Tom Emerson between Zurich and London the 16th of June 2017 by Vincent Bianchi and Yann Salzmann.

Critical Knitting
Paola De Martin

«Die Kämpfe der Arbeiter sind viel weniger gewalttätig als die, welche in ihrem Namen geführt werden.»[1]

Ich hatte von meiner Mutter, einer italienischen Arbeiterin, stricken gelernt bevor ich in die Schule kam. Die Handarbeitslehrerin in Zürich wandte dann allerdings eine andere Technik an. Meine Hände versteckte ich beim Stricken unter dem Tisch, um nicht aufzufallen. Gerade deshalb schöpfte sie Verdacht.

Ich musste ihr gegen meinen Willen zeigen, wie ich die Nadeln halte und die Maschen miteinander verknüpfe. Sie sagte: «Das geht nicht so», ich solle stricken, wie sie es uns beibringt. Und nach einem kurzen Schweigen schob sie nach, wie um mich überzeugen zu wollen: sie könne mir nicht helfen, wenn ich einen ‹italienischen› Fehler mache. Ich beugte mich im Unterricht ihrem Diktat. Zuhause kombinierte ich beide Techniken. Schon bald konnte ich komplizierte Jacquardmuster stricken. Diese habe ich der Lehrerin nie gezeigt, ich dachte, sie würde das nicht verstehen. Meine Fehler korrigierte ich ohne weiteres selber. Die kombinierte Technik habe ich als junge Erwachsene weiterentwickelt, dank peruanischen und norwegischen Vorbildern, die ich auf Reisen kennenlernte und die auf eine ähnliche Art funktionieren. Als ich Textildesignerin wurde, entwarf ich auf dieser Basis meine Muster an der Strickmaschine.

Eine Studentin der ZHdK sprach mich kürzlich in meinem Interkulturalitäts-Modul auf meine Handschuhe an. Sie gefielen ihr, wo ich sie gekauft hätte? Sie konnte kaum glauben, dass ich selbst sie hergestellt hatte. Ich sagte, halb im Spass, wenn Mark Terkessidis, von dem wir gerade ‹Interkultur›[2] gelesen hatten, die postmigrantische Gesellschaft als eine Gestaltungsaufgabe bezeichnet, dann sollte ich vielleicht ein Modul an der ZHdK anbieten, das ‹Postmigrantisches Stricken› heisst? Wenn sie da solche Techniken lernen würden, gab die Studentin scherzend zurück, dann wäre der Kurs garantiert voll.

Aber es geht mir, im Ernst, um mehr. Es geht darum, die Vorstellung zu kritisieren, dass soziale und kulturelle Differenz durch Anpassung der Einen an die sogenannte Leitkultur der Anderen zu überwinden sei. Darum, eine konstruktive Kritik an Integrationsmodellen zu artikulieren, die sich an scheinbar essentiellen Werten orientieren – als ob es eine allgemeingültige Beurteilung von Angemessenheit gäbe, die losgekoppelt von gesellschaftlichen Interessen existiert. Es geht mir um den Fokus auf die soziale Übersetzungsarbeit der Gestaltung. Eine Arbeit, die kleine Unterschiede laufend als Ausgangspunkt für Myriaden von nachvollziehbaren Neuschöpfungen aufgreift, damit Differenz nicht zur grossen Bedrohung eskaliert. Und schliesslich geht es darum, dass wir als Gestalter neue Formen, Muster, Räume und Oberflächen suchen, die von Bildungsfernen und Bildungsnahen geteilt werden können, indem wir so über uns selbst hinauswachsen, dass möglichst viele andere sich darin wiedererkennen. So oder anders können wir, wenn wir wollen, als ästhetische Experten eine Virtuosität entwickeln, die sozial nach unten offen und zugänglich ist. Das mag in der praktischen Umsetzung «verdammt harte Arbeit» sein, wie ein Designstudent an der ZHdK es kürzlich formulierte – aber die Künste, so meine ich, sind das ideale Terrain für diese Versuche. Wer, wenn nicht wir, Designer, Architekten und Kunstschaffende, können die gestalterischen Freiräume in dem Sinne nutzen, dass Expertise nicht in die Sackgasse der Exklusivität führt?

Ich war acht Jahre alt, als ich meine eigene Art zu stricken erfand. Das war 1973, zur Zeit der Schwarzenbach-Initiativen gegen die sogenannte Überfremdung der Schweiz. Meine Mutter ertrug diese Jahre schlechter als mein Vater. Sie gab ihre

Angst vor den Attacken der Fremdenfeinde an uns Kindern weiter. Von meiner Erstklasslehrerin erfuhr sie, dass ich Linkshänderin bin. Es genügte, dass meine Mutter mich fragte, ob das wirklich wahr sei, damit ich von dem Tag an wie von selbst sofort auf rechts umstellte. Aufzufallen war etwas vom Schlimmsten, was man den eigenen Eltern antun konnte als Kind von ausländischen Arbeitern. Hunderttausende von ihnen wurden damals vom rassistischen Diskurs in aller Öffentlichkeit der Verachtung, der Abwertung und dem sanktionierten Schweigen über die Verletzung ihrer Menschenrechte preisgegeben. Meine soziale Scham war deshalb gross, wenn ich als Italienerkind identifiziert wurde. Und dazu kam die Angst, daß man mich als solches potentiell wieder von der Familie trennen würde, wie in den Jahren, als mein Vater Saisonnier gewesen war. Aufgrund dieses Aufenthaltsstatus war ihm per Gesetz verwehrt worden, zusammen mit seinen Kindern in der Schweiz zu leben, wo er als Bauarbeiter doch erwünscht war.

Oft zitierte meine Mutter während der Abstimmungskämpfe gegen die Überfremdung Max Frischs berühmt gewordenen Satz: «Man hat Arbeitskräfte gerufen, und es kommen Menschen.»[3] Mit unterdrückter Wut in der Stimme zischte sie dies, wie um sich Luft zu verschaffen. Ich begriff als Kind den ironischen Sarkasmus von Max Frischs Kritik nicht. Zu abstrakt. Was sind «Arbeitskräfte»? Und meine Mutter übersetzte: «Man hatte Hände gerufen, die arbeiten, weisst Du, und es kamen ganze Menschen. Wir kamen.» Seither träume ich, mir oder meinen Liebsten seien die Hände vom Rest des Körpers abgetrennt worden. Die Träume, in denen wir mit einbandagierten, schmerzenden Armstümpfen oder mit steifen Schaufensterpuppenhänden versuchen, irgendwie weiterzukommen – solche Träume sind ein verlässlicher Indikator für die Konjunktur der Fremdenfeindlichkeit im Land. Vor und nach der Annahme der Masseneinwanderungsinitiative am 9. Februar 2014 häuften sie sich wieder.

Stricken, das tue ich auch deshalb wieder häufiger. Es ist ein motorischer Segen gegen die verbale und politische Zerstückelung des Selbst in Arbeitskraft und Mensch. Jede Masche, die ich mit der nächsten verknüpfe, hält der Verletzung durch den politischen Diskurs eine Kritik entgegen, indem sie den analytischen Verstand mit den tätigen Händen, der Rechten und der Linken, verbindet. Strickend produziere ich Handschuhe und vieles mehr, aber vor allem produziere ich die eigene Unversehrtheit. Je nach Blickwinkel habe ich mehr Glück als Verstand gehabt, oder mehr Talent als Pech. Wenn mich heute politische Krisen in Bedrängnis bringen, kann ich noch immer auf nachwachsende, mitunter sogar auf sorgsam gehegte und am Widerstand erprobte schöpferische Ressourcen zurückgreifen.

Aber was wäre, wenn die Ressourcen sich erschöpfen? Wenn die Angriffe zunehmen? Diese lästigen Fragen drängen sich mir neuerdings hartnäckig auf. Ich vermute, dass das mit der zunehmenden gesellschaftlichen Polarisierung zusammenhängt, die eine gefährliche Spannung angenommen hat. Ich betrachte mich in diesem größeren Kontext wie in einem Spiegel und sehe, wie zerstörerisch-selbstzerstörerisch mein kritisches Potential wäre, wenn ich die eigene Unversehrtheit nicht immer und immer wieder herstellen könnte – die eigene Unversehrtheit, dieser verletzliche, sinnliche Grundstoff der konstruktiven und fruchtbaren Kritik.

1 Harun Farocki, Arbeiter verlassen die Fabrik, 1995.
2 Mark Terkessidis, ‹Interkultur›, Berlin 2010.
3 «Ein Herrenvolk sieht sich in Gefahr: man hat Arbeitskräfte gerufen, und es kommen Menschen. Sie fressen den Wohlstand nicht auf, im Gegenteil, sie sind für den Wohlstand unerläßlich. Aber sie sind da.»
Max Frisch, in: Alexander S. Seiler, ‹Siamo Italiani. Die Italiener. Gespräche mit italienischen Arbeitern in der Schweiz›, Zürich 1965, S. 7.

Eine Übersetzung dieses Textes ins Italienische erhält man auf Anfrage bei der Autorin unter der folgenden Emailadresse: paola.de.martin@gta.arch.ethz.ch

Critical Knitting

©Paola De Martin, 2016.

The Review as a Project
trans Redaktion

★   Professor
▲   Assistant
◆   Jury
●   Student

Chairs

1. Angélil
2. Brillembourg / Klumpner
3. Caminada
4. Caruso
5. Christiaanse
6. de Geyter
7. Deplazes
8. Eberle
9. Emerson
10. Fujimoto / Kerez
11. Gigon / Guyer
12. Girot
13. Kerez
14. Lehnerer
15. Meili / Vogt / Conzett
16. Peter / Dumont d'Ayot
17. Schwartz
18. Sik
19. Spiro
20. Swinnen
21. Topalovic

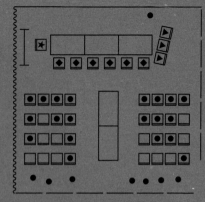

18

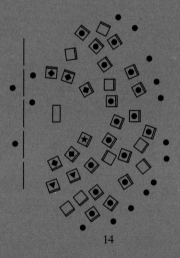

14

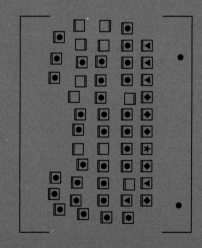

9

This mapping is based on our observations and photographs of the final reviews at ETHZ on the 30th and 31st of May 2017.

The Review as a Project

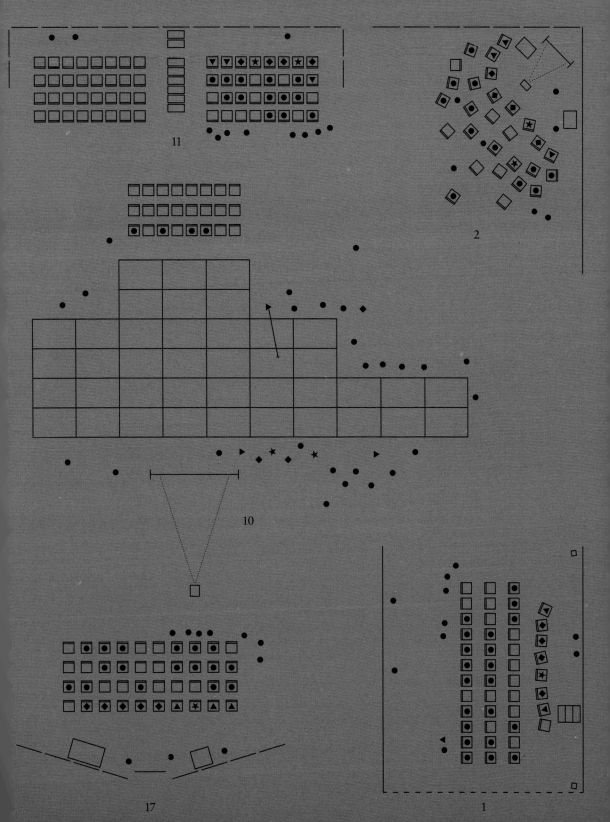

The Review as a Project

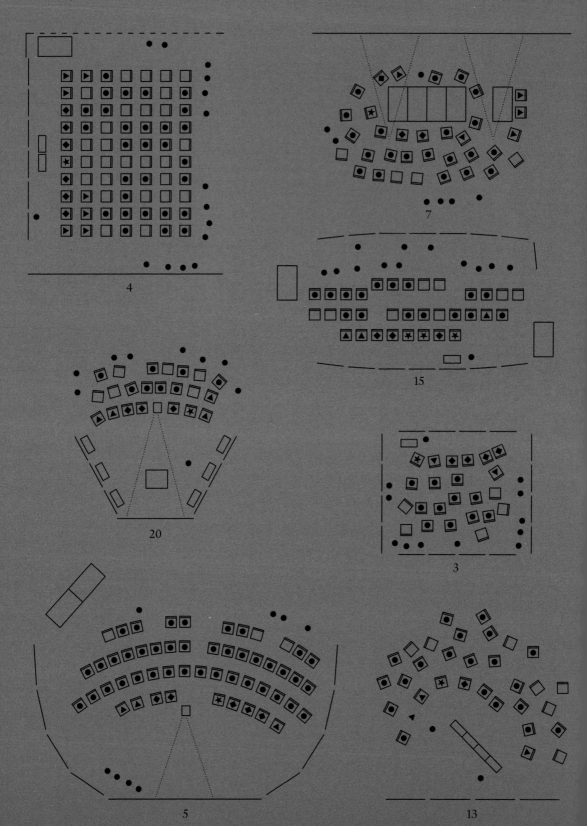

The Review as a Project

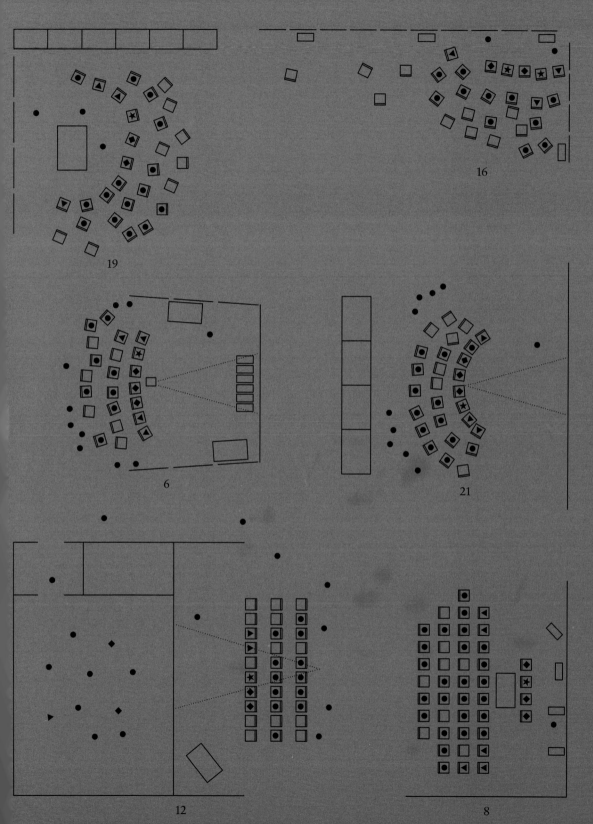

«What is the role of critique in your pedagogy, Mr. Lehnerer?»

«We could easily stop here by saying ‹yes, of course, we want critical architects›, however the ‹how› and ‹what for› seem to remain as itchy as they are. First of all, I think there are different ways of understanding criticism. I was socialised with an architectural discourse in the US, where critique is not necessarily understood as a negative thing. Here, however, criticism tends to be associated differently: To criticise means to oppose—whereas the beauty of criticism is that it can be proactive. It has the potential to produce work.

There are two things that I can mention that we try to do within the chair in that regard. When we set a task, we never argue out of necessity. We never say that Zürich needs such a building or a program because there is a lack of it. We never argue out of the idea that we need to provide the city or the context with a certain solution. Otherwise you can just say: ‹I am fulfilling a task›. That's what practice is full of—in competitions, in serving clients, etc: you are asked for a solution and you deliver it. However, a good school also exists to experience the opposite.

In 2016, we asked our students to design a church; there are already 72 churches in the city of Zurich, it does not need another one. However, we wanted them to make another one because they could no longer safely argue that another piece of that program is needed. They had to find some other justification, which could be the opposite of necessity: desire. ‹I want this›. Then you can no longer hide behind other people's wishes or commissions. This creates a certain discomfort, leading people to wonder: ‹Why should I do this? What else can I express with that project?›. You cannot fulfill a task anymore but you have the opportunity to raise your own question. That is one way of getting into a critical architectural project. I believe that it is more important for the project to be critical than it is for the student to be a critical person. Don't get me wrong, what I mean is that I do not want criticality or self-criticality to be expressed through doubt rather than action. The doubt, the questions, and this self-critical approach should be expressed projectively. Furthermore, once a project starts to speak with itself, it naturally gains a certain ‹autonomy› that our discipline looks for so eagerly.

The most beautiful piece on criticality I have ever read is a text by Jorge Silvetti, called ‹The Beauty of Shadows› from 1977. He has this idea that criticism emerges from the act of design itself. He talks about ‹criticism from within›, that is, your own doing is criticising the core of the discipline. You do not point at something outside your world but at something that is deeply intriguing to you within your own work. I find it very nice to understand criticism as an act of doing. Not as a statement or a commentary. You take something that appears utterly normal and ubiquitous, then you try to subvert it. There are certain techniques you can employ to do that. Exaggeration is one. You can exaggerate something you dislike in an extreme way to turn it into something beautiful. This counter-intuition creates a certain friction to our overly intuitive world. Thereby it turns a project into a manifesto with an antithetical value.

There is a difference between studio teaching and diploma teaching. When I started teaching at ETH, I was opposed to the set diploma. I received my education in schools where there were only free diplomas. Ironically, over the last few years, I started liking the form of set diploma, huh! That almost rigid question gives you the first precondition to challenge it, to try and subvert the task. Which allows for a critical and self-conscious contribution. A school is an institution and provides boundaries. So called ‹total freedom› from the beginning isn't helpful, it is much rather extremely boring. Certain ties and conditions have to be established, so that you can then work against them. It is something that works quite well in the admittedly deterministic mode of our diplomas. Everybody receives the same task. What will they do with it? It allows you to act in a subversive way, to be productive within the range of your skills and sensibility. It has now developed into a game. It's almost a little counter productive that the diploma projects are becoming increasingly freely set. I never thought I would ever say things like this…

There is a certain truth that architecture cannot escape; it always serves power. We are obliged to capital. Nothing works without funding, you need a client. It is when we capture private investments for public pleasures, that we can make a contribution. There has to be this counter-intuitive subversion of the task, in order to smuggle in other qualities, that might be missing in the brief. This is very beautiful as a project. It does not matter whether it's a small object or a big plan, as long as you have that kind of ambition. I fully agree with the idea that a school should create room for that in the students' minds. The statement that architecture serves power cannot be abolished or ignored. You have to trick it somehow. It is only then that the critical architecture we are all interested in can take place.»

This text is taken from the interview with Alex Lehnerer led at ETH Hönggerberg the 13th of June 2017 by Vincent Bianchi and Yann Salzmann.

Postästhetische Architektur
Sebastian Linsin im Gespräch mit Armen Avanessian

Armen Avanessian ist Philosoph, Literaturwissenschaftler und politischer Theoretiker. Seine Arbeiten rund um den ‹spekulativen Realismus› und den ‹Akzelerationismus› haben ihm in den letzten Jahren Aufmerksamkeit verschafft. Nun hat er sich der Architektur zugewandt. Gemeinsam mit Markus Miessen initiierte er eine Gesprächsreihe unter dem Titel ‹Xenoarchitektur›. Der von ihm geprägte Neologismus ist dabei Ausgangspunkt, das Potential von Architektur aus unterschiedlichen fachlichen Richtungen zu erforschen. Sebastian Linsin (SL) nahm dies zum Anlass, Avanessian (AA) für ein Interview zu treffen.

SL Warum interessiert dich Architektur?

AA Mich interessiert Architektur nicht als Einzelobjekt, sondern Architektur als Feld. Dabei steht nicht die Frage im Vordergrund, welche ästhetische Erfahrung ich bei einem spezifischen Raum habe, eher wie sich Architektur zum ökonomischen und politischen Machwerk verhält. Die Figur des Architekten kann – ganz im Gegensatz zu vielen Künstlern – nicht behaupten, ausserhalb des Marktes zu stehen. Künstler tun oft so, als ob sie nicht Teil eines ökonomischen Zusammenhangs wären: *Das machen die Galeristen, das machen die Anderen*. Der Architekt hingegen inkorporiert quasi zugleich den Kreativen, den Galeristen, den Museumsleiter und den Kunstmessenkurator.

SL Dein Zugang zur Architektur spiegelt einerseits die Faszination für Ökonomisches wider, andererseits liest du Räumliches, seien es Landschaften, Städte oder Architektur, durch die Linse der Temporalität, also deren Zeitlichkeiten.

AA Diese zwei Perspektiven haben miteinander zu tun. Philosophen beschäftigen sich schon lange mit dem Wesen der Zeit. Mich interessieren, aus der Literatur kommend, schon eher fiktions- oder erzähltheoretische Fragen. Das ist ein Unterschied. Nicht, *Was ist die Zeit?*, sondern *Woher kommt die Zeit?*, *Wie wird etwas entwickelt?* und *Wie kommt eines aus dem anderen?*. Das sind eher Richtungsfragen, also in gewissem Sinne Fragen nach einer vektoriellen Logik der Zeit. Ich halte dies für relevanter denn je, weil ich einen dramatischen paradigmatischen Wechsel diagnostiziere, den wir noch nicht ausreichend begriffen haben, obwohl die digitalen Infrastrukturen, die Offshore-Architekturen und die Räume dieser neuen Ordnung schon gebaut werden. Daher ist es nur ein konsequenter Schritt diese spekulativen zeitlichen Fragestellungen auch an Architektur heranzutragen. Was würde es bedeuten, über sie nicht nur räumlich, sondern auch topologisch oder zeitlich nachzudenken? Rein etymologisch hat Architektur schon eine zeitliche Dimension.

SL Wie äussert sich dieser (Zeiten-)Wechsel?

AA Wir haben Jahrtausende chronologisch gedacht. Und wir können als lebensweltliche Subjekte vielleicht gar nicht anders als chronologisch denken. Das Problem ist aber, dass wir heute – sowohl als Individuen als auch als Gesellschaft – feststellen müssen, dass vieles nicht mehr chronologisch funktioniert. Jetzt ist es nicht, wie viele Postmoderne sagen *Alles steht still* oder wie Konservative (auch viele sogenannte Linke) *Es geht zu schnell*. Meiner Meinung nach verdeckt der Eindruck, dass wir keine Traktion, keinen Halt mehr in der Gegenwart gewinnen, den tatsächlichen Wandel. Die vorherrschende Richtung der Zeit hat sich geändert. Meine, auf den ersten Blick konterintuitive oder leicht paradoxe These dazu ist, dass die Zeit nicht mehr aus der Vergangenheit kommt, sondern aus der Zukunft. In meinem Buch ‹Miamification› versuche ich dies anhand von Präemptionsphänomenen zu plausibilisieren. Beispiel: Präventivkrieg oder Drohnenkrieg. Einer angeblichen oder tatsächlichen Bedrohung in der Zukunft, soll in der Gegenwart zuvorgekommen werden. Es ist eine Offensive mit defensiver Absicht. Meistens fussen solche Entscheidungen auf Prognosen, die sich auf Modelle und Wahrscheinlichkeiten berufen. Es geht dabei um die Minimierung von Risiken, was in vielen Fällen gleichbedeutend mit der Sicherung von ökonomischen Vorteilen ist. Beispiel: Präemptive Persönlichkeit in der Onlinewerbung. Basierend auf Wahrscheinlichkeiten und Statistik schlagen uns Algorithmen Produkte für zukünftige Einkäufe vor und erzeugen in der Gegenwart ein Begehren, dass wir ohne sie nie gehabt hätten. Es geht dabei nicht nur um eine weitere Transaktion, sondern auch darum, die freie Wahl des Käufers einzuschränken. Durch die Digitalisierung werden nun eine Vielzahl – vielleicht sogar eine Mehrzahl – von Entscheidungen von nicht-menschlichen Agenten (Algorithmen, Computer, Automatisierungsprozesse etc.) gefällt. Entscheidend dabei ist nun, dass ihre Annahmen über die Zukunft unsere Gegenwart mitkonfigurieren. Dabei fasziniert und erschreckt mich gleichermassen die Tendenz, dass wir immer weniger Mitspracherecht haben.

SL Du nennst dies auch ‹derivatives Paradigma›. Wie beeinflusst diese Denkweise die Architektur?

AA Vielleicht macht es Sinn, in diesem Kontext zwischen Wahrscheinlichkeit und Kontingenz zu unterscheiden. Ohne dies freilich zu wissen leidet die Finanzwissenschaft darunter, dass sie innerhalb eines probabilistischen Kalküls funktioniert. Sobald man über die Zukunft mit Hilfe von höheren und tieferen Wahrscheinlichkeiten nachdenkt, verbleibt man immer innerhalb der vermeintlichen Gesetzmässigkeiten. Im Bezug auf Architektur entspräche dies Fragen nach Rentabilität, Nachhaltigkeit, Stadtentwicklung etc. Dieser Diskurs dominiert das Architekturgeschehen. Ich hingegen glaube, dass wir eher über Kontingenz nachdenken sollten. Kontingenz ist alles, was weder notwendig noch unmöglich ist. Somit ist sie viel grösser und viel mehr als das, was uns nur als wahrscheinlich erscheint. Wir sollten über die Möglichkeit nachdenken, dass sich Spielregeln wirklich radikal ändern oder radikal geändert werden können. Dieses Potenzial hat Architektur, sofern man sie als Infrastruktur und nicht nur als Form oder Oberflächen versteht.

SL Man hat den Eindruck, dass Kontingenz in verschieden Kontexten unterschiedlich besprochen werden. In den Naturwissenschaften macht ‹Cutting Edge Technology› im wortwörtlichen Sinn Grenzen poröser und vergrössert so Möglichkeitsräume von Innen. In politisch-ökonomischen Sphären erscheint immer weniger möglich (beispielsweise TINA-Politik in der Banken- oder Griechenlandkrise). Gibt es so etwas wie Kontingenzpolitik?

AA Spannende Frage. Die Alternativlosigkeit ist klar eine Ideologie, es geht hier eher um die Sicherung von Interessen als angebliche Naturgesetze. Eine Ideologie beruht eigentlich darauf, nicht als solche erkannt zu werden. Genau genommen ist dies aber nicht einmal mehr wirklich der Fall. Das Problem ist ja eher, wir wissen, dass etwas falsch läuft,

time-complex

past and future equally important in the organization of the system

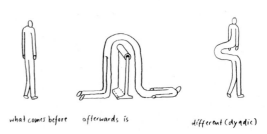

what comes before   afterwards is   different (dyadic)

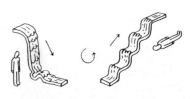

apparent reversal of the flow of time

nur haben wir es nicht geschafft – oder hoffen wir noch nicht – Organisationsformen zu finden, um dieser Kontingenz auch einen Handlungsspielraum zu geben. Hier beginnt auch mein Problem mit der Kritik. Historisch gesehen hatte die Kritik die Funktion, gegen Spekulation vorzugehen. Die Vernunft sollte sozusagen vom ungesunden Drang, über sich hinausschiessen zu wollen und sich ausserhalb eines festen Rahmens auf unsicheres oder unwissenschaftliches Terrain zu begeben, gesäubert werden. Es ist falsch zu denken, dass wir uns von der Krise erholen würden, wenn wir eine kritische Distanz einbauen. Wir brauchen tendenziell nicht mehr additives Wissen. Wir müssen die Frage beantworten, welche anderen Möglichkeiten wir haben. Es geht um die Integration von Wissen in Handlungsformen, und die Übersetzung von Handlungsformen in Praktiken und so weiter. Es geht nicht um die Reflexion und kritische Distanz, sondern um Spekulation und Rekursion. Dieser Zugang verändert auch, was als Theorie verstanden wird. Meine Begegnung mit Architektur war nie, dass ich Theorie als ihren Metadiskurs verstanden habe. Auch in diesem Gespräch geht es meines Erachtens nicht darum, über Architektur als architekturkritische Praxis zu sprechen. Viel mehr interessieren mich Wege zur Verzahnung unterschiedlicher Wissensproduktionen, um anschliessend zu sehen, zu welchen Ergebnissen und neuen Fragen man kommt. Theorie ist so gesehen etwas Vorläufiges und nicht etwas Abschliessendes. Das ist ein wichtiger methodologischer Unterschied.

SL Wie entwirft man spekulative Architektur und wie sähe sie aus?

AA Um nochmal auf das temporale Argument vom Anfang zurückzukommen, ich denke wir brauchen einen spekulativen Move, um uns bzw. unsere Gegenwart aus der Zukunft zu betrachten. Entwerfen hiesse vielleicht aus dem Anderswo auf die Gegenwart zurückzublicken. Nicht im Jetzt Utopien zu entwerfen, das wäre weiterhin das Modell kritischer Melancholie, sondern uns die Algorithmen als Individuen einzuverleiben, eine Art Mimesis der Computer, und eine Zukunft zu schaffen, die tatsächlich in die Gegenwart eingreift. Was würde es heissen, Konzepte zu entwickeln, die sich aus der Zukunft betrachtet bewahrheiten und nicht nur eine akkurate Beschreibung der Gegenwart sind. Vielleicht hat das mit meiner Faszination für ‹Hyperstition› zu tun. Dieser Begriff verbindet ‹hype› und ‹superstition›, Aberglaube, und bezeichnet Phänomene, die etwas beinhalten, dass ihre eigene Realisierung mit sich bringt. Ich vermute, dass wir in einer Gegenwart leben, die selber ‹hyperstitional› ist. Es passieren ständig Dinge, von denen wir sagen, es könne nicht wirklich ernst sein, es können nur eine Erfindung sein oder es müsse eine Fiktion sein. Dennoch werden sie real. Die Wahrwerdungen von unmöglich Gehaltenem fallen uns schwer und sind schwierig zu verarbeiten. Die ‹Hyperstition› kann und muss aber auch als Chance verstanden werden. Denn der Reflex zu einem vergangenen Modus der Architektur zurück zu wollen ist verständlich, aber nicht realistisch. Architekten tun gut daran mit neuen Herausforderungen umzugehen, ihnen etwas entgegenzusetzen, denn nur wer die technologischen Herausforderungen aufnimmt, kann sie auch progressiv mitgestalten. Eine Konzentration auf ästhetische Äusserlichkeiten und ein Festhalten an althergebrachten Arbeitsweisen kann das vermutlich nicht leisten. Entscheidend ist die Art und Weise, wie mit Informationstechnologien umgegangen wird und nicht, ob sie überhaupt eingesetzt werden. Darum habe ich in dem Aufsatz über ‹Mereotopolitik› etwas gegen parametrische Architektur polemisiert. Es geht mir darum mit Hilfe neuer Technologien poröse, xenophile statt glatte, xenophobe Oberflächen zu erschaffen. Quasi eine ‹Xeno-Architektur›, die sich öffnet für Anderes oder Fremdes.

SL Verstehst du Porosität als Materialeigenschaft oder als Metapher?

AA Ich verstehe Porosität nicht primär als ästhetisches Argument. Es ist auffällig, dass viele Architekturen mit glatten Oberflächen einen gewissen Kontrollzwang aufweisen. Dass beispielsweise Grossprojekte für Diktatoren von Zaha Hadid, die ich natürlich für eine große Architektin halte, im Nahen Osten, die teilweise reaktionären Ansichten von Patrik Schumacher und die Art und Weise, wie ihre Algorithmen jegliche Porosität schliessen, eine gewisse Verwandtschaft aufweisen, ist auffallend. Die geschwungenen Formen sind nicht unschuldig, nur weil sie natürlich anmuten. Diese Art von Architektur hat viel mit dem Klassizismus gemein. Viele klassizistische Ästhetiker teilten ein Begehren jede Pore zu schliessen. Da gibt es richtig amüsante Texte, die das Problem mit den Nasen- und Ohrenlöchern bei klassizistischen Plastiken bearbeiten. Es geht einerseits darum, dass sich nichts absetzt, aber auch alles Körperliche, alles Humane zu bändigen. Welche Prozesse würden dagegen eine poröse ‹Xeno-Architektur› produzieren? Wie können wir uns Glitches, Kontingenz und Brüche zu Nutze machen? Kann es einen Umgang mit neuen Technologien geben, der nicht nur Daten sammelt, sondern in dem die eingegebenen Daten den Code selbst umschreiben? Das sind gewissermassen offene Fragen und vielleicht müssen wir dabei einige alte Konzepte über Bord werfen. Was würde es beispielsweise bedeuten, Architektur poetisch, statt ästhetisch zu denken?

SL Worin unterscheidet sich ein poetischer zu einem ästhetischen Zugang?

AA Ich glaube, wir haben allzu lange in einem ‹ästhetischen Regime› gelebt, gedacht und gebaut. Jacques Rancière, der diesen Ausdruck geprägt hat, meint damit, nicht nur über Kunst oder Architektur nachzudenken, sondern quasi ein allgemeines Paradigma. Es betrifft alle Massstäbe, vom Design, über die Architektur bis hin zur Politik. Smartphones ändern alle paar Monate ihr Design ohne wirklich mehr zu können. Alle wollen in einem Design Loft oder in einer entsprechend designten Altbauwohnung wohnen. Städte stehen in einem Wettkampf um Wahrnehmungserlebnisse und Reichhaltigkeit um Touristen anzulocken. Auf allen Ebenen ist Ästhetik, beziehungsweise die Oberfläche dominant. Meistens allerdings nur im Sinne eines Gadgetismus, eines Innovationfurors ohne einen tatsächlichen sozialen Fortschritt. In unserem ökonomischen System spielen offensichtlich ästhetische Kriterien eine unglaubliche Rolle. Meiner Meinung nach gibt es kaum eine Veränderung durch Gestaltung. Zeitphilosophisch hat Ästhetik zudem immer das Problem, dass sie von ‹aisthesis›, also Wahrnehmung ausgeht. Wahrnehmung setzt ein Vorhandenes voraus und wie dieses auf mich, den Betrachter, wirkt. Um meinen vorherigen Ansatz nochmal aufzunehmen: Denken aus der Zukunft kann nicht auf Vorhandenes bauen und also nicht ästhetisch sein. Gebannt aus der Gegenwart auf die Gegenwart zu starren und Veränderung zu erwarten ist illusorisch. Das heisst nicht, dass ich nicht schöne Architektur hässlicher Architektur vorziehe. Aber Schönheit alleine oder schöne Formen alleine sind kein Kriterium. Doch was sind Alternativen dazu? Poetik ist nicht an die Gegenwart gebunden. Was mich interessiert, ist ‹poiesis› als radikale Praxis. Sie kreist um die Erschaffung von Neuem, denn das meint ‹poiesis› ursprünglich: Das In-die-Welt-Kommen, die Her-stellung oder Pro-duktion von etwas tatsächlich Neuem. Die Frage, wie man Neues in die Welt bringen kann, wäre auch der Punkt, in dem sich eine poetische Philosophie und die Architektur träfen. Wir stehen vor massiven Umwälzungen. Wir wissen nicht, ob unsere Demokratien noch funktionieren werden. Wir wissen nicht, ob unsere Ökonomien noch funktionieren werden. Wir wissen nicht, ob wir nicht schon längst in einem post-kapitalistischen System leben, das vielleicht besser als Finanzfeudalismus gefasst werden kann. Die einschneidenden Konsequenzen der Digitalen Revolution haben wir weder in unser Denken noch in unser Handeln eingespeist. Klar ist nur, dass Ästhetik, Kritik und die kritische Distanz dem nicht gewachsen sind. Poetik, Spekulation und Rekursion scheinen mir dagegen vielversprechende Alternativen.

Alle Abbildungen gezeichnet von Andreas Töpfer, entnommen aus: Armen Avanessian, Andreas Töpfer, ‹Speculative Drawing: 2011–2014›, Sternberg Press, 2014.

Armchair activism
Ben Summers

The relative comfort of our homes and their subtly introduced webcams and microphones offer us the possibility to think freely and broadcast our thoughts to the world; our enjoyment of apparent freedom distracting from the fact that even when we are not speaking we are being heard. It is only when Siri speaks out of turn that she gives the game away.

Critique as understood from its Ancient Greek root ‹kritikē tekhnē› (critical art) has arguably been largely a preserve of the bourgeoisie, and this argument seemed no more apt than in a recent private talk by Benno Tempel (General Director of the Gemeentemuseum, Den Haag) when he suggested that «the gallery is one of the few remaining spaces in contemporary society where the general public is invited to be critical.»[1]

This almost archaic demarcation of a bourgeois public sphere does on the one hand sound plausible, considering the general disenchantment with our current forms of democracy. But on the other hand, isn't everyone welcome to say whatever they want, wherever and whenever they want, even if nobody is listening? The small bubble of invited criticality in the gallery is just one enclosure in a foaming mass of separate spaces that make up the human environment.[2] Built or unbuilt, these physical and social enclosures are sometimes adjacent and often overlapping, each with their own rules and conventions to be adhered to. Their varying conditions of decorum and normality determine how we are most likely to interpret or understand which ‹facts› are true and which are false.

Critique is in itself post-fact (in the sense of coming after the topic of discussion); a construction that responds rather than autonomously generates. So in a post-modern, post-fact reality (in the Trumpian sense), where does critique stand? Critical statements— although often assertively positioned as such—are rarely bare facts but instead a handful of facts mixed with opinions; observations tinged with artistic tendency and poetics. In essence the game of critical conversation is one of improvisation where one must rely on the other players of the game to set the context. Now more than ever, this game of critical debate is open to the average internet user, although the chaotic and impermanent nature of internet culture makes serious and meaningful debate increasingly implausible.

It feels a little too easy to reference Donald Trump's tweets, but their position of poignancy in the fact versus non-fact and public versus private debates makes them difficult to exclude. His widespread success at ignoring facts and getting away with it is impressive to the point of evoking a spontaneous standing ovation. It is the kind of bewildering instant where you are not sure if the game has been won or lost… Are you dreaming or has the world actually just decided that it has been flat all along?

These are the conditions in which contemporary debate takes place; a topsy-turvy arena of critique that one might refer to as the public sphere. However, it is in the removal from the debating chamber that one finds space to deliberate and form opinion rather than voice it, withdrawing from the necessary presentation of oneself either as a speaker or listener.

Corporate appropriation of the private realm

In her work ‹The Human Condition›, Hannah Arendt understands the home as a private sphere necessary to preserve and rejuvenate the vitality of human life. This process of private rejuvenation, she claims, is so important because it provides respite from the bright and withering light of the public sphere in which one must present oneself to society, understanding the public sphere in the Ancient Greek sense as the political forum where each citizen speaks to and is heard by their peers. In fact, the word private in its Latin origins of ‹privare› means to deprive, and the later iteration ‹privatus› means to be withdrawn from public life, thus it is the ‹deprivation› of public attention that appears as the defining characteristic of life at home.

However, as Arendt goes on to argue, «[i]n our understanding, the dividing line [between public and private] is entirely blurred, because we see the body of peoples and political communities in the image of a family whose everyday affairs have to be taken care of by a gigantic, nation-wide administration of housekeeping. The scientific thought that corresponds to this development is no longer political science but ‹national economy› or ‹social economy›.»[3]

This assertion of all private interests being analogous to a kind of household administration takes root in the very word company (‹companis›[4]), and such phrases as «men who eat one bread,» and «men who have one bread and one wine». Understanding modern economy as a realm increasingly dominated by private interest, Karl Marx's observation of a «withering away of the state» corresponds directly to the withering away of the public realm, such that in the present situation we are confronted with an ever-increasing conflict of interests where ‹the common good› and the personal profit are practically indiscernible.[5]

To give a recent example, in 2010 the US Supreme Court of Justice upheld the right of corporations to make political donations as a form of lobbying, by attaching the First Amendment (right to free speech) to the Law of Corporate Personhood, saying «Corporations are people, and money is speech»[6].

Mark Cousins proposes an alternative interpretation of the conventional public versus private dichotomy, asserting that perhaps administered versus un-administered space is a more useful ontology.[7] For him, ‹administered space› is a realm where conditions of conduct are impressed upon the individual, thereby dispossessing them of the space. Through this largely social mechanism of ‹normalisation›, standardisation, efficiency and thus homogeneity are established as desirable goals, revoking an alternative view where diversity gives cause for celebration and freedom to be oneself is paramount.

What is clear in either ontological view is that a redefinition of threshold is necessary, in order to shelter the individual once again from constant politicisation, so that the dominant political tools of action (‹praxis›) and speech (‹lexis›) yield, and thus to offer space for the practise of intellection (‹nous›), an act that Aristotle viewed as man's highest capacity.[8]

Whether viewed as unadministered or private space, it is the home that reveals itself as a last bastion of both, preserving the contemplative and critical functions of the individual mind, despite the best attempts of the local municipality to drown the occupants in a deluge of ‹life admin› mail.

fig.a: Auguste Toulmouche, Vanity, 1890

Virtual apertures: two-way glass or black mirror?

In her study of primitive settlements Julienne Hanson asserts that there is, in fact, a kind of binary elemental state of the building: either closed or open. If the closed cell is the domain of the inhabitant, then the open space is «the locus of the interface between inhabitant and user»[9], defining the home as «a certain ordering of categories, to which is added a system of controls»[10].

In the context of the contemporary home it is clear that the ‹virtual apertures› into the home—which have over time developed from a simple one-way audio connection (radio) to an open audio-visual-textual system (internet)—accentuate now more than ever the virtual capacity to open or close the unit of the residence, acting as a kind of metabolic enclosure. The relative comfort of our homes and their subtly introduced webcams and microphones offer us the possibility to think freely and broadcast our thoughts to the world; our enjoyment of apparent freedom distracting from the fact that even when we are not speaking we are being heard. It is only when Siri speaks out of turn that she gives the game away.

«My house is diaphanous, but it is not of glass. It is more of the nature of vapour. Its walls contract and expand as I desire. At times, I draw them close about me like protective armor … But at others, I let the walls of my house blossom out in their own space, which is infinitely extensible.»[11] Georges Spyridaki

It has always been the function of the imported artefact to symbolically link the resident in his home to the outside world, either in the age-old relation to the elements of earth, wind and fire, or in the 19th century tradition of a cultured collector of icons. But it is only in the last few years that virtual connection has made an adaptable geo-spatial adjacency quite so explicit, close, real-time and adaptive. One thing that links all these iterations of artefacts within the home is their propensity to evoke in the inhabitant both an exploration of the external, and a moment of reflection, a glimpse of self-recognition in the artefact that the individual has chosen in their curation of the interior. It is this duality that Charlie Brooker plays upon in the title of his popular television series ‹Black Mirror›, referencing the capacity of the digital screen (mobile phone, laptop or television) to reflect the countenance of the user, or open a window into a distant world.

Jean Baudrillard's observation of the mirror's disappearance from the modern domestic living space—relegated to the bathroom in frameless form as a functional object—could well be explained by the rise of the virtual aperture. However, while bourgeois décor may have evaporated from the majority of homes, «bourgeois consciousness' cross-eyed view of itself»[12] is far from dissolved. The material-focused culture of the bourgeoisie is in many ways proliferating rather than suffering natural deselection, just as the contemporary individual is not even close to attaining release from existential crisis… Modernity has supposedly evolved into a bigger and better cousin, but there remains a lingering suspicion that in our introverted relationship with ourselves we confuse leaps forward with a Concorde-like crash into our past.

‹Unheimlich› homes

Proclaiming criticality as a human resource retained by domestic enclosure, it makes sense that we should consider the retention of control over our physical boundaries as tantamount to control over our mental boundaries.

The overall point is that without privacy we tend to become overexposed to the light of public attention, a little like a photograph;

losing sight of our own edges. As we live our lives more and more in digital space, it is important that we are aware of the external interest we invite into the very heart of our homes through the delights of predictive services that learn from our habits. On the one hand Facebook, Amazon, Netflix and so on are responding to us, listening to our needs and desires. But on the other hand they are responding according to their parameters alone, shaping us through their suggestions, placing us in isolating spheres of their own choosing. Slowly but surely our range of possible actions (and therefore thoughts) becomes limited to those suggestions, until we are no more than actors in centrally scripted narratives.

For all its homely comforts and stable appearances the home is in a precarious position, and as architects we have to engage in the battle to retain—or even reclaim—it as a sanctuary, as a place of mental as well as physical shelter. Perhaps, in consideration of the arguments outlined, it might be a case of designing a place of residence that more thoroughly inverts the atmosphere ‹against› the flow of a public life indoctrinated by the private interest. Or at least this appears to be the solution in respect to today's conditions, where we are increasingly encouraged to feel at home at work; where corporate mentality is the only mentality; where business knows our pleasures. The solution is to make our homes ‹unheimlich›[13], render ourselves not ‹homeless› but still displaced; necessarily delirious and invisible so that we might best rediscover our security.

In the words of Constant Nieuwenhuys, «it is vital that ‹normal› behavioural patterns be interrupted, that a short circuit should occur between ‹daily habits› and an environment so designed as to exclude all compulsive behaviour from the outset, in other words, a ‹disorienting environment›[14]. Within this disorienting environment, «‹straying› [would] no longer have the negative sense of ‹getting lost›, but the more positive sense of discovering new paths»[15].

In a bizarre turn of events it seems we have ended up arguing for a return to one or more of the various modernist failures, creating disconcerting dwellings and pulling apart work and living in the functionalist sensibility; a kind of riff on J. G. Ballard's ‹High-Rise›. Not, of course, because it seems like a genuinely good idea… But because it feels like otherwise we are destined to drift through life in a state of reverie, never-endingly tumbling from one nightmare to another. We are so embedded in the various spiders' webs of human constructions, so deeply conditioned by society and the various ideas of what is ‹normal› and what is ‹appropriate› that it has become increasingly difficult to determine which way is up. At the root of it all is a deep-seated unwillingness to be critical in our thinking, and I'll be damned if the anarchist in me should succumb to slumber in my armchair.

1 Private talk by Benno Tempel for TU Delft students participating in a Methods & Analysis workshop with Anne Lacaton at Gemeentemuseum, Den Haag, February 2017.
2 Peter Sloterdijk, Bubbles: Microspherology, 2011, p.28.
3 Hannah Arendt, The Human Condition, 1958, p.28.
4 ‹Companis› is derived from the Latin words for together (‹com›) and bread (‹panis›), relating more strongly to the military or theatrical application of ‹company› than the more widely used legal-commercial term.
5 Ibid, p.60.
6 A company is called a ‹corporate›. The Latin word ‹corpus› means ‹body› in English. A corporation is thus a ‹legal person› created by means other than human birth.
7 Mark Cousins, ‹The Joylessness of Administered Space›, in: Fulcrum #4, February 16, 2011.
8 Aristotle, Nicomachean Ethics; Book X. Chapter 7, Section 7.
9 Julienne Hanson, Decoding Homes and Houses, 1998, p.6.
10 Ibid, p.7.
11 Georges Spyridaki, ‹Mort lucide›, 1953, p.35.
12 Jean Baudrillard, ‹The System of Objects›, 1996, p.23.
13 ‹Unheimlich› as the linguistic echo of the English antonym to homely: ‹unhomely› but also uncanny; perturbing.
14 Constant Nieuwenhuys, ‹The Principle of Disorientation›, 1974.
15 Ibid.

fig.b: Caruso St John, Brick House, London, 2001–2005. Fotografie: Hélène Binet

Verhältnisse

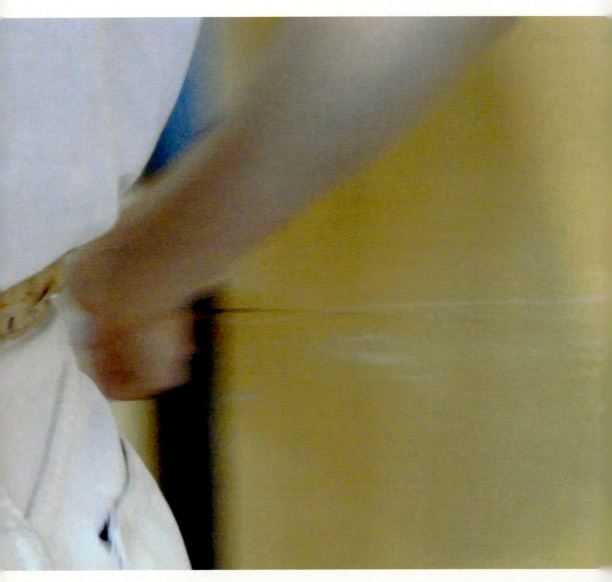

Verhältnisse
Sophie Keel

Ein Torso, eine Hand, ein Kreidestift, Wände. Sie läuft durch die ETH, an den Wänden des HIL-Gebäudes entlang, den Kreidestift auf Hüfthöhe, fest umgriffen in der Hand. Der Abstand zur Wand ist exakt so gross, dass sie mit der Spitze der Kreide die Wandfläche berührt. Die Kamera folgt ihr, einmal nur einige Zentimeter von ihrer Hüfte entfernt, einmal mit etwas mehr Abstand, so dass ihr Oberkörper vor der Wand sichtbar wird. Das Kratzen der Kreide über die verschiedenen Oberflächen ist unangenehm und setzt sich in den Ohren fest. Als sie eine negative Ecke erreicht, gerät sie ins Stocken, die Kreide bleibt in der Furche hängen. Doch es geht weiter: über die perforierten Holzwände der Vorlesungssäle, die gemauerten Wände der Kellergänge, immer weiter, während die Kreide kürzer wird und ihre Hand immer fester zudrücken muss.

‹Verhältnisse› ist eine performative Auseinandersetzung mit der Abstumpfung des Körperempfindens bis hin zu dessen Verlust. Das intensive Arbeiten und der Produktionsdruck im ersten Jahr des Architekturstudiums an der ETH waren Hintergrund dieser Beobachtung der Studentin Sophie Keel an ihrem eigenen Körper. Als kritisches Abbild dieses Verlustes wählte sie die Reibung ihres Körpers mit den Wänden der Architekturschule mittels eines Stiftes. Zum einen ist diese Reibung Abreibung und steht damit unmittelbar für den Verlust von Körper. Zum anderen ist die Reibung aber auch ein Kräftespiel zwischen dem Druck des Stifthaltens und dem Widerstand, die die Wand der Kreide entgegenbringt, bei dem es niemals einen Gewinner geben kann. Die Linie auf der Wand ist die Spur ihres Körpers: Eine Hinterlassenschaft auf einer spezifischen Höhe, und damit Ausdruck der Suche nach einer Bezugsgrösse, nach der eigenen Verortung in der umgebenden Architektur.

Die Arbeit ist im Rahmen des Kurses ‹Intervention und Körper› bei Matthias Wermke an der Professur für Architektur und Kunst ETH Zürich entstanden.

Dorothee Hahn

https://youtu.be/9znkZrCsF3s

«Est-ce que l'architecte possède un regard suffisamment critique, M. Ortelli?»

«Quand j'étais étudiant nous ne regardions pas tellement la production architecturale contemporaine. Nous allions chercher les textes, les contributions théoriques à partir desquelles nous produisions des projets qui étaient, de manière peut-être trop mécaniquement déductive, liés à une vision idéologique. Nous abordions, à l'université, des manières de concevoir l'architecture plus ou moins conscientes, explicites ou critiques vis-à-vis de la profession. J'ai été éduqué dans une prise de distance critique par rapport cette dernière. Aujourd'hui, c'est exactement le contraire. Les étudiants du monde entier regardent le dernier bâtiment de Herzog et De Meuron ou de Tadao Ando. C'est triste parce qu'apparemment, il n'y a plus de production théorique et très peu de critique architecturale, notamment à l'intérieur des universités.

Serait-ce une réaction à l'époque glorieuse des années 70 et 80 du siècle passé, durant lesquelles on produisait des théories mais aucun édifice? D'où la critique virulente contre l'architecture dite postmoderne, considérée architecture de papier? On a aujourd'hui une qualité, si on regarde l'architecture en tant que production d'objets, qui est très élevée. Qu'on aime ou pas, il y a des bâtiments extrêmement bien maîtrisés. Il me semble néanmoins qu'il n'y a pas de grands progrès au niveau des transformations de la ville et du territoire. C'est notre condition. La théorie a été remplacée par une attention à mon avis excessive pour des aspects phénoménologiques de l'architecture. Ils sont essentiels, mais l'architecture a aussi le potentiel de dire des choses, de résoudre des problèmes. Quand je regarde la manière dont se développent les villes africaines, chinoises ou celles des pays soi-disant émergents, perdre la tête parce qu'une surface rugueuse ‹vibre sous la lumière› me semble un discours d'un académisme insupportable.

Je parlais de l'idéologie. Il en existe encore aujourd'hui malgré tous ceux qui ont théorisé sa mort. Certains acquis provoquent des situations de passivité extrême de notre profession par rapport au potentiel qu'elle possède. Le succès de la construction en pisé, lui aussi, est idéologique. C'est un retour en arrière d'un siècle et demi. Un refus d'une certaine manière de concevoir l'architecture et les productions industrielles. Vous, la génération qui occupez actuellement les écoles, possédez une sensibilité et des exigences différentes qu'il y a dix ans. Il y a de plus en plus d'intérêt pour des situations autres que la Suisse et l'Europe, ou encore pour la question du logement. Il y a plein de signaux positifs, y compris le fait que vous soyez là aujourd'hui.

La question fondamentale réside dans le fait qu'on a tellement parlé des rapports entre l'architecture et la politique dans les années 80, qu'aujourd'hui on n'ose même pas affirmer une seule grande vérité: l'architecture est un acte politique. Je suis conscient de défendre une position délicate, difficile et critique parce que la mort des idéologies a été célébrée avec la chute du mur de Berlin. «Maintenant le monde est liquide», pour reprendre une expression de Zigmunt Baumann. «Nous sommes des individus et chacun cultive sa propre individualité.» Les idéologies sont identifiées avec tous les aspects négatifs que les pays communistes ont produits. Nier cette vision est pour moi une posture critique vis-à-vis du monde et du rôle que l'architecture occupe et pourrait occuper dans le monde, particulièrement par rapport à un horizon plus vaste possédant un contenu politique. C'est concevoir l'architecture en tant que série d'actions, de décisions et de connaissances dont l'objectif est le bien-être du plus grand nombre.

On n'a jamais autant parlé d'architecture qu'aujourd'hui. Herzog et De Meuron, Zaha Hadid ou Rem Koolhaas sont connus par tout le monde. Ce grand théâtre autour de l'architecture nous fait perdre notre capacité à analyser et critiquer. Cela ne signifie pas forcément dire du mal de quelque chose mais assumer une position critique par rapport à la production architecturale, parce qu'on a l'impression que le monde va dans une autre direction.

Il y avait, il y a deux semaines, une table ronde sur l'enseignement avec Eric Lapierre, Oliver Lütjens et moi-même. Un étudiant qui a fait son bachelor à Vienne a fait une intervention. Il disait qu'à Vienne il était surpris par la multitude de bâtiments magnifiques qu'il n'avait le droit de considérer que comme produits historiques. C'est également quelque chose qui nécessite une prise de position critique. L'histoire n'est pas la chronique du temps passé, elle est un segment temporel à l'intérieur duquel les architectes ont produit des édifices qui sont encore là et qui participent à notre vie quotidienne. La cathédrale de Lausanne est encore présente. On peut encore en discuter aujourd'hui. On doit en discuter, en tant qu'architectes. Les historiens de l'art ne sont pas les seules personnes autorisées à tenir un discours critique là-dessus. Nous le ferons sûrement de manière un peu barbare, parce qu'on l'est un peu en tant qu'architectes. On n'est pas très cultivés. Mais nous avons un point de vue complémentaire à celui de l'historien de l'art, un point de vue qui redonne aux bâtiments historiques leur rôle et leur vie à l'intérieur de la ville actuelle.»

Ce texte est extrait d'un interview de Luca Ortelli le 24 mai 2017, à l'EPF Lausanne, par Vincent Bianchi et Yann Salzmann.

Solo House
Saida Brückner and Adrien Meuwly

There is no client to be convinced, no built context to consider and no important financial restrictions to accept. Rather the condition of the laboratory leads to an architecture, that has to reference back to the discipline itself. The parameters of design are limited to cultural, constructive and historical influences.

© Office KGDVS, Solo House #2

There is no inside

It is a Circle with its inside that is the outside. Viewed from outside the building is a layering of insides and outsides: the inside is followed by the outside which is inside the circle, then another inside and the outside on the other side of the building.

The concrete floor is the threshold between the house and the landscape. It demarks the house from the landscape but it does not demark an inside space from an outside space. When you are inside then you are outside. And when you are outside you are inside at the same time.

Four walls, placed within the circle, create two sides. Both sides are insides and outsides. They are the same. The reflections of insides and outsides are superimposed. There is no being inside and there is no being outside at any time, there is always both, the inside and the outside.

There is only one place that lets the confusion rest: the only inside is the toilet—but it is not the inside of a house but the inside of a closet.

83

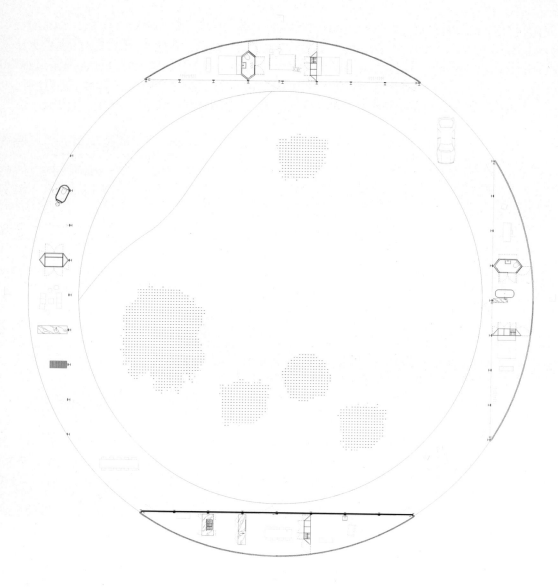

‹go (a)round in circles›

1. Lit. to move over and over on a circular path. *The model plane went around in circles until it ran out of fuel.*
2. Fig. to act in a confused and disoriented manner. *I've been going around in circles all day.*
3. Fig. to keep going over the same ideas or repeating the same actions, often resulting in confusion, without reaching a satisfactory decision or conclusion. *We're just going round in circles discussing the problem.*
(http://idioms.thefreedictionary.com/)

The Laboratory

The Solo Houses project invites a selection of architects to design exceptional houses within a laboratory context. All profane circumstances are minimized to provide the architect with the most creative freedom possible. It is an experiment that provides an ideal context to develop new architectural ideas and to test them on an unrestricted site.

The Gallery. The Solo Houses is an on site project by the Solo Gallery, developed and curated by Christian Bourdieu. The gallery focuses on the experimental work being produced by architects. By placing architecture within the context of the art gallery, it allows it to become more autonomous in conception and production.

The Site. A remote piece of land in the region Matarrana in Spain is the site of the laboratory. Two hours from Barcelona, the untouched natural landscape offers a context in which nature is the only defining element. The Solo Houses are placed within an independent environment, untouched by man.

The Collection. Fifteen houses will make up the first architecture collection in Europe. The selection of architects focuses on renowned international architects, selected by invitation only. Each house will be placed on its own within an untouched landscape, but the collection will be a singular accumulation of inventive architectural ideas on a single piece of land. The houses will be sold individually as pieces of architecture but remain part of a complex of holiday homes that will be rented out at certain times of the year.

The context created by the Solo Houses project puts architects in a new situation in which architecture is no longer primarily a problem solving exercise. The architecture is free of the constraints imposed by established conditions. There is no client to be persuaded, no built context to consider and no important financial restrictions to accept. Rather the condition of the laboratory leading to an architecture, that has to reference back to the discipline itself. The parameters of design are limited to cultural, constructive and historical influences. This gives the chance and challenge to rethink the inherent forms, elements and uses of architecture in order to put in question traditional ways of practising architecture. The laboratory allows the freedom to experiment with something new. It can be a catalyst for a critical reflection of architecture and the architect's own work. It is research put into practice.

Walls are replaced by distance

Walls create a practically complete isolation from the outside world. Thinking about a wall, the image of a package of many layers comes to mind—the sandwich: bricks, an unknown number of plastic sheets, insulation glued on the whole, covered by a nice uniform colour. Thus, walls provide privacy to the different rooms of a house; they permit the direct juxtaposition of antagonistic activities and produce very dense living places. What is happening on the other side of the wall, even so close, remains unknown.

In the Solo House, there are no walls. The model of the house made of walls has been expended, the concentration of its different rooms distributed around an empty core. The walls have been replaced by distance. Placing the different functions of the home far away from each other produces privacy. You glimpse at the distant living room as you would glimpse at your neighbours' TV across the street to know what program they follow.

Two people on the opposite side of the house can be seen in the distance, but neither their activities nor their discussions are distinguishable. Only their strong exclamations are perceptible

Solo House

through the forty meters of emptiness. These fragments of intrusion, which would be understood as disturbances through a badly insulated wall, create a tension between the parts of the home. Solo House is a series of open private spaces.

Champagne

We are strolling around in a circle, passing people sipping champagne and sitting in the sun. Others are walking around following the architects on every step with black notebooks in their hands. We observe the group that are meticulously jotting things down. It feels that the day is too sunny, the house too beautiful and the situation too exceptional to stare onto a piece of paper.

Everyone seems to know each other and yet it is a curious combination of people. There are the friends of the architects: beautiful intellectuals that came to celebrate the opening of the new building. For them it is a relaxed gathering of old and new friends, an opportunity to come together, drink champagne and talk about new projects. On the other hand there are the journalists enjoying the champagne with care, they pay attention and take notes—documenting the architectural masterpiece that was created in this far off place. Neither famous friends nor professional journalists, we are the odd ones out.

As we do not have to catch up on old stories and we do not have to report every word the architects say, we walk around the house and observe the architecture and the people. It feels as if the house was designed for precisely this situation: a collection of 50 privileged people drinking champagne in the sun.

Appetizers and small bites of food are served together with more champagne. A blond woman skips the line to go around the bar and ask for a «glass of white wine for the architect, please». Another women talks about last Saturday's dinner with «Pezo and Sofia*». Some people start lying around the pool on sun loungers designed by the architects' brother.

The more champagne we drink the more we feel part of the scenery—maybe you need a state of slight delirium to step over the threshold of the inner circle. To be part of it you need to feel part of it. The sun, the reflections, the champagne and the mise en scene of the assembly lets everyone drift away in a dreamlike befogged state.

There is no outside anymore, there is just being in the moment at the place. We are not observing anymore, we are talking, laughing, discussing, drinking. We are a small community in a beautiful place. No one is coming or leaving, everyone just moves within the infinity of the house. The perfect circle has no direction and time passes without anyone noticing. The sun wanders but for us, there is no more east or west. We stay in a delirium of complete bliss. It is the epitome of hedonism. We admired the architecture when we arrived but now we live it.

Gottfried Semper visiting the Solo House

GS Foundation: check. Structure and roof: check. Even though the roof looks quite similar to the floor. What about the enclosure? (Kersten Geers goes away and comes back dragging a heavy metal panel with him.)
GS OK, fine. In the centre of the house is the fire. Where is your fire?
KG Well… The house has no centre.

* von Ellrichshausen

Insulae

The Solo Houses park is a remote place with a limited accommodation capacity. The gallery invites architects to rethink the model of the holiday home: a retreat away from the problems of the troubled world, an ideal place glorifying the bond between people and nature. The Solo Houses project thus finds its roots in its restrictive character. The amount of houses, as the amount of people is limited, in order for the park not to be turned into a Club Med. To stay in one of the Solo Houses is the privilege of a wealthy society.

    The project brings up the recurrent question of the architect's role in society. Architecture is intrinsically a social practice; architects are responsible for the production of liveable built environments for social cohabitation. Solo Houses however is taking a distance from society. With its remoteness it is far from touching social problems.

    It creates a context only for the sake of architecture. Thus, the progress it generates is exclusively architectural and will be experienced only by the small amount of its privileged inhabitants. However this context allows to produce new ideas, which are contributions to the general cultural wealth.

    The question arises whether the ideal design context of Solo Houses could be taken as an example to also reflect on other programs: it has to be seen if Solo Supermarket or Solo Social Housing has any to chance to exist or whether exclusivity is an inherent condition of Solo.

The Storm

September, late in the afternoon. The day has been hot. It is amazing how heavy the air feels in this region. Sitting at the swimming pool, he is reading the last chapters of his book: a holiday novel he had bought in a gas station on his way from Paris. But he is not concentrating on his reading. He appreciates the moment, that stunning silence and the sun on his skin.

    A light breeze gets up and refreshes the air, blowing on the light silver curtains that are now dancing in the air. He had completely opened the sliding facade earlier in the day, hoping for this wind to come and ventilate the house. He empties his glass, drops his book on the table and jumps into the pool.

    Climbing the few steps to get out of the water he realizes that the sun is now swathed in clouds. He feels a little cold but remains optimistic: the weather forecast was indicating a few drops of rain, but not before nine. But as he returns to his *chaise longue* a sudden gust of wind tips over the small table away, breaking the glass on the floor. This violent mass of air raising dust, leaves and small tree branches now crosses the entire house. A few seconds later it starts to rain. There is no time to collect the glass splinters. He rushes to the first piece of sliding façade—the one he had used as a sun shade in the afternoon—and starts closing it. He runs to the second one and drags it to the first. Only one third of these huge panels are now in place and the sky is getting darker and darker. On the horizon, thunderbolts are already dropping out of the sky.

    As he arrives in his room the rainwater has already reached the bed. He steps off the floor onto the soggy earth to pull the next heavy panel. He slowly moves it to its place, barefoot, slipping in the mud. He still has to close the kitchen on the opposite side of the house, forty meters away. He wants to cross diametrically through the centre of the house, but the vegetation is definitely too dense. The wet and slippery terrazzo slows down his run along the curved way. Arriving there, the floor is covered with water, sand and leaves, but he

has no time to think: the thunderstorm is getting closer. He uses his last strength to close the panels and finally finds himself safe in the kitchen, freezing, wearing nothing but his speedo.

The Architecture of Objects

The connection between landscape and inhabitants is the strongest parameter of Office's Solo House design. The minimization of the architectural elements' physicality aims to let the architecture vanish in the surrounding nature. There are walls, columns, a floor and a roof, but they have no visual importance. The floor and the roof are two simple concrete slabs, the walls are made of glass and the columns are lost between the outside trees. The house is almost nothing.

In contrast the geometric objects staged upon the slab of the roof create a sculpture exhibition. Containing the technical devices, the sculptures objectify what is usually hidden. The technical devices are the only elements of the house that have a physical and visual mass. At the same time they are the only elements that the inhabitant does not directly interact with.

The objects on the roof are not merely a demonstration of technics. It is not simply about showing on the outside what is usually hidden inside. No ducts or ventilation shafts are exposed. The technical elements were rather given abstract geometric shapes that are designed as all the other elements in the house. They become thus an even more important part of the architecture. The objects become stylistic devices that are the only volumetrically defining parameters. The architecture is no longer an architecture of elements, but an architecture of objects.

© Bas Princen

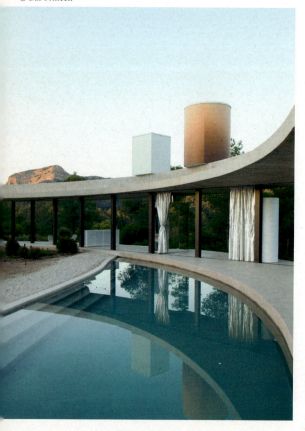

Unkritische Nähe.
Erik Wegerhoff

Reflexionen über Peter Zumthors und Juhani Pallasmaas Konzepte einer Architektur der Empfindsamkeit

Architektonische Qualität bedeutet, «von einem Bauwerk berührt» zu sein. Peter Zumthor zumindest meint das, gleich zu Beginn seines 2006 erschienenen Büchleins mit dem Titel ‹Atmosphären›. Darin propagiert Zumthor eine Architektur der Empfindsamkeit, haptisch und körperlich erfahrbar und nicht intellektuell.

Ganz ähnliche Gedanken äussert der finnische Architekt Juhani Pallasmaa. Sein 2012 herausgekommenes Buch ‹The Eyes of the Skin› spricht schon in seinem Titel der Haut die Fähigkeit des Sehens zu, verleiht dem Spüren also die Qualität von Einsichten.[1]

Eine solche Sinnenfreude kann einem kaum anders als sympathisch sein. Tatsächlich haben derlei Ideen im jüngeren Architekturdiskurs einen solchen Nachhall gefunden, dass man von einer ‹Neuen Sinnlichkeit› sprechen kann. Zumthors und Pallasmaas Bücher gehören zu den erfolgreichsten Architekten-publikationen der letzten Jahre, ihre Gedanken wurden und werden auflagenstark vervielfältigt.[2]

Doch diese Neue Sinnlichkeit hat Schattenseiten. Ihr impliziter Mystizismus und ihr expliziter Anti-Intellektualismus verorten den Architekten in einer Position der Unangreifbarkeit. Ein Hinterfragen ist nicht vorgesehen in diesen Gedanken zu einer Architektur, die empfunden anstatt verstanden werden soll. Die einfühlende Nähe, die ein solches Architekturempfinden voraussetzt, lässt keinen Raum für reflektierende Distanz. In anderen Worten: Die Neue Sinnlichkeit kennt keine Kritik. Das offenbart eine – kritische – Lektüre der beiden Texte. Diese ist längst überfällig, um diese Konjunktur der Empfindsamkeit zurückzuholen dorthin, wo architektonische Qualität sich eigentlich entwickelt: in einem kritischen Diskurs aus geschriebenen wie gebauten Beiträgen.

Zumthors Mystizismus

Peter Zumthor ist streng genommen nicht der Autor des Buchs Atmosphären, sondern der Erzähler der Worte in dem von Brigitte Labs-Ehlert herausgegebenen Band. Dies ist nicht irrelevant, was Ton und Position von Zumthors Zeilen anbelangt. Im Vorwort der Herausgeberin nämlich erfährt man, dass es sich bei dem folgenden Essay um einen 2003 auf einem Kunstfestival in der norddeutschen Provinz frei gehaltenen Vortrag handelt, der im gedruckten Text wortwörtlich wiedergegeben werde.[3] Tatsächlich meint man, den Architekten reden zu hören, wenn man die von spontanen Einschüben und etwas wundersamem Satzbau charakterisierten folgenden Zeilen liest. Die Intention dieser gedruckten Tonspur liegt zweifellos darin, die Sinnlichkeit des Hörens gegenüber dem abstrakteren Lesen herauszustellen. Allerdings erinnert diese unveränderte Aufzeichnung einer Stimme auch an die Evangelien. Matthäus, Markus, Lukas und Johannes notierten bekanntlich auch, was ihnen vom Himmel kommend eingeflüstert wurde, ein häufiges Motiv in der christlichen Ikonographie.[4] Es handelt sich also, darf man schliessen, um eine Notation oder auch: Übersetzung eines Wissens aus einer anderen Sphäre. Das muss auch der Grund für die ungewöhnliche Illustration des Vorworts sein (Abb. a). Abgebildet ist da nämlich ebenfalls eine Übersetzung: Arnold Böcklins ‹Toteninsel›, ein zypressenbestandenes rätselhaftes Eiland, zu dem ein Kahn mit einem Sarg und einer daneben stehenden Figur übersetzt. Noch bevor man Zumthors Text liest, weiss man also, dass es sich um gewichtige Worte handelt und das Buch die Übersetzung auratischen Wissens darstellt, das in Bereiche des Religiösen vordringt. Die Herausgeberin deutet hier bereits einen Mystizismus an, den der Architekt im Folgenden zu einer sehr persönlichen Architekturtheorie ausbaut.

Nachdem Zumthor eröffnend architektonische Qualität als von einem Bauwerk Berührtsein definiert hat (wie oben dargestellt), sinnt er in neun kurzen Abschnitten darüber nach, wie Architektur rezipiert wird und wie er sie kreiert. Dem Menschen schreibt Zumthor dabei die Fähigkeit zu, Architektur zu empfinden. Zentral ist ein emotionaler Zugang. In seinen Worten:

«[…]die Wahrnehmung, die unglaublich rasch funktioniert […]. Wir werden ja nicht jedesmal, in jeder Situation irgendwie lang denken wollen, ob uns das gefällt oder nicht […]. Da ist etwas in uns, das uns sofort viel sagt. Sofortiges Verständnis, sofortige Berührung, sofortige Ablehnung.»[5]

Diese sowohl emotionale als auch tatsächlich physische Berührung werde hervorgerufen durch sinnlich erfahrbare Materialien. Die Zusammenstellung verschiedener Baustoffe schliesslich steigere diese Erfahrung ins Transzendente. Der Architekt nennt das weihevoll die «Magie des Realen».[6] Auf diese magische, nur der Empfindung zugängliche, intellektuell nicht begreifliche Dimension der haptisch greifbaren Architektur spielt der Redner an, indem er immer wieder gewisse Wendungen in seinen Vortrag einstreut, die die Grenzen menschlichen Wissens und die Existenz einer höheren Wahrheit andeuten. Zunächst ist das die stete Formel «ich weiß [sic] nicht». So sagt er beispielsweise über den Klang von Bauten: «Ich weiß [sic] nicht, was es ist. Es ist vielleicht der Wind oder so».[7] Ein weiterer Topos der Zumthor'schen Rede über eine auch ihm verborgene Dimension der Architektur ist das Geheimnis. So nennt er das Kombinieren von Materialien «Großes Geheimnis, große Leidenschaft, große [sic] Freude».[8] Dieser in einem sinnlich-emotionalen Zugang zur Architektur begründete Mystizismus steigert sich letztlich ins Religiöse. Den Abschluss des letzten, neunten Kapitels über Architektur, eine Hommage an das Licht, bildet das Eingeständnis, dass auch dieses sich dem Begreifen entziehe und auf die Existenz eines Göttlichen verweise: «Ich verstehe dieses Licht nicht. Ich habe da das Gefühl, es gibt etwas Größeres [sic], das ich nicht verstehe».[9] Es wird kein Zufall sein, dass diese Passage illustriert ist mit einem Foto des Oculus' der Bruder-Klaus-Kapelle, das mit den Reflexionen entlang der fluchtenden Kanneluren im Beton unübersehbar an Darstellungen des Heiligen Geists erinnert – an das die Taube umgebende Strahlenbündel, beispielsweise bei Gianlorenzo Berninis Cathedra Petri im Petersdom. Die Religiosität Zumthor'schen Architekturdenkens spiegelt sich auch in der Gliederung der Rede, ergänzt er die neun Abschnitte zuletzt doch um drei kurze Unterpunkte. Die unvollkommene Zahl Neun spiegelt menschliche Imperfektion wider, die sich letztlich mit Nichtwissen bescheiden muss; zur Perfektion bedarf es der Erweiterung um die Dreifaltigkeit. Hier eine solche Zahlenmystik zu erkennen, dürfte kaum überinterpretiert sein, wenn Zumthor den ersten seiner drei Anhänge als Transzendenz[10] bezeichnet.

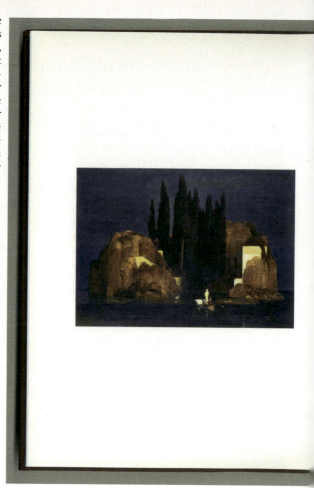

Abb. a: Vorwort zu Peter Zumthors Text ‹Atmosphären› (2006) von Brigitte Labs-Ehlert, illustriert mit Arnold Böcklins ‹Toteninsel›

Pallasmaas Über-Sinnlichkeit

Zumthors sinnlicher Mystizismus findet einen Vor-läufer und zahlreiche Parallelen in Juhani Pallasmaas seit den 1990er Jahren publizierten Gedanken zu einer Architektur, die eine umfassende sinnliche Wahrnehmung ansprechen will. Ähnlich wie der Schweizer sich von Architektur «berührt» fühlt, schreibt auch der finnische Architekt: «Every touching experience of architecture is multi-sensory».[11] Die konventionellen fünf Sinne ergänzt Pallasmaa schon in seinem 1994 erschienenen Aufsatz ‹An Architecture of the Seven Senses› um eine Empfindung von Skelett und Muskel und damit um eine Körperlichkeit, die auch bei Zumthor so bedeutend ist. Pallasmaa wendet sich in einem historischen Rundumschlag vor allem gegen eine Kultur der Dominanz allein visueller Wahrnehmung, deren Ursprünge er schon in der Renaissance erkennt, die vor allem aber im 20. Jahrhundert mit den technischen

Vorwort

Zwiegespräch mit der Schönheit

Es ist ein Wechselspiel, eines von Nehmen und Geben, zwischen Peter Zumthors Bauten und den vorgefundenen Umgebungen. Ein Aufmerken. Ein Anreichern. Beim Umgang mit seiner Architektur fällt unweigerlich und sofort der Begriff der Atmosphäre, eine Stimmung, eine Gestimmtheit des gebauten Raumes, die sich direkt den Betrachtern, Bewohnern, Besuchern und eben auch der Nachbarschaft mitteilt und an sie weitergegeben wird. Peter Zumthor schätzt Orte und Häuser, die den Menschen aufheben, ihn gut wohnen lassen und unauffällig unterstützen. Das Einlesen in den Ort, das Herausarbeiten von Zweck, Sinn und Ziel des Auftrages, das Entwerfen, Planen und Gestalten des Bauwerks ist deshalb ein vielfach verschränkter, nicht einfach linearer Prozeß.

Atmosphäre ist bei Peter Zumthor eine Kategorie der Ästhetik. Welche Rolle der Architekt ihr zumißt und wie er sie beachtet, darüber gibt dieses Buch Auskunft. Es enthält den Vortrag ‹Atmosphären. Architektonische Umgebungen – Die Dinge um mich herum›, den der Schweizer Architekt während des Literatur- und Musikfestes ‹Wege durch das Land› am 1. Juni 2003 an einem passenden Ort

Die Toteninsel
(erste Fassung), Arnold Böcklin 1880, Kunstmuseum Basel

Medien visueller Reproduktion (der Kamera) vorherrschend geworden sei.[12] Inwiefern Architektur und deren Erfahrung jedoch auch andere Sinne als nur das Sehen allein ansprechen könne, skizziert er in den folgenden Abschnitten jeweils anhand von Beispielen. Deren Wahl und implizite Aussage zeigt wiederum eine gewisse Nähe zu Zumthor und ist in Bezug auf die (mangelnde) Kritikfähigkeit des Rezipienten von Architektur vielsagend. So konstatiert Pallasmaa beispielsweise zum Hören in der Architektur:

«Sight makes us solitary, whereas hearing creates a sense of connection and solidarity; the gaze wanders lonesomely in the dark depths of a cathedral, but the sound of the organ makes us realize our affinity with the space. […] The sound of church bells through the streets makes us aware of our citizenship.»[13]

Beispielhaft für die hier herausgehobene integrative Kraft des Klangs ist ein Sakralbau, dessen innenräumliches und stadträumliches Erlebnis. Hören löst hier ein Zugehörigkeitsgefühl aus, einmal eine Wesensverwandtschaft mit dem Kirchenraum, einmal die Bürgerschaft. Auch wenn er diese Integration weitgehend entsakralisiert, die Glocken also nicht an die Religionszugehörigkeit und die Rhythmisierung des Tages und Jahres durch die Kirche, sondern an die Verortung in einer Stadt erinnern sollen, ist die Präsenz des Sakralen auffällig – und wird mit dem einschliessenden uns («us», «our») wie selbstverständlich vorausgesetzt. Pallasmaas Glaubensgemeinschaft des Hörens ist keine so deutlich christliche wie diejenige Zumthors, aber auch seine Über-Sinnlichkeit kennzeichnet eine Affinität zum Heiligen. Stille in der Architektur etwa konnotiert Pallasmaa allein mit Religiösem: ägyptischen Tempeln, einer gotischen Kathedrale, gregorianischen Gesängen und dem Pantheon.[14]

Unkritische Nähe:
Der Distanzverlust der Neuen Sinnlichkeit

Man ginge an die Grenzen wissenschaftlicher Legitimität, träfe aber durchaus eine Kernaussage, würde man Peter Zumthors oben herausgestelltes Zitat reduzieren auf «Wir werden ja nicht […] denken wollen». In Zumthors Vorstellung zählt der (körperliche) Reflex, nicht die (intellektuelle) Reflexion. Architektur nimmt man ihm zufolge intuitiv sensuell und physisch wahr, ohne dass ein Denkprozess involviert wäre. Dass ihm kritisches Reflektieren zweitklassig ist, machen solche Äusserungen deutlich wie «dieses lineare Denken, das wir auch haben und das ich auch liebe, von A nach B mit dem Kopf»[15]. Denken wird hier auf das Zurücklegen einer Strecke reduziert, eine Unterkomplexität, die dadurch nicht besser wird, dass der Redner bekennt, er «liebe» es auch. Selbst Denken ist bei Zumthor offenbar nur mit Gefühlen zu umschreiben. Das ist keine zufällige Formulierung, wie an späterer Stelle deutlich wird, wo er meint, er «kenne sehr wohl die Magie des Gedankens. Und die Leidenschaft des schönen Gedankens», auch wenn ihm die «Magie des Realen» wichtiger sei.[16] Abermals wird Denken verniedlicht und der Emotion untergeordnet. Und letztlich ist offenbar selbst das Denken Teil einer Magie, als deren Apologet Zumthor sich präsentiert. In diesem Zusammenhang betrachtet, wird auch offenbar, warum der Redner so oft betont, dass er nicht wisse. Wissen ist, als Nebenprodukt der abgelehnten Reflexion, überflüssig.

Die Neue Sinnlichkeit, die durchaus ihre gewinnenden Seiten hat, indem sie zurecht auf die auch sensuellen Seiten der Imagination und Rezeption von Architektur hinweist, sie geht in dem Moment zu weit, wenn sie sich zum Anti-Intellektualismus steigert. Pallasmaa diagnostiziert eine «current over-emphasis on the intellectual and conceptual dimensions of architecture».[17] Das mag vor allem in den 1990er Jahren und damit zu Hochzeiten dekonstruktivistischer und postmoderner Theorien nachvollziehbar gewesen sein.

Doch was meint er, wenn er diesem vermeintlichen Über-Intellektualismus einen «wisdom of the body»[18] entgegensetzt? Für ihn ist tatsächlich ein nicht sprachlich und nicht intellektuell vermitteltes Wissen im Körper vorhanden, das sich als Tradition fortsetze. Das sollen wohl Sätze aussagen wie «The essence of a tradition is the wisdom of the body stored in the haptic memory.»[19] Eine solche Sichtweise auf Architektur aber bewegt sich allein auf dem Niveau von Instinkten. Pallasmaas «touching experience», Zumthors «sofortige Berührung», sie suggerieren eine Nähe, die ihre erotischen Reize hat – aber es gibt kein Entkommen mehr daraus. Abweichende Positionen sind ausgeschlossen. Tatsächlich beschreibt Pallasmaa den Prozess des Entwerfens und des Rezipierens von Architektur als Liebesakt von Architekt und Bewohner:

«[A]n architect internalizes a building in his body; movement, balance, distance and scale are felt unconsciously through the body as tension in the muscular system and in the positions of the skeleton and inner organs. As the work interacts with the body of the observer the experience mirrors these bodily sensations of the maker. Consequently, architecture is communication from the body of the architect directly to the body of the inhabitant.»[20]

Eine solche Nähe[21] aber erlaubt keine divergierenden Empfindungen, geschweige denn Ansichten – vielleicht ist Sehen auch deshalb vermeintlich überbewertet. Dem Rezipienten bleibt nichts als nachzuempfinden, was der Architekt fühlend entworfen hat. In Pallasmaas Worten muss er sich beschränken aufs «Widerspiegeln». In der engen Umarmung von ‹ob-server› und ‹maker› aber erstickt der Kritiker.

Reflexion und Distanz als Voraussetzungen von Kritik

Zumthors wie Pallasmaas wie selbstverständlich vorausgesetzte undefinierte höhere Macht setzt Glauben voraus und schliesst Hinterfragen aus. Der Preis für die komplette körperliche Integration in eine Welt der Nähe voll sensualistischer Erfahrungen ist der Verlust von Distanz. So verortet und inszeniert die Neue Sinnlichkeit den Architekten in einer Position der Unangreifbarkeit. Ein gewisser analytischer Abstand aber und ein auch intellektueller Zugang zu Architektur sind unverzichtbare Voraussetzungen von Kritik. Natürlich kann man etwas auch intuitiv ablehnen, Kritik aber erfordert einen komplexeren Prozess, sie kann nicht aus Intuition entstehen. Denn: «Kritisieren ist […] nicht Negation, sondern ein In-Frage-stellen», wie es beispielsweise Ole W. Fischer 2015 in einem Beitrag für ‹werk, bauen + wohnen› klarstellt.[22] Dabei ist nicht Kritik um der Kritik willen das Ziel. Sondern es geht darum, überhaupt eine Debatte in der Architektur zu ermöglichen. Architektur und ihre Entwicklung kann man begreifen als einen dauernden kritischen Diskurs aus geschriebenen wie gebauten Beiträgen. In dieser ständigen Interaktion verschiedenster Ansichten, mit Statements und Einwänden aus Worten wie aus Werkstoffen, kommt der Architekturkritik eine herausragende Rolle zu. Der Kritiker ist ebenso wie der Entwerfer ein unverzichtbarer Akteur in einer dauernden gesellschaftlichen Debatte über Architektur und ihre Qualität.

Fruchtbar kann eine solche Debatte aber nur sein, wenn die Akteure innerhalb dieses Diskurses in einem Spannungsverhältnis der Unabhängigkeit stehen, in einer Situation, die kreative Konflikte erlaubt. Das geht nicht ohne Abstand. Die grosse Bedeutung von Distanz als Grundvoraussetzung einer Kultur des reflektierenden Hinterfragens stellt beispielsweise einer der wichtigsten Beiträge heraus, die in jüngerer Zeit über Architekturkritik verfasst worden sind, Françoise Fromonots 2011 in der ‹archithese› erschienener Artikel ‹Der richtige Abstand. Über die Beziehung zwischen architektonischer Praxis und Architekturkritik›. Der Beitrag der französischen Kritikerin und Publizistin liest sich weitenteils wie eine Entgegnung auf Juhani Pallasmaas «communication from the body of the architect directly to the body of the inhabitant» (obwohl er nicht als solche verfasst wurde). Symbiose, Fusion oder Schizophrenie nennt Fromonot Spielarten einer Architekturpublizistik, in der Kritiker und Architekt sich zum gegenseitigen Vorteil in den Vordergrund rücken, Architekten selbst vorgeblich kritisch schreiben, oder aber mal als Entwerfer, mal als Kritiker auftreten. All diesen Varianten bescheinigt sie einen Mangel an Distanz. Der einzige Ausweg aus diesem Dilemma einer zu grossen Nähe – und also einer zu grossen Freundlichkeit, einer gegenseitigen Abhängigkeit – ist ihrer Ansicht nach die Wahrung eines bewussten Abstands zwischen Kritiker und Architekt. Nur das garantiere die Autonomie der Kritik. Wer den Kontakt mit dem Entwerfer meide, so Fromonot, «kann sich besser auf die Kritik des Werkes konzentrieren und diese Kritik […] besser begrifflich erfassen».[23]

Allerdings wurden hier zwei Diskurse wiedergegeben, die bislang kaum miteinander in Beziehung gekommen sind. Fast keine der Publikationen der letzten Jahre, die sich dem Sinnlichen oder den oft damit assoziierten «Atmosphären» in der Architektur widmen, kommt ohne Pallasmaa und Zumthor aus – Exzerpte aus den hier untersuchten und anderen Schriften, wohlwollende Interviews oder Portraits der Bauten.[24] Doch fast ausnahmslos gebärden sich solche Publikationen als Sprachrohr der hier beschriebenen

Neuen Sinnlichkeit, ohne deren Anti-Intellektualismus und Kritikfeindlichkeit zu erkennen und zu thematisieren. Der französische Architekt Jacques Lucan ist einer der wenigen, die diesen Diskurs jüngst skeptischer beäugt haben. Er problematisiert Zumthors Wissensabneigung und attestiert ihm eine «alles in allem romantische Haltung», die ihn zu einem «antimodernen» Architekten mache.[25] Es ist Zeit für eine Kritik an der Kritikfeindlichkeit der Neuen Sinnlichkeit.

1   Peter Zumthor, ‹Atmosphären. Architektonische Umgebungen; die Dinge um mich herum›, Basel 2006, das Zitat S. 11.
    Juhani Pallasmaa, ‹The Eyes of the Skin. Architecture and the Senses›, Chichester 2012.
2   Grundlage von Pallasmaas Buch war sein Aufsatz ‹An Architecture of the Seven Senses›, in: ‹a+u› [‹Architecture and Urbanism›], Juli 1994, S. 27–37. Das Buch erschien in jeweils neuen Überarbeitungen London 1996, Chichester 2005 und Chichester 2012. Zumthors ‹Atmosphären› erfuhr zahlreiche Übersetzungen: ins Englische und Spanische (2006), Französische (2008), Tschechische (2013) und Chinesische (2014).
3   Brigitte Labs-Ehlert, ‹Zwiegespräch mit der Schönheit›, in: Zumthor: ‹Atmosphären›, 2006 (wie Anm. 1), S. 6-9.
4   Vgl. beispielsweise Caravaggio: ‹Matthäus und der Engel› (1602), Rom, San Luigi dei Francesi, oder Rembrandt: ‹Der Evangelist Matthäus und der Engel› (1661), Paris, Louvre.
5   Zumthor, ‹Atmosphären›, 2006 (wie Anm. 1), S. 13.
6   Ebd., S. 17 und 19.
7   Ebd., S. 31. Ähnlich, über Musik: «[N]ach zwei Sekunden ist das Gefühl da! […] Und ich weiß [sic] nicht warum», S. 13; über Intimität: «Ich weiß [sic] aber nicht so viel darüber […], aber es ist da», S. 49.
8   Ebd., S. 23. Ähnlich: «[D]as erste und größte [sic] Geheimnis der Architektur [ist es], daß [sic] sie Dinge aus der Welt, Materialien aus der Welt zusamenführt», S. 23. Zu seiner Tätigkeit: «Ich liebe diese Arbeit, und je länger ich sie mache, umso geheimnisvoller wird sie irgendwie», S. 25.
9   Ebd., S. 61–63.
10 Ebd., S. 63.
11 Pallasma, ‹An Architecture of the Seven Senses›, 1994 (wie Anm. 2), S. 30. Der Kürze halber wird hier aus dem Aufsatz von 1994 zitiert, der die Grundlage für ‹The Eyes of the Skin›, 2012 (wie Anm. 1) bildete, wo die Zitate sich leicht umformuliert wiederfinden.
12 Pallasma, ‹An Architecture of the Seven Senses› (1994, wie Anm. 2), S. 29.
13 Ebd., S. 31.
14 Ebd.
15 Zumthor, ‹Atmosphären›,2006 (wie Anm. 1), S. 13.
16 Ebd., S. 17 und 19.
17 Pallasma, ‹An Architecture of the Seven Senses›, 1994 (wie Anm. 2), S. 29.
18 Ebd.
19 Ebd., S. 34.
20 Ebd., S. 36.
21 Nähe ist ein stetes Thema bei Pallasmaa, vgl. etwa: «Beyond architecture, our culture at large seems to drift towards a distancing, a kind of chilling, de-sensualization and de-eroticization of the human relation to reality.», ebd., S. 29; den Kapiteltitel ‹Acoustic Intimacy›, S. 30; «[T]ouch is the sense of nearness, intimacy and affection», S. 34.
22 Ole W. Fischer, ‹Architektur, Theorie, Kritik?›, in: ‹werk, bauen + wohnen› 102 (2015), April, S. 47f., hier 48.
23 Françoise Fromonot, ‹Der richtige Abstand. Über die Beziehung zwischen architektonischer Praxis und Architekturkritik›, in: ‹archithese› 41 (2011), Juli/August: Architekturkritik›, S. 62–65, das Zitat S. 64. Fromonot ist Gründungs-Mitherausgeberin der 2008 etablierten französischen Zeitschrift ‹criticat›.
24 Beginnend mit der die Therme von Vals und Zumthor mystifizierenden Publikation ‹Peter Zumthor: Thermal Bath at Vals›, London 1996 (Architectural Association: Exemplary Projects, 1). Siehe etwa auch Christian Borch (Hg.): ‹Architectural Atmospheres. On the Experience and Politics of Architecture›, Basel 2014; ‹OASE› 91 (2014): ‹Sfeer bouwen/Building Atmosphere›; ‹Architectural Design› 78 (2008), Nr. 3, Mai/Juni: ‹Interior Atmospheres›.
25 «Zumthor privilégie ainsi constamment ce qui est de l'ordre d'une connaissance intuitive, au détriment d'une connaissance ‹savante›. Jacques Lucan: ‹Précisions sur un état présent de l›architecture›, Lausanne 2015, S. 165, die «posture somme toute romantique» S. 166, das Prädikat «antimoderne» S. 129f.

Die Fleischwerdung des Katasterplans

Kritik als Methode
oder Die Schönheit des Katasterplans
Jan Engelke und Lukas Fink

Architektonisches Entwerfen ist in der Regel lösungsorientiert. Meist bildet ein reales Problem den Ausgangspunkt des Projekts und dieses dient als Veränderungsinstrument, als ein Werkzeug zur Herstellung erstrebenswerter Zukünfte. Unser Projekt ‹Die Schönheit des Katasterplans› geht von einem kritischenEntwurfsverständnis aus, das vielmehr erkenntnis- als lösungsorientiert ist.

Die kritische Methode als Werkzeug

Dabei verstehen wir die Architektur als eine Disziplin, deren Grenzen sich nicht im Gebauten, in der Form erschöpfen. Der Entwurf ist eine Praxis, welche nicht primär Antworten gibt, sondern selbst kritische Fragen stellt und dadurch ihren eigenen Möglichkeitsraum erweitert. Er ist eine experimentelle Untersuchung bestehender Situationen. Dabei wird der Status Quo nicht blind akzeptiert, sondern aktiv hinterfragt.[1]

Wie die Wissenschaft zu einem bestimmten Gegenstand forscht, wie ein Roman von gewissen Dingen handelt, verhandelt die Architektur auch gewisse Themen. Und diese Themen sind in einer gesellschaftlichen Realität verankert. Deshalb ist die Stadt das Spielfeld unseres Experiments. Denn hier treten einzelne Architekturen in einen Dialog und bilden gemeinsam das kollektive, gesellschaftliche Projekt: die Stadt. Das Vorhaben des architektonischen Entwurfs dient dazu, die Mechanismen, die diesem Projekt der Stadt zugrunde liegen, zu durchdringen und besser zu verstehen. So können durch das Entwerfen Erkenntnisse über unsere Gesellschaft gewonnen werden. Das Entwerfen wird somit zu «Quelle und Mündung»: Wir gelangen vom Spezifischen zum Allgemeinen und der Entwurf ist Ausgangspunkt «einer Theorie der Praxis».[2]

Das Spekulative ist dabei Methode, die Frage «was wäre wenn?» Mittel zum Zweck. Es ermöglicht uns aus Bestehendem Neues zu erschaffen. Dieses Neue sind überraschende räumliche Konfigurationen und architektonische Figuren. Die spekulative Methode, der Vorstoss ins Unbekannte, lässt uns neue räumliche Welten erschliessen, die wir mit reiner ‹Kreativität› nicht erreichen. Der Beitrag zur Disziplin liegt folglich in einer Verhandlung gesellschaftlicher Zustände, die der Architektur inhärent sind, und der gleichzeitigen Produktion neuer architektonischer Form. Wir möchten die gebaute Welt nicht nur formen, sondern zugleich verstehen und hinterfragen.

Der Fehler als kritische Methode

Fehler sind «durch ein vorgegebenes System bedingt, von dem sie abweichen, das sie unterlaufen oder überschreiten»[3] Sie stellen scheinbar Gewohntes in Frage, zwingen uns hinzusehen und Fragen zu stellen; sie stellen selbst Fragen. In diesem Sinne haben Fehler per se ein kritisches Potential. Ein Beispiel für solch einen kritischen Fehler, der auf der formalen, architektonischen Ebene stattfindet, stellen die berühmte Triglyphen in Giulio Romanos Palazzo del Te dar: «Die von Giulio Romano verübte Häresie gegen die Sprache der klassischen Architektur scheint mehr als ein blosser Verstoss oder eine triviale Spielerei zu sein: Wir werden

Der Fehler als kritische Methode: Die verschobenen Triglyphen in Giulio Romanos Palazzo del Te.
Fotogragfie: Maria Ida Biggi, ‹Giulio Romano›, Electa, 1989

notwendigerweise auf die Architektur selbst zurückverwiesen, da uns die gestörte Ordnung in der Ordnung verstört.»[4] Der kleine Fehler, die Verschiebung der Triglyphen, stellt hier also einen Bruch mit der Sprache der klassischen Architektur dar und stellt sie in ihrer Gewöhnlichkeit bloss. Der Fehler tritt als ein subversives Element auf und übt eine «Kritik von Innen»: Eine Kritik die die disziplinären Gesetzmässigkeiten in Frage stellt aber noch nicht in ihrem Akt sondern erst in ihrer Wirkung einen gesellschaftlichen Einfluss hat.[5]

Durch den Zwang zum Hinsehen, die Aufforderung das Einzelne, aus seiner Ordnung verrückte Objekt zu durchdringen wird, der Fehler in seiner kritischen Natur zum Produzenten von Erkenntnis und Wissen. Doch der Fehler dient nicht nur der Reflexion des Bestehenden, sondern ebenso als Katalysator für Neues: «Durch das Abweichungsmanöver vom Kanon fördert der Fehler das Experimentieren, um dadurch dem System einen ästhetischen und perzeptiven Innovationsschub zu bescheren, neue Stilkonfigurationen zu bilden und gänzlich neue Deutungen zu ermöglichen.»[6] Und dies geschieht, ohne dem System etwas von aussen hinzuzufügen, sondern lediglich durch eine Störung desselben.

Die Verschiebung des Katasterplans

Die Kraft des Katasterplans ist gewaltig und kaum zu überschätzen. Er ist die Grundlage jedes architektonischen Projekts und formt deshalb ganz massgeblich die physische Form der gesamten Stadt. Seine Macht und die gestalterische Kraft seiner Linien wird oftmals als ein Hindernis verstanden. Wir möchten diese Kraft mit unserer Arbeit freilegen und produktiv machen. Wir möchten den Katasterplan verschieben!

Ausgangslage
Alles in gewohnter Ordnung. Parzelle und Haus bilden eine Einheit.

Gleichzeitig bedeutet die Idee der Verschiebung ein kritisches Hinterfragen der Parzellengrenze. Das architektonische Objekt selbst wird durch die Verschiebung zum Kritiker der Linien, deren Produkt es darstellt: Gebautes besetzt nach der Verschiebung die Parzellengrenzen und unterwandert somit die Abstandsregeln. Dieser Akt der Verschiebung des Katasterplans bedeutet, anders als eine reine ‹Kritik von innen›, eine Kritik von ‹aussen› nach ‹innen› nach ‹aussen›: Das gesellschaftliche Konstrukt des Grundeigentums wird über das Medium der Architektur mit verhandelt und stellt wiederum in seiner Wirkung disziplinäre Konventionen in Frage.

Die Operation der Verschiebung
Der Katasterplan wird verschoben. Das Grundstück verfügt nur noch über Gebäudefragmente.

Bei der Verschiebung des Katasterplans werden die abstrakten Linien der Parzellengrenzen in ihrer Gesamtheit bewegt. Die physische Substanz der Stadt, Gebäude, Landschaft und Strassen, bleibt zunächst unberührt. Mit den verschobenen Linien verschiebt sich auch das Eigentum sowie die durch den Katasterplan wirkenden Zonenordnungen und Baugesetze. Die genaue Distanz der Verschiebung beträgt 47m vom Goldbrunnenplatz stadtauswärts. Diese Distanz entspricht dem 1,5-fachen einer mittleren Parzellenlänge im Perimeter. Sie ermöglicht häufig, zwischen den Bestand zu bauen und somit ganz ohne Abriss nachzuverdichten. Damit stellt die Katasterplan-Verschiebung eine Kritik an aktuellen Trends der Stadtverdichtung dar: Sie ist eine Alternative zum Ersatzneubau mit höherer Ausnutzung oder der Arealüberbauung auf zusammengelegten Parzellen.

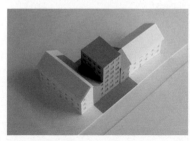

Das neue Ganze
Zuvor unabhängige Bauten werden durch Dazwischenbauen zu einem neuen Ganzen.

Doch nach der Verschiebung befindet sich die Stadt zunächst in einer unmöglichen Situation: Die verschobenen Grenzen zerteilen, was zuvor zusammengehörte und fassen zusammen, was zuvor nichts miteinander zu tun hatte. Es ist jedoch nicht Ziel dieser Operation einen anarchischen Zustand herzustellen, der jegliche gesellschaftliche Normen und Vorstellungen negiert. Vielmehr soll die Verschiebung des Katasterplans ein Moment der Un-Ordnung herstellen und damit die Möglichkeit eröffnen, die bestehende Ordnung in Frage zu stellen. Die Verschiebung wird zum selbst gestellten Problem, das es zu lösen gilt. Deshalb erfordert diese unmögliche Situation neue Regeln, um mit den Konsequenzen der Verschiebung umzugehen. Ihre scheinbaren Probleme sollen in neue

Kritik als Methode

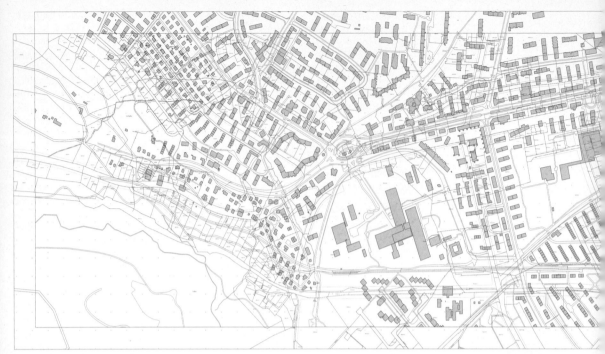

Die Verschiebung des Katasterplans

Der Perimeter Goldbrunnenplatz-Triemli vor und nach der Verschiebung des Katasterplans

Qualitäten verwandelt und so ihre produktive Kraft nutzbar gemacht werden.

Nach der Verschiebung wird jede Parzelle einzeln untersucht: Verfügt sie über mehr oder weniger Gebäudesubstanz als zuvor? Hat sich ihre Grundfläche durch Bereinigung der Strassen verkleinert? Der Verlustwert von Gebäudesubstanz und Grundstücksfläche lässt sich nach einem bauökonomischen Schlüssel durch Erhöhung der Ausnutzungsziffer für das betroffene Grundstück – gleichbedeutend einer Erhöhung des Grundstückswertes – kompensieren: Wer verloren hat, darf dafür mehr bauen. So erhält jede Parzelle ein potentielles Neubauvolumen, das im Rahmen der Bauregeln in ein konkretes Gebäude übersetzt werden kann.

Durch diese Kompensationsregeln erhöht sich die Dichte im Perimeter von zuvor 0,6 auf 1,3 nach der Verschiebung. Dadurch verfügt die Stadt über eine differenzierte Höhenentwicklung, die das vorherrschende Zonen-Denken unterwandert, sowie durch das Zusammenspiel von bestehender und neuer Bausubstanz über eine neue figürliche Vielfalt. Dies wiederum provoziert vielfältige Grundriss- und Wohnungsformen, sowie überraschende Details.

In dieser neuen Stadt nach der Verschiebung des Katasterplans prallen unterschiedliche Formen und Zeitebenen unmittelbar aufeinander, ohne dass das Ergebnis Produkt der anachronistischen und akontextuellen Methode der Collage ist. Es entsteht aus der Verschiebung des grösseren Ordnungssystems: Der Text der Stadt wird mittels der ihm eigenen Gesetzmässigkeiten auf neue Weise fortgeschrieben. Die kritische Frage – die Verschiebung des Katasterplans – befreit die gestalterische Kraft der Parzellengrenze, wird zum Katalysator der Stadtentwicklung und zeigt das Verhältnis der Morphologie der Stadt und der Idee des Grundeigentums auf.

1   Berthold Brecht hatte es sich zur Aufgabe gemacht mittels des Theaters gesellschaftliche Konflikte durchschaubar zu machen. Er schreibt zu seiner kritischen Methode des epischen Theaters folgendes: «Es war die Entfremdung, welche nötig ist, damit verstanden werden kann. Bei allem ‹Selbstverständlichen› wird auf das Verstehen einfach verzichtet. Das ‹Natürliche› mußte das Moment des Auffälligen bekommen. Nur so konnten die Gesetze von Ursache und Wirkung zu Tage treten. Das Handeln der Menschen mußte zugleich so sein und mußte zugleich anders sein können. Das waren große Änderungen.» Berthold Brecht, Schriften zum Theater I, Gesammelte Werke, Band 15. Frankfurt a.M., 1968.
2   Simon Kretz, Abstract zur Dissertation «Der Kosmos des Entwerfens, eine methodologische Forschung»
3   Felix P. Ingold, Yvette Sánchez, Einleitung. In: Ebd. (Hg.), Fehler im System. Göttingen, 2008, S.10.
4   Jorge Silvetti, The Beauty of Shadows. In: K. Michael Hays (Hg.), Architecture Theory since 1968. Cambridge (Massachusetts), 2000. S.269-270. (Übersetzung der Autoren)
5   Jorge Silvetti schreibt über die gesellschaftliche Relevanz einer internen disziplinären Kritik folgendes: «This peculiar discourse, as is obvious to many and disturbing to most, concerns mainly the most hermetic level of meaning that architecture can articulate. What may be read in this architecture of ‹criticism from within› pertains only to the closed domain of architecture itself as a discipline, and requires a trained reader, one who knows the symbolic universe proposed and instituted by it, and one whose intimate knowledge of the universe of, for instance, classical and modern architecture enables him to decipher the depth of the critical message […]. Thus, this ‹hermetic› language of ‹criticism from within› must be understood and used as an internal disciplinary mechanism, whose social value is pointless by the boundaries that any specialized language establishes in society. […] However, that they are only as hermetic as any internal criticism of any contemporary discipline is a fact that we can easily test, for example by attempting to decipher the communication among physicists. But if we can refrain from discarding physics for its seemingly ‹hermetic› quality, we should at the same time demand that its products have a more positive collective value. This also goes for architecture where the issue seems even more pressing because of the unavoidable impingement of its products upon the public realm. […] The two discourses, the hermetic and the collective, seem to define the two poles of the scale of possible discourses that architecture is capable of handling. Considering these terms as dichotomic and exclusive is an error that seems to explain much of the confusion and poverty pervading architectural discussion […].
    Jorge Silvetti, ‹The Beauty of Shadows›, in: K. Michael Hays (Hrsg.), ‹Architecture Theory since 1968›, Cambridge (Massachusetts), 2000, S.278.
6   Felix P. Ingold, Yvette Sánchez, ‹Einleitung›, in: Felix P. Ingold, Yvette Sánchez (Hrsg.), ‹Fehler im System›, Göttingen, 2008, S.12.

Zuvor isolierte Zeilenbauten können zu einer Einheit verbunden werden.

Einzelne Zeilenbauten werden zu vielfältigen Hoffiguren zusammengefasst. Die Einheit von Haus und Wohnung wird aufgelöst. Es entstehen Wohnungen, die sich in mehreren Gebäuden gleichzeitig befinden.

Durch die Verschiebung können bestehende Gebäude in alle Richtungen erweitert werden. Es wird durch verschiedene Häuser hindurch und über die Strasse hinweg gewohnt.

«How can students be critical today, Mr. Dietz?»

«In my view we should start with questions rather than with answers, and work in a way that they remain open and do not close upon themselves. Very often we are confronted with situations where questions are already set as fixed problems. You may have a client who thinks he or she knows his or her needs. But those needs may be complex, and other than what he or she truly believes they are. This also goes for competitions. Many of the briefs would deserve further questions to be asked of them. Actually, any architectural project deserves to be questioned. I personally believe that being critical is about raising the right questions rather than solving problems.

Most students come from a system where they are taught how to solve problems to given questions. If you have to raise questions yourself, the mindset that you have to be engaging in is very different. Visions also come from there: they are not just answers to problems, they are new configurations of questions. If we engage in real problems we must rather treat them as potentials. Questions are not simply an individual's domain. This implies that we have to communicate with other people, and we have to find the languages that enable us to do so. They're not always the same. I'm not talking about different nationalities such as French, English etc., I'm talking about much more diverse cultures – especially between disciplines. Often it can prove difficult to build up an understanding between different groups.

In any pedagogical process, in architecture or other types of education, what matters fundamentally is civic engagement. You have to find ways to take part, to share, and to participate actively as one of many, with your own personal responsibility. What can be misunderstood is that voting, which is of course important in a democracy, is an engagement—but it is only a minimal one. You can do it at home or just go to any letter box in the city. That takes about ten minutes. Real engagement demands much more. What is unfortunately quite a sad development in recent times is that certain movements in many countries, including our own, have hijacked democracy in a negative manner. They use disengagement and disinterest as justifying forces. The worst about it is that they legitimize not being interested. That is, of course, the downfall of democracy: when disengagement and not caring about the other outweighs engagement. We have to engage and we have to share—with the public, with anyone.

Sometimes I am surprised that there is not more engagement, interest in engagement or care about what could be a bigger picture or vision. You have to be fairly blind not to be aware of how fragile the values are that are at stake today. I'm not just talking about architecture. In general, we are living in a very critical moment and I think the coming 2-5 years will be decisive in a way that will demand our entire engagement. As architects, we have the responsibility to propose spaces that are capable of taking on their own mission. Spaces can actually do that, and sometimes it requires only a few simple gestures for people to begin to appropriate them.

What we are trying to do with ALICE* is to collapse hierarchies to become as flat as possible. The roles that are usually installed in institutions are not fostering engagement, they're rather hindrances to it. They predefine hierarchies, and create linear and unidirectional ways of communication. Horizontal structures do not always work and sometimes people may find a lack of clarity in them. However, if processes are well structured, most often they are valuable. On the other side, totalitarian regimes are very clear. I don't want to be too blunt but they are. There are other ways to live together, which are not always easy but we have to work them out. I truly believe that the biggest mistake that is occuring right now, including in Europe as a whole, is that we are closing borders. We should have had open borders ten years ago and we would not have the problem that we are facing today. I am totally convinced about that.

Finally, it's also about curiosity. It's very sad sometimes to see that some people simply are not curious. It's sad for any person, not for me but for themselves. What a dull life that must be, if you're not curious.»

*Atelier de la conception de l'espace, EPFL

This text is taken from the interview with Dieter Dietz led in front of the installation ‹HOUSE 2› at Pfingstweidstrasse Zurich the 6th of June 2017 by Vincent Bianchi and Yann Salzmann.

To Miss the Desert: Architecture, Site and Writing
Jane Rendell

A hot tent, the swathes of sheet are close enough to make me sweat. I rush headlong into the redness, with sultry breath and a swollen tongue. Down and down, round and round … swirling in the shallows. The waves rise up and over me. I sink into a world beneath the sand. Towards me, staggering, comes a soldier, left, right, left, right … I open my eyes. I am in a palace of lilac silk, a cool object is on my chest and something metal in my mouth. A smooth brown hand holds mine.

In my own architectural design research, as a spatial writer and critic, I have suggested that, with his/her responsibility to convey an experience of the work to another audience, the critic occupies a discrete position as mediator and that his or her situatedness conditions the performance of his/her interpretative role.[1] I have described this form of situated criticism as ‹site-writing›, arguing that the location of the critic with respect to his/her object of study or subject matter is a determining factor in the construction of a critical interpretative position.

Site-writing questions the terms of reference that relate the critic to the work positioned ‹under› critique, and instead proposes alternative positions, so functioning as a mode of practice in its own right. This is an active writing, which enacts its interpretative function, aiming to perform the spatial qualities of an artwork or piece of architecture through textual and spatial strategies, reconfiguring the sites between critic and work, essay and reader, as an ‹architecture› of criticism.[2] Here site-writing operates as a form of architectural design research exploring how architectural processes of structuring and detailing spaces can work through textual media, offering new insights into what architecture is and might be.

To Miss the Desert[3]

Around the Centre

Surrounding her house is a moat of flints with furrows running through it at regular intervals like a ploughed field. When you run up and down these slopes, you can lose your footing and slip, and that is when you know the sharp-looking stones really can cut your knees. Still it is safer here than beyond the walls in the waste-ground of dry bushes and stinging insects, where hyenas cry in the night.

A hallway forms the centre of the house. It has a tiled floor, hard and shiny, at night she comes here to catch insects. Many creatures skulk across it, ants and spiders, and some more sinister, whose names she does not yet know. But as long as she is careful to catch them under her glass jar with its smooth edge, the one that meets the marble without making any gaps, she is safe to sit and watch the trapped insects inside.

14 Floor Finishes
Location G6
Lay new flooring 300 mm × 300 mm terracotta unglazed tiles with sandstone colour grout 10 mm widejoints. All tiles to be laid out from centre line. Finished floor level to match G5.

A small pig and a spider; the tin roof drums with yet more rain. The rains have come early this year, and they are heavy. She lies tucked up in bed, reading about Charlotte and her web. Her tummy aches. It is swollen, a bit yellow, and worse still, it sticks out. Today she has had her tenth injection, thankfully the final one. Each time the fat needle went into her it made another mark, making a circle around her tummy button, first at mid-day, then at six o'clock, then at three o'clock, then at nine o'clock, and then all the way around again, until she felt bruised and sore.

Big injections had been talked about ever since Bobby the dog got a tick on the rim of his eye. The tick would not come free, not even with a burnt match and ghee. Poor Bobby, with his sad eyes and velvet brown ears, got sicker and sicker. He lay on his side in the shade, panting, his ribs heaving in and out. Sometimes his tummy shook. Finally, he was taken away, to the vets, and never came back.

They kept on talking about big injections. No one seemed to know why Bobby had been sick, was it from tick fever or rabies? Tick fever was not a worry, they said, but rabies certainly was. It turned you mad, frothing at the mouth and running screaming from water, until it got you in the end. Everyone agreed it was the vets' fault; they had burnt Bobby's body. Anyone knows that you should keep the head and take a slide from the brain before burning it. Only then, when you look at that slide, can you tell whether or not the dog had rabies.

Had Bobby licked her hands, they wanted to know. They looked at all the scratches. She always had cuts on her hands from stone hunting and mud-pie baking, she told them. Of course Bobby had licked her hands, especially when she tried to comfort him at the end, poor Bobby.

On an Ethiopian airlines plane, a DC3, with their ‹13 Months of Sunshine› posters, all the way from Addis Ababa, came the special cool box. She knew the route well; it took you past Gondar, Lalibella and the place beginning with D. You could get out there for a bit to play on the grass by the lake. For eating your snack of bread and jam, the stewardess gave you a bright orange cushion.

The cool box was delivered right to her door by the nice Dutch Doctor. It was packed with jars of a plum-coloured syrup and big plastic syringes, ‹horse syringes›, the Doctor said and laughed. To keep them cold, everything else had to be taken out of the fridge.

I swing back and forth, higher and higher, watching my dark shadow on the dirt. As mid-day approaches, my shadow grows smaller, and then it disappears. Everything is grey but it is not a shade I have seen before. It is not a dull grey, like the light on a cloudy day when shadows cover up the sun, but bright and dazzling, a grey that hurts my eyes. I look up. The sun has disappeared. Instead there is a black hole. Around the centre is a halo of white light.

Along the Edge

The bathroom has a floor of polished marble, black, interwoven with white veins. Perched on the toilet, with her feet dangling off the ground, she traces the white lines with her gaze. She keeps alert for cockroaches, at any time an intruder might crawl through the cracks along the edge of the room and into the blackness.

Nathan Coley's art work ‹Black Tent›, ‹Art in Sacred Places›, Portsmouth, 2003. Photography: Nathan Coley and Peter Langdown

Inside her house all the floors are marble, smooth and cool, laid out in careful grids, except for the big golden rug. In the evening when the sun is in the west, the rug glows. At this time of day she likes to follow the intricate patterns with her feet, like paths around a secret garden. But if you dance along the edge of the squares, you must be careful not to fall in, who knows what could lie in wait for you in such an enchanted place.

> Our initial proposal is for a one-storey building with a courtyard at the centre and the accommodation along the edge of the site. This means that the building will be fully accessible without the additional cost of a lift and there will be no problems of overlooking. The main entrance leads to a central courtyard, covered and top lit. All the other facilities are to be accessed off this space.

Along one edge of the garden are the homes of two men. Gullum is tall and fair skinned, with light hair and green eyes; and Kareem shorter, stockier, darker. They have fought each other in the past, and will again when the Soviets come to Kabul, and then again, when her own people search the Hindu Kush to wipe out all evil. But for now, there is no fighting, once the sun has gone down, they sit and eat together.

On weekday mornings she has to wait by the gate for the yellow school bus. She goes to a Catholic school, but the Italian Priest who teaches her has not noticed yet that she never reads the bible. They call him a real revolutionary, a man who fights for the people of Afghanistan. On days when she does not have to go to school, she swims in the streams of the Hindu Kush, looks at blue pots in Istalif, wooden chests in Peshawar, plastic boots in the Kabul bazaar, and one day, she goes south, to visit Kareem's home.

He is a man with property: land and wives. Inside the walls of his house are sunlit orchards full of dark purple fruit. Among the trees his wives sit. Dressed in shades of red, some of the women have covered their faces, others have painted their toes nails pink. From a distance, the women watch them arrive, disappearing inside as they draw closer.

The guests are taken upstairs to a long veranda overlooking the garden. The only furniture here is the carpet laid out in a long line down the middle of the room. Men in turbans sit cross-legged along the edge and eat from the dishes laid out in front of them. They are invited to sit down and eat—the only women—her mother, her sister, and herself.

After the meal, as they walk back down through the dark house to leave, she sees a pair of eyes watching her from behind a screen. The eyes belong to a girl, a girl with the hands of a woman, a woman who glints with silver. Later she learns that this is Kareem's youngest wife, once a nomad, who carries her wealth in the jewels on her fingers.

My own dress is set with tiny mirrors and a handsome square of embroidery at the front. It is hard work to get on, with no fastenings and a fabric so thin it could rip. In this dress I feel just like all the other Afghan girls. Except that they wear their dresses a bit softer, sometimes black. I wonder whether it is to match the black around the edges of their eyes.

At the Threshold

A hot tent, the swathes of sheet are close enough to make me sweat. I rush headlong into the redness, with sultry breath and a swollen tongue. Down and down, round and round … swirling in the shallows. The waves rise up and over me. I sink into a world beneath the sand. Towards me, staggering, comes a soldier, left, right, left, right … I open my eyes. I am in a palace of lilac silk, a cool object is on my chest and something metal in my mouth. A smooth brown hand holds mine.

  Her mother tells her a story of how she taught the Sheik's niece English. She was allowed to go inside the harem, and saw that underneath their burqas the women wore make up and perfume. For her labours, she was offered a gift. She asked for a gold leaf burqa, the costume only the wives of the sheik can wear.

  Her mother's labour is not easy; she refuses to come out. Her mother walks the dunes along the creek, back and forth, past the apartment block where she lives, but still she waits inside, for a night and a day. The chance of infection is high. There is no glass in the hospital windows. A caesarian section might kill them both, one of them for sure, certainly her mother if she turns out to be carrying a son.

  Fortunately there is a woman who is willing to take a chance. On the second night of her mother's labour, the hospital is almost empty; everyone who can has gone, to feast, to break the fast. A nurse runs a drip to encourage her out. But she holds her ground. The nurse turns the drip up. Still she refuses to budge. The drip is turned up again, faster, until she has no choice but to leave her warm waters and enter the world. For her entrance, and her mother's bother, the sheik sends his apologies. «Sorry», he said, «so sorry it isn't a boy». For a boy he would have sent a watch, but for the girl, a tiny gold coffee pot on a gold chain.

> 14 Floor Finishes
> Location 1.5 and G5
> Forbo Nairn lino sheeting 1.5 mm to be laid
> on 6mm wbp ply sub floor.
> Ply and lino to run under appliances and around
> kitchen units.
> Colour tba by client.
> Aluminium threshold at junction
> with G2, G6 and 1.1.

Nathan Coley's art work ‹Black Tent›, ‹Art in Sacred Places›, Portsmouth, 2003. Photography: Nathan Coley and Peter Langdown

Born on the eve of the haj, I am a hajia. I will never have to make the journey to Mecca.

In the Middle

Two concrete paths lead away from the gate, with a long line of zenias in the middle. A small girl in an orange dress comes here often in her search for special stone. Before she crouches down to pick one out, she checks for scorpions.

  On the window cill is a row of large tins that have once contained milk powder. Now they hold a collection of carefully chosen and prized items. She takes her stones out and covers them in water so that they glisten. Then she sorts them according to their colour. Her favourites form the most important group, seven in number, one for each colour of the rainbow. She puts them in a safe place, on a small piece of cloth on the table next to her bed. On certain days she takes the stones out into the garden and lays them on a soft patch in the rough grass. Right in the middle she places the violet one. Put right there, it will bring her luck when looking for four-leafed clovers.

  She has been told to always shake her shoes out before putting them on, in case a scorpion might be hiding in the toes. And she must make sure to check for them too beneath the ground sheet of

tents. Scorpions like nothing better than a warm dark place to nest.

Once when she was small, she and her mother went to camp with her father as he checked wells. They slept in a tent, with their daughter between them. Later as they broke camp, under the ground sheet, right in the middle, a large yellow scorpion was found.

They say the way to make a scorpion suffer is to build a circle of fire, place the insect in the middle and watch the poor thing sting itself to death.

> There is an option of making a partition in the middle, between the crèche and the café, a flexible one. The partition we have suggested would be half-hour fire resisting and provide equivalent acoustic separation to that of a standard brick wall.

One hot day, she takes the lids off the tins, and pours out her stones over the floor. There is a scuttling sound. She stands firm and watches; in the warm moist interior of the tins, a family of yellow scorpions has hatched and is coming to the surface. She screams. Kareem comes running. He kills each scorpion calmly with the bare of his heel. She hates camping, almost as much as she hates churches. She finds them both boring. But the soft black of a Bedouin tent, that is different...

It is a scorching hot day in San Francisco. Anyone with any sense is on a rooftop or in a park. Instead I force myself through the modern art collection. The gallery is badly lit; each room is a different shade of grey. They say they are going to renovate soon. I stop at another tedious canvas square. This time it is black. I stare hard. Nothing happens. Then I scrunch up my eyes and look out to the middle distance from between the fringes of my lashes. And remember what it feels like, to miss the desert.

To Miss the Desert was a site-writing written in response to Nathan Coley's ‹Black Tent› (2003), curated by Gavin Wade.[4] Black Tent had developed out of Coley's interest in sanctuaries in general, but particularly the evocative and precise description of the construction of the tabernacle given in the bible.[5] Wade had read a piece of my writing, where I questioned whether it was possible to ‹write architecture› rather than to ‹write about architecture› and so he asked me to ‹write a tabernacle›. I felt that the text in the bible had already written the tabernacle, so I decided to write Black Tent.

Black Tent consisted of a flexible structure, a number of steel-framed panels with black fabric screens stretched across them, and smaller ‹windows› inserted into them. Black Tent moved to five sites in Portsmouth reconfiguring itself for each location. My essay echoed aspects of Black Tent; each of its five sections was composed around a different spatial boundary condition, such as ‹around the edge›. Yet in order to critique Coley's choice of sanctuary as a specifically religious and Judaeo-Christian one, my choice of spatial motif was the secular sanctuary of home.[6] Like the squares, the voice of my text was two-sided, setting up a dynamic between private and public sanctuary. One remembered a childhood spent in various nomadic cultures in the Middle East. The other adopted a more professional tone by taking texts from construction specifications I had written when designing contemporary sanctuaries—a series of community buildings for different minority groups.[7]

A couple of years later, for an exhibition entitled ‹Spatial Imagination›, I selected ‹scenes› from this essay and reconfigured them into a text three by four, in response to the grid of a window, where I wrote the word ‹purdah› on the glass in black eye liner from Oman. This two-part text installation ‹An Embellishment: Purdah›—one part sited in a book and the other in a building—responded to the window as a boundary condition, performing the interface between inside and outside.[8] Here writing, by responding conceptually, emotionally and spatially, to the conditions offered by the specific site of a window, reconfigured architectural design and space through new conceptualizations of positionality, subjectivity and textuality.

1. For a discussion of the politics of spectatorship see for example, Umberto Eco, ‹The Poetics of the Open Work›, [1962] in Claire Bishop (ed.), Participation: Documents of Contemporary Art (London and Cambridge, Mass.: The MIT Press and the Whitechapel Art Gallery, London, 2006) pp. 20–40 and Claire Bishop, Installation Art: A Critical History (London: Tate Publishing, 2005) p. 13 and p. 131.
2. Jane Rendell, Site-Writing: The Architecture of Art Criticism (London: I. B. Tauris, 2010).
3. The following text is based on Jane Rendell, ‹To Miss the Desert›, Gavin Wade (ed.) Nathan Coley: Black Tent (Portsmouth: Art in Sacred Spaces, 2003) pp. 34–43 but radically shortened and reworked.
4. Jane Rendell, ‹To Miss the Desert›, Gavin Wade (ed.) Nathan Coley: Black Tent (Portsmouth: Art in Sacred Spaces, 2003) pp. 34–43.
5. Nathan Coley's fascination with places of religious worship runs through his practice. An early work, Fourteen Churches of Münster (2000), comprises a street plan and the view from a helicopter circling fourteen churches in the city: in the Second World War allied bomber pilots were issued with an order to target them. The Lamp of Sacrifice, 161 Places of Worship, Birmingham (2000) and The Lamp of Sacrifice, 286 Places of Worship, Edinburgh (2004) consist of cardboard models of all the places of worship in the towns listed in the Yellow Pages, have been argued to express the premise of Coley's work—that architectural forms remain empty contained until socially occupied. See Martin Herbert, ‹Nathan Coley, Fruitmarket Gallery Edinburgh›, Art Monthly, n. 278 (July–August 2004) pp. 35–37, p. 36. More recent projects, such as There Will Be No Miracles Here (2006) Mount Stuart, Isle of Bute, question the passivity of architecture especially in current religious conflicts. One part of the exhibition—Camouflage Mosque, Camouflage Synagogue, Camouflage Church—comprises three models covered in ‹dazzle› camouflage, a technique applied to ships during both World Wars as protection from attack. See Andrea Schlieker, ‹Negotiating the Invisible: Nathan Coley at Mount Stuart› at http://studionathancoley.com/works/camouflage-mosquesynagoguechurch (accessed 2 September 2012).
6. Coley's interest in sanctuaries has been related to their role as places of refuge outside state control. See Nathan Coley, Urban Sanctuary: A Public Art Work by Nathan Coley (Glasgow: The Armpit Press, 1997) which comprised a series of interviews with eight people including a policeman and a fen shui practitioner where the artist asked each person what the term sanctuary meant to them and documented their answers.
7. Coley's work has examined the representation of architecture through different kinds of media simultaneously, for example, Minster (1998) an installation in The Tate Gallery Liverpool, consisted of slide projected images of a non-conformist chapel in Liverpool's Toxteth, a recorded lecture and a guided tour of York Minster and an explanatory pamphlet describing the correct procedure for establishing a tabernacle or portable sanctuary. See Nick Barley (ed.) Leaving Tracks: Arttranspennine98, an International Contemporary Visual Art Exhibition Recorded (London: August Media Ltd., 1999) pp. 78–81.
8. See Jane Rendell, An Embellishment: Purdah (2006) Spatial Imagination, domoBaal contemporary art, London with an associated catalogue essay Jane Rendell, ‹An Embellishment›, Peg Rawes and Jane Rendell (eds) Spatial Imagination (London: The Bartlett School of Architecture, UCL, 2005) pp. 34–35. See www.spatialimagination.org.uk. (accessed 8 July 2008). For a longer discussion of this installation see Jane Rendell, Site-Writing, pp. 103–109.

Findling
Johanna Muther und Claudio Schneider

Erratische Blöcke, Findlinge, ortsfremde Felsblöcke in Gebieten ehemaliger Vereisung; sie wurden durch Gletscher oder Inlandeis, oft hunderte von Kilometern weit, vom Ursprungsort an ihre Fundstätte transportiert; sie sind daher Indizien für die Ausdehnung und Herkunft von Eismassen. – Im Volksglauben wurde die Verbreitung erratischer Blöcke vielfach auf den Teufel oder auf Riesen zurückgeführt.[1]

[1] Definition für ‹Findling› aus der Brockhaus Enzyklopädie, 2017.

The Fox and the Lion
or the Perpetual Habit of ETH Students to Romanticise the Past

Up on the hill lived a great lion, casting his shadow on the woodlands below. In these woods lived a quiet community of animals of all shapes and sizes. There were badgers, squirrels, wolves, rabbits, sheep, owls and many others. It was well known that the climb to the top of the hill was treacherous, and none dared undertake it. Their days were spent in solemnity, in stubborn worship for the great lion on the hill. They looked up to him for guidance and direction. It was not always an easy way of life, with many cumbersome traditions and customs. Each of these animals wore their own lion's mane, a sign of respect for their leader.

There was one disruption in their small community; the fox. Always a little different, always a little difficult. He did not hunt the same way as the others, did not eat with them, did not follow their lifestyle. But most of all, he showed a flagrant disregard for the worship of the lion. He did not wear a false mane. He did not strive to become the lion. For he was the fox, and such was his nature. The fox was perceived as cunning and arrogant by the other animals. They did not understand why he could not just follow them in their worship. Everyone wore the prescribed costume, they all looked alike and lived alike.

One day, the bravest of the group decided to confront the fox about his wayward ways. «Why do you not wear the mane of the great lion?» asked the badger. The owl added, «Why do you flout convention?» The fox replied, «You all look ridiculous with your false manes. You are neither a badger nor a lion, just bastards. You let your worship for him cloud your judgment—do you even know the lion?» Angered by his answers, the badger threatened the fox to tell the great lion of his disrespect and arrogance. The fox boldly laughed at his proposition, «Go ahead».

The badger plucked up all his courage to embark upon the journey. To his surprise, the crest of the hill was closer than what he had been told and he reached it with barely a drop of sweat on his brow. He squinted his eyes, excited to finally meet his master. As he approached he saw to his dismay, that the great lion was indeed not what they had expected. His mane was a mass of ragged, overgrown hair. Their deity had never been a lion, but simply an old fox.

by Axel Chevroulet and Anna MacIver-Ek

Architectural Criticism on the Art Market: A US-American Debate
Martin Hartung

As Paul Goldberger put it in 2005: «An architecture critic has a lot of authority but not much real power. Power is a much more raw and direct force. Authority is respect and trust. I don't think architecture critics have the power. It used to be said that ‹The New York Times› critic can close a Broadway show. Well, that's power. But nobody tears down a building if an architecture critic doesn't like it.»

One of the hottest debates touching on some core issues of architectural criticism in the last two years was triggered by a defamation lawsuit the architect Zaha Hadid filed against the New York Review of Books architecture critic Martin Filler in August 2014. To recall the prominent case: in a review of Rowan Moore's ‹Why We Build: Power and Desire in Architecture›, published on June 5, 2014, Filler accused Hadid that she «unashamedly disavowed any responsibility, let alone concern, for the estimated 1000 laborers who have perished while constructing her [Al Wakrah] project [in Qatar].»[1] Filler also quoted Hadid as having commented: «I have nothing to do with the workers […] It is not my duty as an architect to look at it.»[2] Even though Hadid's lawsuit was regarded by many as morally questionable, Filler had to face the problem that he didn't check his facts. Not only was there no proof of any cases of death related to the building site—yet, the even higher number of 1.200 reported deaths of migrant workers in Qatar at the time, was (and remains) an issue. Most importantly, the construction of Hadid's stadium for the World Cup in 2022 had not yet begun when the critic made his statement. Filler apologized, Hadid's New York-based lawyer (Oren Warshavsky, also a lead attorney in the Bernie Maddoff case) released a statement and finally, in early 2015, the architect dropped the lawsuit.[3]

It was, however, not the first time an architecture critic got sued: In 1978, Allan Temko, who had introduced a new form of activist criticism in the 1960s, working for the San Francisco Chronicle, started a review of the local touristic shopping mall ‹Pier 39› with the memorable words: «Corn. Kitsch. Schlock. Honkytonk. Dreck. Schmaltz. Merde.» At the time, ‹Pier 39›'s architect, the San Francisco-based Sandy Walker, sued Temko for two million US-dollars. With the help of the newspaper, the case was finally dismissed. In the mid-1980s, during a time of heavy debates on the legacy of modernism in architecture, it was Filler who recounted another prominent case: that of Donald Trump versus Paul Gapp in 1984. The widely respected architecture critic of the Chicago Tribune condemned Trump, who attempted to build the world's tallest building—a 150-story skyscraper in southern Manhattan—for his imposing egomania. In response, the critic had to face a 500 million US-dollar lawsuit against himself and the newspaper, which was eventually dismissed in court in 1985. Filler's elaborations shed light on the specific mechanisms of criticism in the field of architecture, in which «it is the creator, rather than the critic, who calls the tune».[4] Focusing on the complex power plays in the field, Filler assessed: «Historically, the establishment of a critical voice in architecture in this country has usually depended more on the support given the writer by a publication rather than his or her own evolution of a set of principles and values.»[5] Thirty years later, the lawsuit Hadid vs. Filler, more generally, drew attention to the responsibility of the critic as well as his or her exemplary role, and points us to the boundaries of the field, which the American philosopher, Stanley Cavell, defined as a recurrent «affront.»[6] According to Cavell, «[criticism's] only justification lies in its usefulness, in making its object available to just response.»[7]

I would like to draw attention to one specific field that began to occupy architecture critics in the seventies: architectural representations in the art market; a phenomenon that peaked in the United States in the 1980s, when architects were offered new ways of marketing their businesses in a handful of art and architecture galleries.[8] In 1978, an article in the magazine Architectural Digest concludes a survey of «architectural drawing as an art form» with the observation that it was «still something of a pioneer field for the collector [affording] a dual satisfaction: There is both aesthetic pleasure and intellectual stimulation in having direct contact with art that shapes our manner of living.»[9] Eight years later, the New York Times art critic, Grace Glueck, recapitulated in the ‹Home› section of the newspaper that despite fears over high prices—and a dispersal of documents—from organizations such as the Society of Architectural Historians, «architecture as a subject has become much more accessible, and architects not quite so anonymous.»[10] As a result, the art market for architectural drawings gradually collapsed

‹Architectural Studies and Projects›, The Museum of Modern Art, New York, March 13-May 11, 1975. Installation view.
© The Museum of Modern Art, New York/Scala, Florence.

in the early 1990s, coinciding with a new construction boom since the late 1980s and the institutionalization of more standardized, computer-aided drawing techniques that significantly limited the supply. In the long run, the specialized market proved to be closely related with the actuality of professional polemics as well as the sales and collecting efforts of a few key players, but not so much driven by the potential originality, rarity and standing of its commodities in the context of art.

My focus is on a case study, which relates criticism at the New York Times to activities in the art market at The Museum of Modern Art (MoMA) to contextualize the way in which contemporary architectural drawings increasingly began to be observed as saleable commodities. How did a group of architecture critics serve as a vital source for evaluating this market within debates on disciplinary autonomy, and how intertwined are the markets of criticism with those of publicity?

A comprehensive article by an architecture critic, which directly related to a sales exhibition of drawings by contemporary architects, was written by Ada Louise Huxtable in April 1975. In her piece, Huxtable, who became the highly respected first architecture critic of the New York Times in 1963, featured a drawing of ‹House VI› (1975) by Peter Eisenman. It was part of the exhibition ‹Architectural Studies and Projects›, held at MoMA from March 13 until May 15, 1975. With the help of Emilio Ambasz, then curator at the Department of Architecture and Design at MoMA, twenty-three international architects, including Peter Cook, Michael Graves, John Hejduk, Hans Hollein, Rem Koolhaas, Elia & Zoe Zenghelis, Adolfo Natalini, Cedric Price, and Ettore Sottsass, were each invited to submit between two and five drawings to the informal exhibition at the museum. It was only open to museum members and associates. The majority of the architects pursued teaching activities rather than working on building commissions at the time, mirrored by a shortage of commissions in the course of the oil crisis in 1973, which had increased a refined production of architectural ideas and representations. At the same time, as already evidenced by some architects' activities in the 1950s and progressively throughout the 1960s, a diverse range of elaborate architectural drawings made a comeback in the context of historical revisions after their widespread dismissal by Modernists in the early 20th century, who countered the Beaux-Arts tradition.[11]

It was thus not a coincidence that Arthur Drexler, then Chief Curator of the Department of Architecture and Design, aimed «to re-examine our architecture pieties»[12] through large-scale, nineteenth century drawings in the exhibition ‹The Architecture of the École des Beaux-Arts›. Held from October 29, 1975 until January 4, 1976, the architectural drawing was placed center stage at a critically debated and long-prepared show by the preeminent cultural institution of Western Modernism, which promoted architecture as an art form since the opening of its Department of Architecture and Design in 1932.

Just about five months earlier, the informal, comparatively swiftly assembled, contemporary version of this exhibition in the Members Penthouse marked the humble beginning of a series of more prominent architecture-related art gallery shows; held since the late 1970s in the United States, Europe, and Japan. In the US, the New York-based art galleries of Leo Castelli and Max Protetch ensured broad newspaper and magazine coverage of architectural drawings and models as commodities, which did not provide nearly as much income compared to the sales of artworks, but allowed for recurring profits in a developing attention economy. Protetch was quick to market architects and their image(s) in the most systematic way amongst the interested art gallerists, something which writer Lisbet Nilson recognized as an «important innovative coup for him as an art dealer», in a feature on the gallerist for the lifestyle magazine Metropolitan Home.[13] Nilson also emphasized that «many of the presentation drawings and theoretical sketches produced in the name of new architectural directions, are lovely even to a layman's eyes. As architecture, they are important cultural documents. Viewed as art, they are desirable objects of beauty.»[14] Not surprisingly, this focus on aesthetics with regard to architectural drawings—previously regarded as means to an end—triggered mixed feelings in architecture circles. The majority of commercial art gallerists that exhibited contemporary architectural drawings, shared an interest in positions associated with Minimal and Conceptual art, which featured documentation and administration-based art practices and thus opened up links to the referentiality of architectural drawings.

These unusual activities in the art market, which itself was undergoing structural changes in the wave of Neoliberalism, began with the direct involvement of some MoMA associates and trustees. As an informal exhibition at the Members Penthouse, ‹Architectural Studies and Projects› was orchestrated by the art collector and entrepreneur Barbara Jakobson, who attempted to help her architect friends in a time of scarce commissions.[15] Jakobson served as the head of the museum's Junior Council, an active funding source for the institution with a group of council members managing the institution's Art Lending Service. From 1951 until 1982, when it closed to the public, the Art Lending Service cooperated with a number of art galleries to rent and sell art to museum members in support of institutional affairs. Beginning in the mid-1950s, an exhibition series was programmed for the Members Penthouse. Under this umbrella, Jakobson and Emilio Ambasz, then curator of design at the museum, presented this first international sales exhibition for contemporary architectural drawings in New York.

It served as an occasion for a very personal statement by Huxtable, herself a former employee at the Department for Architecture and Design at MoMA, who became the first architecture critic to receive the prestigious Pulitzer Price in 1970. She remembered her fist years in the profession as «crisis-oriented».[16] In 1964, New York's Penn Station was demolished, a building the critic had called «a monument to the lost art of magnificent construction, other values aside.»[17] A year before the station's demolition, Huxtable emphatically expressed her disappointment: «It's time we stopped talking about our affluent society. We are an impoverished society. It is a poor society indeed that […] has no money for anything except expressways to rush people out of our dull and deteriorating cities.»[18]

‹Architectural Studies and Projects›, The Museum of Modern Art, New York, March 13–May 11, 1975. Installation view.
© The Museum of Modern Art, New York/Scala, Florence.

Left: Architecture critic Paul Goldberger and architect Charles Gwathmey during a dinner in a private dining room of The Four Seasons restaurant on the occasion of Gwathmey's 60th birthday in June 1998. Among the small group of attendees were Richard Meier and John Hejduk (to the right), Peter Eisenman, Michael Graves, and Philip Johnson. A private note to Johnson by Gwathmey's business partner, Robert Siegel, in a photo book, in which this picture is included, reads: «Dear Philip, Knights of the round table gathered; King Philip, Prince Paul, the reunion of the New York Five to celebrate commitment, respect and Charles' 60th birthday. […]». © The Philip Johnson Papers, Getty Research Institute, Los Angeles.

Asked how the role of the architecture critic changed over the years, she replied decades later: «The role is the same, but the emphasis has changed. A critic has a lot of responsibility. It is largely informational and educational—to let the public know what's going on in the large and small issues and to let them know the difference between good and bad, how to distinguish a work of art. Today, I think the emphasis is too much on chasing celebrities, which has emerged all through society.»[19]

In 1975, Huxtable concluded her review of the MoMA show: «Architectural fantasies can be a lot better than building in a bankrupt society.»[20] Her associate Paul Goldberger, who had started to work as an assistant editor at The New York Times Magazine in 1972 at the age of 22 and became a junior critic in 1974, found a clearer tone in judging that the exhibition, «has little real insight into the state of architectural practice today.» He continued: «Its significance, rather, lies in its ability to remind us that architects do, in fact have imaginations, and when these imaginations are permitted to run free of the constraints imposed by actual building programs, the results can be exciting and often extraordinary beautiful.»[21]

Without mentioning that the informal exhibition was only accessible to MoMA members, the critic further stated: «One of the objectives of the show has been to encourage public interest in architectural drawings as art, and on this level it is likely to be successful [...].»[22] Rather than questioning the unprecedented market presence of these architectural representations, Goldberger highlighted, «extremely skilled drawings by more familiar New York architects such as Peter Eisenman, Richard Meier and John Hejduk»,[23] all of which had support of Philip Johnson, who was instrumental in financing Eisenman's Institute for Architecture and Urban Studies (IAUS) in New York. Early on, Goldberger would extensively cover the group of architects that had become known as the ‹New York Five›, but he also focused on newly emerging positions subsumed under the buzzword ‹Postmodernism›. Later, the critic acknowledged that, «one of the problems in perception of my criticism was that I didn't really take an absolute position completely on one side or another.»[24] In 1975, Goldberger's colleague, the Boston Globe's architecture critic Robert Campbell, expressed his disappointment by stating: «After the splashy review in the New York Times and the usual intriguing press release, I had somehow expected more from the new show at the Museum of Modern Art called ‹Architectural Studies and Projects›.»[25] The critic continued: «To begin with, most of the drawings don't even pretend to be visionary architecture as the show promises.»[26] Campbell concluded his review: «It was Ernest Hemingway who said that the most important equipment for a writer is a built-in, tamper-proof, copper-bottom crap detector (or something like that), and a show like this makes you wish the same for architects, who as a group possibly need it more. After you get through everything that hasn't even tried to be ‹visionary architecture› you are left with not an awful lot.»[27] He further stated that «Real architecture is so much more complex, many-layered, exciting, alive, simply by trying to respond to the contemporary world instead of reducing it to someone's personal iconography.»[28] Two years later, during a presentation at IAUS, Campbell's suggestion to mount a different exhibition with buildable projects rather than reactionary drawings in order to «help educate the public in the one visual art it can't help living with», was reflected by the Boston-based critic and editor, Peter Blake, who, like Campbell, was also an architect.[29] In his public talk during the IAUS' spring semester, Blake made the point that «certified architecture critics in the US by large do not understand architecture, discuss it as an abstract art, and write not for an intelligent and interested and aware public, but for each other […].»[30] Campbell took a very different stance to Goldberger—an example of how two critics with different backgrounds and contexts judge their subjects differently. Moreover, New York was Goldberger's «own backyard».[31]

His suggestion that, by encouraging public interest in architectural drawings as art, the exhibition was most likely going to be successful, was met by the critic himself, when he purchased at least one drawing from the show.[32] Although it was not the drawing Goldberger purchased, OMA's ‹Egg of Columbus Circle› (1975), the image featured in the critic's article, was offered at the museum for $780 (a buying power of about $3,600 today).[33] Overall, 43 drawings were for sale in the exhibition and nine clients—private individuals as well as members of corporations—purchased works. Not least, if this early example of criticism around an art market-related exhibition in the 1970s points to anything, then to the question whether any critic, through detachment, can ever be effective. Furthermore, it points to the position of the critic in a multi-tiered, commercial world. Martin Filler remembered with regard to operations of the professional magazine Architectural Record during the 1970s that «they had no sense of criticism. Their attitude was: if it gets built, it's good for the profession; [and] even in a place that permitted criticism [such as Progressive Architecture] there were always internal struggles about that.»[34] Criticism functioned differently in the other arts, «because in architecture the stakes are so much higher than in any of the other art forms.»[35] Likewise, architectural drawings in the art market represented an unusual phenomenon in the context of the profession.

Nevertheless, Goldberger's involvement with a ‹power elite›[36] would in itself trigger criticism from yet another critic: Michael Sorkin. In an article for the New York-based Village Voice in 1984, titled «Why Paul Goldberger is so Bad», Sorkin addressed and criticized the colleague sharply for his stance with regard to the planned re-design of Times Square.[37] Johnson and Burgee's proposal had been commissioned by the Park Tower Realty Corporation and would have featured four granite-color buildings of different sizes. Whereas many professionals opposed the project, Goldberger endorsed the endeavor and earned himself a raving response from Sorkin, who expressed his outrage in his typical writing style—«suspicious of the non-stop lifestyles of the rich and famous, […] beach houses and Disneyland»,—by stating: «The main problem with architecture in this country is the stranglehold that people like Johnson and [Robert] Stern have on its institutional culture, the way in which schools, museums, patrons, and the press call their tunes, excluding so many others. America's architecture is too important to be held prisoner by a bunch of boys that meets in secret to anoint members of the club, reactionaries to whom a social practice means an invitation to lunch, bad designers whose notions of form are the worst kind of parroting. It is for being the unquestioning servant of these that I accuse Paul Goldberger.»[38]

Criticism does not happen in a vacuum. This is equally the case with regard to Sorkin, who, «under the spell of doughty Marxism»[39] would counter any elitist project. Sorkin, who until today is nothing short of criticism for the field, provoked in the early 2000s that, «The majority of critics nowadays are simply flacks: There are too many fashionistas and too few street fighters. We've been taken up into the culture of branding.»[40]

The architecture historian James Marston Fitch (Columbia University, New York), reviewed architectural criticism in the United States in 1976 and came to the conclusion, that «the iron-bound formalism of current architectural criticism is quite as dangerous to favored buildings as to favorite architects.»[41] Not even ten years later, Goldberger, who up to then had supported formalist, post-modern positions in architecture, announced in a headline for the International Herald Tribune that «The Celebrity Architect Arrives».[42]

When evaluating the case of Hadid versus Filler in 2014/15, Goldberger stated that «there is much to be unhappy about the way that the celebrity culture has infiltrated architecture»,[43] a development the critic himself participated in fostering. Accordingly, a market for architectural drawings, which repeatedly focused on the power of images rather than the technical feasibility of projects, was largely made possible through the coverage provided by critics: A solo exhibition of drawings by Massimo Scolari at the Max Protetch Gallery in 1980, which did not sell well, was extended for a week to allow Ada Louise Huxtable to review it. The architecture director of the gallery stated that «naturally we [the Max Protetch Gallery] hope that sales will increase if Huxtable does write about your work.»[44]

Architecture's—and the architect's—entanglement with a global, cultural infrastructure became more and more apparent since the late 1970s.[45] Accordingly, the critics had to adapt and to balance these powers against pure affirmation. As Goldberger put it in 2005: «An architecture critic has a lot of authority but not much real power. Power is a much more raw and direct force. Authority is respect and trust. I don't think architecture critics have the power. It used to be said that ‹The New York Times› critic can close a

Broadway show. Well, that's power. But nobody tears down a building if an architecture critic doesn't like it.»[46] Notwithstanding instances, in which critics had an impact on the built environment, it is fitting then that the ‹powerless› critic was able to flourish by covering the market of architectural representations, which featured hardly any buildings that could have been torn down in the first place.

1 http://www.architectmagazine.com/design/will-retracting-the-defamatory-article-be-enough-for-zaha-hadid_o. Retrieved: June 10, 2017.
2 Ibid.
3 See http://www.architectmagazine.com/practice/zaha-hadid-reaches-settlement-in-lawsuit-against-the-new-york-review-of-books-martin-filler_o. Retrieved: June 10, 2017.
4 Martin Filler, ‹American Architecture and Its Criticism: Reflections on the State of the Arts›, in: Tod A. Marder, ‹The Critical Edge. Controversy in Recent American Architecture›, Cambridge, Massachusetts 1985, 27–32, 28.
5 Ibid, 29. That publishers did not always readily protect critics is issued by Filler on p. 30: «In New York, Carter B. Horsley, whose incisive reportage on the real estate market had long been among the best writing on architecture in the ‹New York Times›, was demoted in 1982 to checking facts for wedding notices on the society page after his investigative coverage […] drew the wrath of the ‹Times› management.»
6 Stanley Cavell, ‹The Availability of Wittgenstein's Later Philosophy›, in: ‹Philosophical Review› 71, 1962, 67–93; quoted by William H. Hayes, ‹Architectural Criticism›, The Journal of Aesthetics and Art Criticism›, vol. 60, no 4, Fall 2002, 325. See also John Macarthur and Naomi Stead, ‹The Judge is Not an Operator: Criticality, Historiography and Architectural Criticism›, in ‹OASE›, vol. 69, 2006, 116–138.
7 Ibid.
8 See 4. In his essay, Filler notes «that because of self-imposed prohibitions of The American Institute of Architects, which remained in effect until only recently, architects in this country were traditionally barred from advertising their services, and therefore had come to view criticism—that is to say positive reviews of their work—as the only ethically permissible form of publicity open to them.» (p. 28) Another form of publicity, which Fuller does not explicitly mention in his essay, was the increasing exhibition of architectural representations in art galleries and museums.
9 ‹Art: Architectural Drawings. The Grace of Fine Delineation›, in: ‹Architectural Digest›, March 1978, 78–83.
10 Grace Glueck, ‹Architect's Drawings Lure Collectors›, in: ‹The New York Times›, February 6, 1986, C1/C10.
11 See Paul Goldberger, ‹Architectural Drawings Make Comeback to Respectability›, in: ‹The New York Times›, September 22, 1977, C16.
12 MoMA press release, published on October 29, 1977. Drexler served as MoMA's Chief Curator for Architecture from 1956 until 1986. He joined the staff in 1951. A debate on the exhibition with architectural professionals was published in Oppositions (Spring 1977:8, 160-175), edited at the Institute for Architectuare and Urban Studies (IAUS), which was founded in New York in 1967 and served as a center for debates on the autonomy of architecture under the directorship of Peter Eisenman.
13 Lisbet Nilson, ‹New Deals in Art: Marketing the architect's fine hand›, in: ‹Metropolitan Home›, February 1984, 34-105, 36.
14 Ibid.
15 Barbara Jakobson in conversation with the author (New York, October 28, 2014).
16 See https://archpaper.com/2005/11/on-criticism-2/. Retrieved: June 10, 2017.
17 http://niemanreports.org/articles/architecture-criticism-dead-or-alive/. Retrieved June 10, 2017.
18 Ibid.
19 See 16.
20 Ada Louise Huxtable, ‹Poetic Visions Of Design For the Future›, in: ‹The New York Times›, April 27, 1975. The article appeared about six weeks after Goldberger's shorter report on the exhibition and less than three weeks before its closing. Huxtable wrote in her carefully crafted critique: «What we get is not a picture of buildable building, or anything remotely resembling it except in the most lyrically perverse way. […] It is a kind of poetry.»
21 Paul Goldberger, ‹Architecture Drawings at the Modern›, in: ‹The New York Times, March 14, 1975. Goldberger remembered that in the 1970s, «The New York Times was so big and so essential and had so much advertising in it and was so thick, they were just desperate to fill space, so that anything I would write they would welcome.» (See 24.)
22 Ibid.
23 Ibid.
24 Paul Goldberger in conversation with the author (New York, January 27, 2016).
25 Robert Campbell, ‹MOMA display weak, timid›, in: ‹The Boston Sunday Globe›, March 23, 1975, F14. In his critique, Campbell did not mention that the drawings in the exhibition were for sale.
26 Ibid.
27 Ibid.
28 Ibid.
29 See 24.
30 Blake further stated that «the architectural profession in the US, individually and collectively, subverts and emasculates all intelligent criticism of architecture», through censorship, which also advertisers executed, if the coverage mentioned their products in a negative way. During his time as an editor-in-chief of Architectural Forum the magazine died three times. It ceased publication in 1974. (Peter Blake on the failure of architecture criticism, public talk at IAUS in the spring semester of 1977. Tape recording, Peter Eisenman fonds (AP143), Canadian Center for Architecture, Montreal.)
31 See Martin Filler, note 4. In his essay, Filler mentions Goldberger with regard to the lawsuit Trump vs. Gapp (Chicago Tribune). Although he «rightly ridiculed» Trump's plan to erect the skyscraper, the critic «nonetheless […] left it to Gapp to take on this development in Goldberger's own backyard.» (p. 28)
32 See Art Lending Service and Art Advisory Service Records in The Museum of Modern Art Archives, New York, ‹Architectural Studies and Projects› [MoMA Exh. #1091b, March 13-May 11, 1975].
33 See 24. From the show, Goldberger purchased a drawing by Ettore Sottsass, titled ‹Rafts for Listening to Chamber Music› (hand colored lithograph, edition of 17) for $340, which was one of the least expensive items in the exhibition. In his article, the critic describes the drawings' content as, «wonderful constructions, named for Mozart and Telemann, which float down a river.» (See 21.) Between 1979 and 1991, Martin Filler and his wife, the architectural historian, Rosemarie Haag Bletter, purchased a total of eight drawings from the Max Protetch Gallery. Asked about a potential conflict of interest, the critic stated: «I would not write a critique on a show and then buy something.» (Martin Filler and Rosemarie Haag Bletter in conversation with the author (New York, February 16, 2017).)
34 Ibid.
35 Ibid.
36 See Charles Wright Mills, ‹The power elite›, New York 1956. See also Kazys Varnelis, ‹The Spectacle of the Innocent Eye. Vision, Cynical Reason, and The Discipline of Architecture in Postwar America›, Dissertation, Cornell University, Ithaca, New York 1994.
37 See Michael Sorkin, ‹Why Paul Goldberger is so Bad: The case of Times Square›, in: M. Sorkin, ‹exquisite corpse. Writing on Buildings›, New York 1991, 101–108. First published in ‹The Village Voice› in April 1985.
38 Ibid, 108. Goldberger later stated: «I rarely saw [the profession] in terms of power, even though, obviously, that existed, that was a force and factor in this job and I was not stupid. I couldn't have been totally innocent of it. But nevertheless, I don't recall feeling that it was terribly important to me […].» (See 24.)
39 See note 16.
40 Ibid.
41 James Marston Fitch, ‹Architectural Criticism: Trapped in Its Own Metaphysics›, in: ‹JAE›, vol. 29, No. 4, ‹Architecture Criticism and Evaluation› (Apr., 1976), 2-3. In his article, Fitch assessed that «architectural criticism seldom if ever deals with the full consequences of architectural intervention. Obsessed with formal rather than functional consequences, it dooms itself to fundamental irresponsibility.» (p. 2)
42 See Paul Goldberger, ‹The Celebrity Architect Arrives›, in: ‹The International Herald Tribune›, January 4, 1985, 7.
43 See note 16.
44 See letter by Fran Nelson to Massimo Scolari, dated May 28, 1980. Max Protetch Gallery Archive. In the end, the exhibition was not reviewed by Huxtable, who nevertheless frequently covered Protetch's exhibitions.
45 Against the backdrop of a rising number of architecture-related sales exhibitions, critics increasingly evaluated the market from different angles. In conjunction with the opening of the German Architecture Museum (DAM) one critic asked: «How much value does a mediocre drawing have?» (Nils ABC, ‹Francfort: ouverture du musée des Post›, in: ‹Libération›, 9/10 June 1984, 32–33.)
46 See note 16.

The Museum of Modern Art

11 West 53 Street, New York, N.Y. 10019 Tel. 956-6100 Cable: Modernart

NO. 14
FOR RELEASE: MARCH 13, 1975
PRESS PREVIEW: March 12, 1975
-11am - 4pm -

<u>Architectural Studies and Projects</u>, an informal exhibition of 50 recent drawings by American and European architects, will be on view in the Members Penthouse of The Museum of Modern Art from March 13 through May 15, 1975. The exhibition is open to the public daily between 3:00 and 5:30.

The majority of the drawings on view are of visionary projects, imaginary creations never intended to be built. The drawings are, in many cases, not the plan or facade for a specific construction, but rather the expression of an idea, or an attitude towards architecture. As Emilio Ambasz, Curator of Design at the Museum, writes: "Paper projects have in many instances influenced architecture's history as forcefully as those committed to stone. Whether their intent is aesthetic, evocative, ironic, polemical, methodological, ideological, or conjectural, their strength has always resided in their poetic content."

Mr. Ambasz organized the exhibition by selecting 23 architects and groups who were invited to submit three works they considered representative of their ideas. Included are Raimund Abraham's ink and watercolor "House with Flower Walls," Friedrich St. Florian's "Himmelbett, Penthouse Version (with Holographic Heaven)," Superstudio's collage "Life/Supersurface--You Can Be Where You Like," and John Hejduk's "Villa of No Consequence." Among other works are Peter Eisenman's "House Six: Transformations #14," Gaetano Pesce's "Project for the Remodeling of a Villa," Peter Cook's "The Urban Mark as City," Cedric Price's "Thinkbelt," and Ettore Sottsass' "Temple for Erotic Dances."

<u>Architectural Studies and Projects</u>, the first of a series of exhibitions, is made possible by a grant from Pernod, and organized by the Museum's Art Lending Service, a project of the Junior Council. All of the drawings are for sale, ranging in price from $200 to $2000.

The Art Lending Service is a sales/rental gallery with selected works in various mediums from galleries and independent artists. Works are on sale to members and non-members; rental is a membership privilege. Rental fees, for a two month period, are approximately 10% of the value of the work and can be applied to the purchase price.

Additional information available from Michael Boodro, Assistant, and Elizabeth Shaw, Director, Department of Public Information, The Museum of Modern Art, 11 W. 53 St., New York, NY 10019. Phone: (212) 956-7504; 7501.

‹Architectural Studies and Projects›, The Museum of Modern Art, New York, March 13-May 11, 1975. Press release.
© The Museum of Modern Art, New York/Scala, Florence.

Architecture Drawings at the Modern

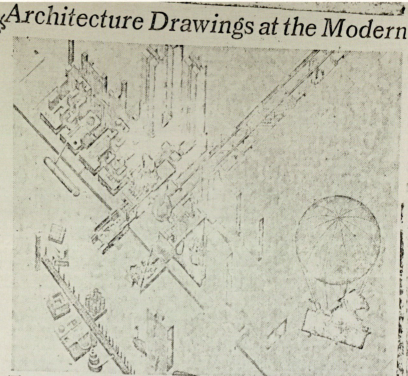

"The Egg of Columbus Circle," by Elia and Zoe Zenghelis, at Museum of Modern Art

By PAUL GOLDBERGER

"Architectural Studies and Projects," which opens today in the Penthouse of the Museum of Modern Art, deals with the most peripheral, yet perhaps the most luxurious, aspect of architecture: the making of purely visionary drawings, schemes that have no connection with reality.

As such, the exhibition, sponsored by the museum's Junior Council and organized by Emilio Ambasz, curator of design, has little real insight into the state of architectural practice today. Its significance, rather, lies in its ability to remind us that architects do, in fact, have imaginations, and when these imaginations are permitted to run free of the constraints imposed by actual building programs, the results can be exciting and often extraordinarily beautiful.

One of the objectives of the show has been to encourage public interest in architectural drawings as art, and on this level it is likely to be successful—even though the most interesting drawings are, in most cases, the ones least related to real building schemes, which has the effect of suggesting that plans and elevations of built works are somehow less interesting as objects on their own.

The exhibition has the European bias that the Museum of Modern Art frequently displays in architectural matters. But the lack of more American representation is less regrettable here than it might be in another type of show, since it has led to the inclusion of some splendid work by a number of visionary architects little known to the American public.

Among the best objects in the show are a genuinely witty set of three projects by Ettore Sottsass from his 1972 series "The Planet as a Festival," including "Temple for Erotic Dances" (a huge fantasy version of a machine); "Rafts for Listening to Chamber Music" (wonderful constructions, named for Mozart and Telemann, which float down a river), and "A Gigantic Work" (a serpentine building winding through a jungle).

Equally notable are Gaetano Pesce's two water-colors of a project for remodeling an Italian villa, which include gutting the house and filling it with a great stair running down to the nearby waterfront, and Raimund Abraham's stunning drawings for his "House With Three Walls" and "House With Flower Walls," a proposal for a house with flowers growing between double panes of glass.

There are also some splendid fantasy views of New York by Elia and Zoe Zenghelis and Rem Koolhaas, as well as extremely skilled drawings by more familiar New York architects such as Peter Eisenman, Richard Meier and John Hedjuk.

The exhibition will be on view from 3 to 5:30 P.M. daily until May 15.

Paul Goldberger, ‹Architecture Drawings at the Modern›, in: ‹The New York Times, March 14, 1975. Art Lending Service and Art Advisory Service Records. © The Museum of Modern Art Archives, New York/Scala, Florence.

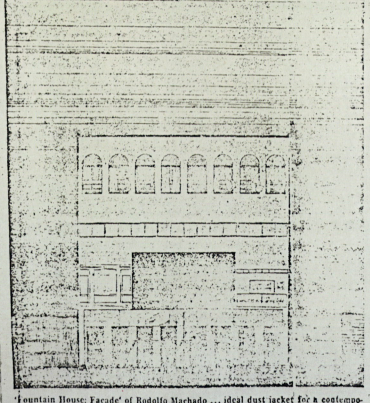

Robert Campbell, ‹MOMA display weak, timid›, in: ‹The Boston Sunday Globe›, March 23, 1975, F14. Art Lending Service and Art Advisory Service Records. © The Museum of Modern Art Archives, New York/Scala, Florence.

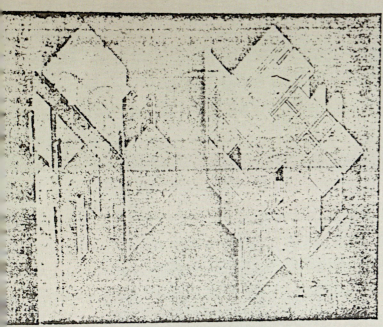

Peter Eisenmann drawing on view at New York's Museum of Modern Art... a game of intersecting transparent planes.

ment for a writer is a built-in, tamper-proof, copper-bottom crap detector (or something like that), and a show like this makes you wish the same for architects, who as a group possibly need it more. After you get through everything that hasn't even tried to be "visionary architecture" you are left with not an awful lot.

A few drawings do qualify, but what they make you realize, paradoxically, is that being a visionary in architecture today means being a member of a very traditional role, like being, say, Georgian Revivalist. Like Georgian Revivalism, visionary-ism is basically reactionary.

The drawing by Peter Eisenmann (reproduced here), for example, is reactionary in the sense of being a throwback, though modified, to works of the Dutch De Stijl group of the 1920s, and it's also a trivialization of architecture in the sense that it leaves out practically everything you might want to see in the actual built environment, except a game of intersecting transparent planes.

As Mark Twain might have put it, the visionary game has been pretty well worked in this century. There isn't much future in it. If this show proves anything it proves that. Real architecture is so much more inclusive, more complex, many-layered, exciting, alive, simply by trying to respond to the contemporary world instead of reducing it to someone's personal iconography.

It would be immensely valuable if some museum would find a way to put that kind of architecture on display, and give it the kind of comparative, interpretive exhibition that the other arts get. It wouldn't be easy, as some recent tries here have shown, but it would help educate the public in the one visual art it can't help living with.

MOMA's show is in the Member's Penthouse, an innovation, and is open to the public from 3 p.m. to 5:30 p.m. daily until May 15. There's also a depressing exhibit in the design section of the museum, of chairs shown, as usual, as if they had been primarily intended as sculptures.

Francis J. McGee, of Marblehead, past president of the Eastern Mass. Chapter of the Society of Real Estate Appraisers, has been appointed vice governor of this region by the board of directors of the National Society of Real Estate Appraisers.

«How important is it that your students are critical, Mr. Kerez?»

«You address a question we have discussed quite intensely at the chair. I taught the first year students for 8 years, and during the 5th or 6th year I wondered, ‹What is the most strongly needed asset for an architectural student today?› We figured that it's exactly critical thinking. I do not believe that the students are not critical anymore, rather the pressure in the field of architecture has increased enormously over the last 10 to 20 years. There is really a change going on in the conditions of architecture that I observe with anxiety. There is in Swiss competitions today an enormous number of things that you have to prepare, to solve and to prove as an architect that did not even exist before.

    I participated in two major international competitions: the Royal College of Art, in London, and the Beyeler Foundation in Basel. In both cases, both juries tried to prevent journalists from debating the result of the competitions or making a comparison between the projects. Architectural juries today are notoriously afraid of any debate, even if there are so many competitions actually that the public lost interest. Whereas it is actually only the debate that makes competitions in architecture interesting. Is a painting by Ad Reinhart better than a painting by Liechtenstein? Is a proposal by Sanaa better than a proposal by OMA? They have both different attitudes, different understandings of architecture and the difference between two proposals comes out of that. The jury has to find criteria to evaluate them and the public has to debate these criteria. In the last 10 years, there has been a total loss of critical debates on architecture together with a dramatic increase in architectural investments, the scale and in the political impact of the buildings. When I went to university, Martin Steinmann would describe competition entries from Jaques Herzog and Pierre de Meuron which were not even winning prizes. Still they were the most interesting projects that were discussed. Times were different, the debate in competition was actually more important than who won or lost them. I remember much better the [sensation] of the Parc de la Villette by OMA than the winning competition entry.

    I think that we are witnessing the end of an era. It is time for a new generation to take over. In this sense, we were thinking: ‹how can we help the students to develop a critical understanding?›, but I honestly wonder if it's really the professor's responsibility to ensure this. Because it's exactly what is not on the agenda of an authoritarian professor-student relationship; Can you imagine the teacher giving the grades and saying: ‹my dear students you were not critical enough, especially not towards me so you only get a low pass›.

    We are to a certain extent successfully helping the diploma students to develop a critical understanding. We have been cultivating a climate of debate with them for several years. As a teacher, my role is not to tell them: ‹please do this› or ‹I think this is bad because it's not classical or not modern› or ‹please do refer more to the buildings of Luigi Caccia Dominioni›. It is rather the meaning of the brief which is important to me. ‹What does it mean that this brief is selected for this context?›, or ‹what does it mean that you now make such a proposal?› In practice, it becomes hard to ask all these basic questions. They are time consuming, difficult and possibly preventing you from winning because they do not put the jury in a comfortable position. In this sense, it is a freedom for them to think about the meaning or the story behind a given program. It helps the students to investigate what they will be doing later in their practice.»

«The model of the studio—the idea of having an experienced architect showing the way to younger students—has a very strong bias towards dogmatism. Could you say that you propose something different to avoid it and actually foster a critical culture?»

«As I have explained you earlier, I am not the master of the student; I do not tell him what to do. This means that they have to come up with ideas and proposals themselves. We insist on this demand especially with the diploma students. We differentiate between an authentic and personal idea and a convention, a generic scheme as you see often in competitions. This has nothing to do with personal or aesthetic preferences. It is hard work to find your own attitude, your personal approach towards architecture. It is very painful and stressful. A Lot of students do not appreciate to be taken out of their comfort zone and say that we do not know what we want from them, which we somehow also do out of conviction. If a student does not find an idea, for whatever reason, He will fail. I am critical in this sense. I do not only wish I could help the students become more critical I am also critical towards what they are doing. They have to convince me that what they present is really their own thought, their own understanding. In the end, It is the statement of a project that matters to me, no matter if this might be politically correct or not.

    Next semester our chair will be doing something new. We will first work on the definition of space, its perception and understanding. With this knowledge, the students will enter Swiss competitions. It will not be about square meters, cost estimation, and all this non-architectural arguments. It will be about space, about architecture; whether or not you can still think about spaces in this very restricted area of Swiss competitions and at the same time do your work as an architect.»

This text is taken from the skype interview with Christian Kerez led the 9th of June 2017 by Vincent Bianchi and Yann Salzmann.

Follow that Big Yellow Duck!
On Jokes and Urban Commons
Marija Marić

June 11th 2016, Belgrade. Only recently has a two meters tall yellow styrofoam duck been sitting here, on the grass plot in front of the City Hall. Now, thousands of people of all age gather here again, well equipped with whistles, hand-made drums, posters and flags with that same duck as the central protagonist.

Like in a ritual, everybody has come to express honor and worship to their God. As young activists loudly address the crowd from the small, provisional stage, a deafening whistling follows. Anger and laughter pervade the atmosphere, naturally collaborating with each other. A few minutes later, a small truck, carrying loudspeakers and a flag with the face of an angry duck, slowly moves down the street, passing by the Parliament building. Everyone follows. As we reach the House of the Constitutional Court, the truck stops. Its followers stop too. The rolls of toilet paper suddenly fill the air, ending on the surrounding trees and street lampposts. Soon, the walk continues. An elderly woman walks next to me, wearing a plastic whistle in the shape of a small yellow duck around her neck, shouting loudly: «Resignations!»

June 17th 2016, Novi Sad. A few meters away from my house, in front of the building of Radio Television of Vojvodina, a small group of people gathers, holding a large poster of the crossed-out yellow duck. A truck is parked in front of the standing crowd, playing loud music. A bit further away, side streets are clogged with a number of parked buses from various parts of the country. After a while, the group moves, soon dispersing throughout the city, some for shopping, others for food and drinks. A police officer stands on the corner, monitoring the event. I approach him, asking what is going on. He says—it's a counter-protest. I ask—what are they protesting against? He says—they are protesting against the protests in Belgrade.[1]

A Bad Joke

But, what is the story behind the big yellow duck? The story of a real estate development called ‹Belgrade Waterfront›, and thousands of people it brought to the streets in what will become a series of the biggest protests in Serbia since the fall of Milošević's regime.

‹Belgrade Waterfront› is a large-scale real estate, urban development project initiated in 2014 by the Serbian Government and Abu Dhabi based private company Eagle Hills. With the total estimated costs of 3.5 billion euros, the project represents the single most expensive venture of the Serbian Government so far. Located on the unbuilt lot of the Sava Riverbank in the center of the city, ‹Belgrade Waterfront› consists of almost two million square meters of mixed-use luxury housing and retail properties, featuring the biggest shopping mall and the highest tower in the region, designed by SOM.[2]

Announced for the first time in 2012, as part of the municipal pre-election campaign of the Serbian Progressive Party, the project was discarded as another ‹grand maquette›, uncannily familiar pitch of the populist political propaganda in Serbia.[3] Abandoning the principles of workers' self-management and societal ownership after the breakup of Yugoslavia, post-socialist political elites opted for ‹vulgar capitalism› in which the market rhetoric, disguised as ‹transition› and ‹democratisation› was exploited to clear the way for corrupted development and economic inequality. Since 1990s, urban space in former Yugoslav republics has been shaped by the rules of private property, legal controversies and what had been often described as ‹investor urbanism›.

During the 2014 parliamentary election campaign, the project appeared again, this time officially branded with the promotional hub, the realistic model and the large billboard. In March 2015, a draft of the ‹Lex Specialis›[4] arrived to the Parliament. The legal revision proposed a quick expropriation of the private land, exempted the investor from paying the obligatory taxes for the usage of the land and proclaimed 1.8 million sqm of luxury housing and office space to be of the «public interest». The urgent legal procedure was justified by the urgency of «the deadline for the end of the project».[5] In April 2015, Lex Specialis was adopted and ‹Belgrade Waterfront› was now legally possible.

Without any public competition, the contract between the Serbian Government and Eagle Hills was signed two weeks later. Published only after a couple of months, the contract showed that, out of the 3.5 billion euros of the project's total value, Eagle Hills is obliged to invest only 150 million euros and provide another

Yellow Duck on the ‹Boat Carnival› held on August 29th 2015, in Belgrade. Photograph by Horda Sage.

150 million euros of loan, while Serbian taxpayers take responsibility for the rest. At the same time, Eagle Hills' participation in the ownership of the company ‹Belgrade Waterfront› is 68 percent.⁶

A year later, in the night between April 24th and 25th 2016, after the parliamentary elections in Serbia were finished and the results announced, with the Serbian Progressive Party as the winning majority, a bizarre event occurred. Several unidentified men, wearing balaclava masks and driving bulldozers without license plates, illegally demolished buildings in the Savamala district, clearing the way for the ‹Belgrade Waterfront› construction. Despite calls, the police did not come. The only witness was a guard, who died in a hospital a couple of days later. As nobody claimed responsibility for the event, the public anger grew. Soon, Aleksandar Vučić, the Serbian Prime Minister at the time, the leader of the Serbian Progressive Party and the father of the project, took the stage and said that «whoever did it, was a complete idiot for not doing it in the middle of the day.»⁷ Rallies started, with protesters calling for the resignation of «complete idiots.»⁸

Big Yellow Duck

Already in 2014, a group of activists with various backgrounds founded an Initiative ‹Ne Da(vi)mo Beograd› roughly translatable into ‹Don't Let Belgrade D(r)own›. The aim of the group was to publicly expose non-transparent processes of the project advancement, with an attempt of including the public opinion into the plan development. In the beginning, their engagement was mostly based on protest letters, complaints and existing participatory tools, which, as they write, were without any significant effect.⁹

When, in November 2014, the General Urban Plan of Belgrade changed according to the investor's model for the future ‹Belgrade Waterfront› location, against legal regulations and without any public consultancy, the Initiative once more filed complaints. They invited citizens to join the public session to be held in November 2015, in the building of the Assembly of the City of Belgrade, writing: «Belgrade floats freely on the water, despite laws and public interest. On Wednesday, November 5th, the last simulation of including citizens into the process of planning will take place. Flood follows. We should be prepared.»¹⁰ As all of their remarks to the plan were rejected, and in the middle of the public session, the activists took out lifebelts and small yellow rubber ducks, in what will become ‹Operation Lifebelt› (Operacija Šlauf).¹¹ This was the first performative action of the group, where absurd and comedy were employed as a means of critique and struggle against absurd and tragedy of the project. A day later, newspapers and social media circulated the story followed by photos of a serious-looking public meeting of the city officials with colorful lifebelts and yellow ducks being spread around the room.

In Serbian language, a duck means both a duck and a dick.¹² Duck as a fraud, but also duck of the resistance that monitors the drowning of a corrupt city. Duck as an official symbol of the protests appeared for the first time in March 2015, when ‹Lex Specialis› for the ‹Belgrade Waterfront› project came into the Parliament.¹³ Made of styrofoam, approximately two meters tall, the duck was now a hack that entered Serbian politics and trolled any seriousness on the side of the political elites. It multiplied as a joke, image and symbol that could fit in anything related to the political corruption, even beyond ‹Belgrade Waterfront› project. It travelled around the city, it was parked in front of the National Parliament, it visited the City Hall, it drove on a boat in the Sava River monitoring the construction site. It was angry. After the night demolitions in Hercegovačka Street, it wore a balaclava mask. Everyone was taking photos of it, photo-shopping it into their profile pictures on social networks. The duck was all around. It was growing.

The power of the duck was in its simplicity and potential for multiplication. Politicians narrating real estate fictions of ‹creative›, ‹green›, ‹smart›, ‹spectacular› experiences for the future residents of the most expensive square meter in the country, now faced a big yellow duck standing in front of the expected audience. The duck became a ‹meme›, a visual, cultural, performative gesture that spreads across the community. It was a «continuation of politics by other memes.»¹⁴ The duck mobilized easily because it transformed the long-lasting and chronic political depression into something funny, and therefore less overwhelming, less absolute. Suddenly, the political arena was not reserved only for those ready to play dirty. Instead, at that point it was actually about playing, and everyone could participate.

The duck also saved activists from over-exposure. Although the most visible ones were misrepresented in the media and connected to various foreign power structures, it still, up to a certain degree, anonymised the group. It was the duck who was angry, it was the duck who was leading the protests, it was the duck who was rebellious. It enabled a kind of positive simplification of the struggle. The duck was a public joke, and not a public art. Its designer was unknown, so it belonged to everybody. In her study of the ‹Anonymous›, the anthropologist Gabriella Coleman looks into the ways the group «underwent a metamorphosis from underworld trolls into public-facing activists.»¹⁵ Built around the anti-leader and anti-celebrity ethics that decentralizes the power within the group and helps its expansion, she argued that collective identity did not homogenize the group. Similarly, the duck as a collective identity, made it easier for many on the outside to identify with, first the group's sense of humor, and then also the real thing—the struggle they set off.

The History of Laughter is Everyone's History

«This history of walking is an amateur history, just as walking is an amateur act. To use a walking metaphor, it trespasses through everybody else's field—through anatomy, anthropology, architecture, gardening, geography, political and cultural history, literature, sexuality, religious studies—and doesn't stop in any of them on its long route. For if a field of expertise can be imagined as a real field—a nice rectangular confine carefully tilled and yielding a specific crop—then the subject of walking resembles walking itself in its lack of confines. [...] The history of walking is everyone's history, and any written version can only hope to indicate some of the more well-trodden paths in the author's vicinity.»[16]

Joke is a critique that operates on a common sense. Jokes are commons, per se. They belong to everybody, both to the powerful and the weak. In order to laugh, you do not need to be an expert. Jokes are anonymous, their maker is unknown, his or her identity gets lost as the joke travels. In the words of Metahaven, the creator of the joke is truly a designer, enabling communication across the distance—«jokes, when politically effective, perform what everybody knew but couldn't say.»[17] As they spread, they also mutate, are edited, are lost. Jokes are a free, and therefore, endlessly accessible resource. They are not about high quality, but about easy distribution, circulation and manipulation. This decentralized network through which jokes disperse, is also its actual production site, and the producers are all those who laugh and retell the funny story.

Jokes make shared history, they unite those who laugh. Already at the beginning of 20th century, French philosopher Henri Bergson took jokes seriously, proposing laughter as the key element for understanding social, collective and popular imagination. He wrote: «You could hardly appreciate the comic if you felt yourself isolated from others. Laughter appears to stand in need of an echo. [...] Our laughter is always the laughter of a group.»[18] Jokes mobilize amateurs and imply collaboration. Still, their histories are invisible.

Jokes as Entry Points

Confronted with large-scale problems or abstract concepts such as global capitalism, inequality, corrupt state—we stand paralysed. How does one affect something ‹global›? How does one work against mechanisms of inequality that evolve and perfect throughout centuries? How does one change a corrupt state? It seems as if our possibilities are infinitesimally small and our actions irrelevant. Thus, we give up.

Jokes help us access large scales and abstract ideas; they are at the same time local and global, particular and universal. In her book ‹Friction›, anthropologist Anna Tsing writes: «Scale is not just a neutral frame for viewing the world; scale must be brought into being; proposed, practiced, and evaded, as well as taken for granted.»[19] Instead of talking about scale as dimensionality, we should rather talk about ‹scale-making›, scale as a way of seeing, a way of talking and a way of entering the problem. Jokes are tools that can reshuffle our ideas of scale, opening an entry point to what would normally be too abstract and what normally we would not be able to enter. Jokes are the means of translating the distant into close, big into small, and too-serious into approachable.

For a joke to be functional, there has to be somebody that will laugh. Travelling the distance from the anonymous creator to the anonymous receiver, a joke has to bridge universal with particular; it has to bring common sense into the relationship to the specific. Thus, jokes work with the knowledge, culture and common sense of a community. This can be a community of two people, but it can also be a global community—in the end, we all laughed at Trump, although he was not really a joke. At the same time, the yellow duck from Belgrade is a language-based joke, and the laughter in this case has limitations. But how hard can we laugh within these limits? «Can we laugh so loudly at those in power that they fall? Can jokes, in fact, bring down governments?»[20]

On Nowness

In her book ‹Extrastatecraft›, architect and a theorist Keller Easterling looks into how repeatable spatial formulas, constituting the global ‹infrastructure space›, play a role in formulating new forms of power and governance beyond the State. Still, she writes, «the things that make infrastructure space powerful—its multipliers, its irrational fictions, or its undeclared consequential activities—are perhaps the very things that make it immune to righteous declaration and prescription.» Proposing ‹An Expanded Activist Repertoire in Infrastructure Space›, Easterling argues for an approach that is «more performative than prescriptive» where architects could learn from «pirates, prisoners, hackers, comedians.»[21]

‹Belgrade Waterfront› was one such ‹extrastatecraft› in action. Still, it triggered urban resistance that quickly exploded into a wider political struggle, larger than the project itself. The struggle over the right to the city opened the door for rethinking politics and citizenship in the environment shaped by social and economic inequality. Gathered in common fight, citizens and activists showed understanding of urban space more insightful than the experts.

Finally, this takes us to the question—what are the positions from which architects speak? Could the future of critical architecture be in designing new subjectivities, new roles architects can occupy, instead of in designing new objects and typologies? In her essay ‹What is a Theorist›, Irit Rogoff looks into the ways (historical) research very often escapes its connection to the worldly struggles: «The answer lies, to my mind at least, in substituting the historical specificity of that being studied with the historical specificity of the he/she/they doing the studying.»[22] Following this, we could say that only by consciously working with one's own ‹historical specificity›, either as an architectural student, as an architect, as a worker, or a class, one can be truly critical. Perhaps architectural critique doesn't have to do as much with what we produce, but as how we do it. And with recognizing and working with our own ‹nowness›.

Follow that Big Yellow Duck!

1. The third public protest of the Initiative ‹Ne Da(vi)mo Beograd› (‹Don't Let Belgrade D(r)own›) held in Belgrade, and the first ‹counter-protest› named ‹Stop anarhiji› (‹Stop the Anarchy›) with anonymous organizers, held in Novi Sad, respectively.
2. http://www.eaglehills.com/our-developments/serbia/belgrade-waterfront. Retreived: 5.8.2017.
3. On the same location of the ‹Belgrade Waterfront›, Slobodan Milošević proposed to build ‹Europolis›, a monumental plan for the new city, never realized.
4. Full title of the ‹Lex Specialis›: ‹Bill on Deteremination of the Public Interest and Special Procedures for Expropriation and Construction Permits for the Realization of the Belgrade Waterfront Project.›
5. Legal analysis of the ‹Lex Specialis› from the official publication of the Initiative ‹Ne Da(vi)mo Beograd›, Issue 2, March 2016, Belgrade, p. 7.
6. https://www.slobodnaevropa.org/a/ugovor-o-beogradu-na-vodi-otkriva-veliku-prevaru/27260571.html. Retreived: 5.8.2017.
7. A press statement from May 10th 2016.
8. https://www.theguardian.com/world/2016/may/26/serbs-rally-against-shady-demolitions-after-masked-crew-tied-up-witnesses. Retreived: 5.8.2017.
9. http://www.eurozine.com/report-from-belgrade-waterfront/. Retreived: 5.8.2017.
10. https://nedavimobeograd.wordpress.com/2014/11/03/ne-davimo-beograd-operacija-slauf/. Retreived: 5.8.2017.
11. Čukić, et al., 2014.
12. Originally ‹duck›, but used in jargon as a ‹dick›, or a ‹fraud›.
13. http://www.vreme.com/cms/view.php?id=1495169.Retreived: 5.8.2017.
14. Metahaven, ‹Can Jokes Bring Down Governments? Memes, Design and Politics›, (Kindle Edition), Moscow 2013.
15. Gabriella Coleman, ‹Hacker, Hoaxer, Whistleblower, Spy: The Many Faces of Anonymous›, (Kindle Edition), London 2014.
16. Rebecca Solnit, ‹Wanderlust: A History of Walking›, (Kindle Edition), New York 2001.
17. Metahaven, 2013.
18. Henri Bergson, ‹Laughter: An Essay on the Meaning of the Comic›, London 1911, p 6.
19. Anna Lowenhaupt Tsing, ‹Friction. An Ethnography of Global Connection›, Princeton and Oxford 2005, p. 58.
20. Metahaven, 2013.
21. Keller Easterling, ‹Extrastatecraft. The Power of Infrastructure Space›, (Kindle Edition), London and New York 2014.
22. Irit Rogoff, ‹What is a Theorist›, in: Katharyna Sykora (Ed.) ‹Was ist ein Kunstler›, Berlin 2003, p. 149.

Tischkritik
Nikolai von Rosen und *Karin Sander*

Eigentlich müssten wir am Anfang um die Angabe spielen und festlegen, wer den ersten Schlag ausführt, und dann zählen. Andererseits spielen wir zwei gegeneinander fast nie um Punkte. Es genügt uns, die Möglichkeiten des gemeinsamen Spielens auszureizen, ohne zu schauen, wer von uns beiden der bessere ist. *Unser Spielen ist wie Armdrücken. Wenn die eine Person drückt, dann drückt die andere auch. Aber sobald eine versucht besser zu sein, verlieren wir beide das Interesse. Wenn es also nicht um Stärke, sondern um das Spielen geht, das weit interessanter ist als das Gewinnen, dann konzentrieren wir uns auf den Dialog.*

Du spielst nur Rückhand. Mit der Folge, je schneller man auf dich spielt, umso schneller kriegt man den Ball auch wieder zurück. Wie ist dein Tischkritik-Stil entstanden? *Ich stelle mich ganz auf die Situation und mein Gegenüber ein, halte den Schläger und gebe den Ball meist so zurück, wie er auf meiner Seite ankommt. Meine Art des Tischtennis ist ein Zurückspielen von dem, was der andere mir präsentiert.*

Dadurch entsteht selten ein Angriff, sondern eher eine Abwehr, ein Zurückgeben dessen, was ich empfange. Ich weiss, das ist seltsam, aber nur so kann ich mich voll und ganz auf das einlassen, was da an der Platte vor sich geht. Das hat dann auch etwas damit zu tun, wie ich arbeite und lehre. Und genau so ist das mit der Tischkritik. Je mehr von den Studierenden kommt, je mehr sie ihre Persönlichkeit zeigen, desto mehr Rückspiel. Ich sehe dabei nicht meine Meinung im Vordergrund, sondern vielmehr das, was die Studierenden in das Spiel einbringen. War das auch von Anfang an dein Stil, also zu Beginn, als du Professorin an der ETH geworden bist? Dass du dich hingestellt hast mit deinem Schläger und geschaut hast, was kommt von Seiten der Studierenden und auch von Seiten der Architekturprofessuren? *Als ich an der ETH zu unterrichten anfing, habe ich für die 300 Studienanfänger dieses Jahrgangs ein leeres Buch binden lassen. Das führte zu einer ersten Irritation.*

Das Buch hatte 365 Seiten … und die Studierenden sollten jeden Tag eine Idee, eine Überlegung, eine Beobachtung oder einen Satz in das Buch schreiben oder zeichnen, jeden Tag üben, sich auf einem Papier zu artikulieren. Die Überlegungen eines Jahres als Buch. Das ist eine Möglichkeit, den Studierenden erst einmal Raum zu geben, sich und ihre Fähigkeiten kennenzulernen und sich von Zwängen und Vorgedachtem freizuschaufeln, ihre eigene Position zu finden. Das ist etwas anderes, als sich durch etwas Vorgegebenes inspirieren zu lassen. Der Grundgedanke dahinter wäre: Man lernt in der Kunst Erfahrungen zu machen, die exemplarisch sind. Also wie es sich anfühlt, überhaupt ein Themenfeld zu finden, das es vorher so noch gar nicht gegeben hat. Oder die Erfahrung zu machen, wie man zu so etwas wie einer Position, zu einem Thema oder einem Medium kommt, in dem man sich ausdrücken möchte. Ja, künstlerisches Denken lernen heisst, sich erst mal auf etwas einzulassen, wofür es keine Regeln gibt. Auf welche Art von Spiel wollen wir uns einlassen? Welche Spielregeln wollen wir dafür entwickeln? Wie kann der Studierende dabei zu dem finden, was ‹seins› ist? Von hier aus starten wir dann in freie künstlerische Überlegungen, die sowohl auf die Überlegungen im Entwurf als auch übergeordnet auf das Studieren übertragen werden können.

Dein Lehrstuhl heisst nicht mehr ‹Professur für bildnerisches Gestalten› oder ‹Grundlagen der Gestaltung› wie noch bei deiner Übernahme, seit einigen Jahren heisst er ‹Lehrstuhl für Architektur und Kunst›. *Ein Name wie ‹Grundlagen des Gestaltens› schränkt ein. Bei einer künstlerischen Ausbildung geht es wahrlich um mehr, am wenigsten jedenfalls um das Gestalten. Es geht um etwas viel Komplexeres. Das Gestalten wäre nur eine Dimension. Vorletztes Jahr habe ich uns auf einem Kongress der Kunstlehrstühle an Architekturhochschulen in Stuttgart vertreten. Die meisten Lehrstühle haben etwas mit ‹Gestaltung› im Namen, und natürlich gibt es verschiedene Methodenansätze. Es gibt die einen, die basierend auf der Annahme von Prinzipien der Gestaltung unterrichten, und es gibt andere, zu denen wir gehören, die Methoden des künstlerischen Arbeitens lehren und sich auf kontextuelle und konzeptuelle Strategien konzentrieren. Dabei geht es nicht nur um das Denken, sondern um ein kontinuierliches, selbstbestimmtes Arbeiten. Wir leiten die Studierenden an, aus dem, was sie tun, Konsequenzen zu ziehen. Dass dieses Vorgehen nachher auch Aspekte der Gestaltung berührt, ist möglich, aber das darf nicht das Vordergründige sein.*

Bei Kritiken habe ich oft an solchen methodischen Bruchstellen aufgemerkt. Also wenn in der Argumentation aus dem konzeptuellen Modus in einen gestalterischen gewechselt wurde. *Ja, wobei der konzeptuelle Modus am Ende zwangsläufig auch ein gestalterischer wird. In mir drin regt sich dann das Temperament und ich weiss, genau da war ein Punkt, den ich so* nicht durchgehen lassen darf. *Das sind solche Beobachtungen, die im Laufe des Arbeitsprozesses dann plötzlich keinen Sinn mehr ergeben. Es wird langweilig. Und das natürlich ist auch beim Tischtennis ein ganz wichtiger Punkt. Wenn wir nur bemüht sind, den Ball auf der Platte zu halten – das könnten wir lange durchhalten –, ist das nicht interessant. Das Spiel wird erst dann aufregend, wenn wir überrascht werden, wenn eine gewisse Spannung aufgebaut wird.*

Als Kind war ich sehr fasziniert, als ich erfuhr, dass die besten Tischtennisspieler aus China den Schläger ganz anders halten. Die haben den ganz locker zwischen zwei Fingern hängen. *Damit gibt es natürlich auch keine Vor- und Rückhand mehr.* Eine verblüffende Schlägertechnik. Als Kind fühlt man sich sogar ein wenig verhöhnt. Da hält man den Schläger ganz brav und richtig, und dann merkt man, dass die Leute, die viel, viel besser Tischtennis spielen, den Schläger ganz anders halten. *Ja, und damit sind wir bei der Technik. Wie viel Technik sollte vermittelt werden, und hilft die Technik wirklich? Ich würde sagen ja, als Einstieg, aber dann kommt das Üben, Trainieren und Ausprobieren, das Arbeiten am Eigenen. Es gelten dabei Regeln, die aber genügend Raum geben, um sich zu bewegen, und dem Spiel Dynamik verleihen. Genau das ist für uns interessant, nämlich die Kriterien für unser Agieren innerhalb der Regeln zu verstehen und individuell zu definieren. Oder aber die Regeln in Frage zu stellen. Das ist ein heikles Terrain, weil es zunächst einmal mit Unsicherheit verbunden ist.*

Es ist kein Wissen, das man in dem Sinne erlernen kann, kein reproduzierbares Wissen. Man kann sich nur darin erproben. *Genau, man kann sich erproben, sich darauf einlassen, am besten ohne Hintergedanken, möglichst unvoreingenommen, und wach sein, sich dem Spiel stellen. Unsere Tischkritik gibt einen Rahmen vor, der dann mit Ereignissen gefüllt wird. Für eine Architekturhochschule ist das eine starke Aussage, Kunst in dieser grösstmöglichen Ergebnisoffenheit zu unterrichten, und nicht der Annahme zu folgen, dass es so etwas wie Regeln, Techniken oder eindeutige Kriterien für gutes künstlerisches Arbeiten gibt. Oder zumindest Handlungsanweisungen, wie einem die Kunst in schwierigen Situationen helfen kann.*

Es gibt Kriterien in der Kunst, aber man kann sie nicht so klar abhaken. Man kann sich immer nur annähern. Grundlagen bringen die Studierenden mit. Und davon muss ich ausgehen können, wenn sie sich an einer Hochschule für ein Studium einschreiben. Dabei spielt das Sprechen als Grundfertigkeit eine nicht zu unterschätzende Rolle. Das Sprechen, das Denken, das Sehen, das Verstehen, das Reagieren und das Handeln. Dass der Studierende das, was er sieht, auch richtig interpretieren kann. Es hilft ihm nicht, kenntnisreich zu sein, wenn er keine Schlussfolgerungen daraus ziehen kann.

Deine offene Sicht auf die Dinge, diese akademische Freiheit hast du an uns Kollegen deines Teams weitergereicht und uns immer den Rücken freigehalten, damit wir selbst die zu uns passenden Formate finden und entwickeln konnten. So habe ich insbesondere durch die Diplombegleitungen die Möglichkeit

‹Tischkritik› im Ausstellungsraum Maria HIL-F 46 am 17.12.2013.

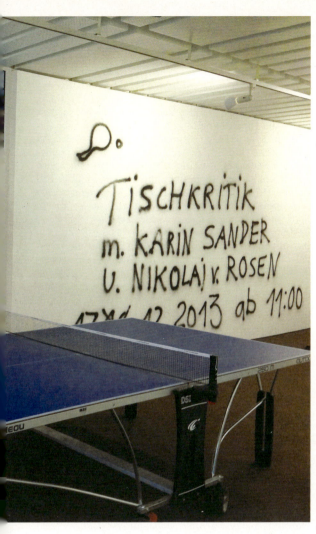

bekommen, beinahe wie ein Studierender agieren zu können. Ich konnte mich quer durch die ETH bewegen und mich mit allen Professuren und ihren verschiedenen Methoden auseinandersetzen. *Du hast über diese zehn Jahre an der ETH wahrscheinlich mehr Architektur studiert als deine Studierenden. Du hast dich auch deswegen so hervorragend in diesem Terrain bewegen können – weil du dich als Lehrender und zugleich als Studierender darin bewegt hast. Und dadurch hat eine ganz andere Form von Dialog zwischen dir und den Studierenden stattfinden können. Du hast den Studierenden das künstlerische Denken direkt und als aktiv Kunstschaffender sehr authentisch vorgeführt, indem du sie zum freien und kreativen Sprechen eingeladen hast. Weit über den Abschluss hinaus hat dein Kontakt zu ihnen gehalten, was zeigt, wie erfolgreich sich deine Arbeit bei ihnen eingeschrieben hat. Gute Lehre findet immer dann statt, wenn die betreffenden Personen das weitergeben, was sie sind, wenn sie als Künstler in ihre Fragestellungen verstrickt sind. Das funktioniert aber nur, wenn ich ihnen die – du nennst es die akademische Freiheit, ich würde es die künstlerische Freiheit nennen – gebe, so, wie ich sie selbst auch für mich fordere.*

Dann funktioniert die Lehre auf Augenhöhe und die Studierenden haben auf diese Weise sehr viel von dir gelernt. Das ist eigentlich genau das, was man jedem Studierenden mitgeben möchte, diese Form des Denkens und des Dialogs. Oft kam es mir so vor, dass ich durch meine Begleitfachtätigkeit eine Art von Architekturausbildung erhalte. Vielleicht ähnelt meine Kompetenz der eines Dramaturgen, aber eben nicht am Theater, sondern beim Entwerfen in der Architektur. Mich hat das Auf-Augenhöhe-kommen, wie du sagst, das in einer gelungenen Kritik stattfindet, immer getrieben. Und dabei geht es nicht darum, dass man den Studierenden hilft, ihre Arbeit fertig zu denken, sondern jedes Mal erneut den Punkt findet, ihnen Möglichkeiten des Weiterdenkens aufzuzeigen und sie zu stimulieren, ihre Arbeit weiter zu schärfen und sich mit ihrer ganzen Energie darin zu verlieren. Die Kritiken, die Semesterkritiken ebenso wie die Diplomkritiken, waren für mich sehr schöne Momente an der ETH.

Es ist intensiv, den Studierenden seinen Kopf zu leihen, seine Kategorien, seine Erfahrungen. War das bei dir in der Kunstausbildung ähnlich, du hast ja vorher an Akademien unterrichtet, oder ist dort der Umgang mit der künstlerischen Position der Studierenden rigoroser? *Kritik kann genau so funktionieren. Man denkt sich ein, sehr fein, weil jeder mit seiner Arbeit dasteht und du musst dich reinfinden. Im Laufe der Zeit merkst du dann auch ganz genau, wann der Punkt gekommen ist, an dem der Studierende sehr selbstbewusst weiss, wohin seine Reise geht, wann die Schmetterbälle wie gesetzt werden oder auf welche Art gespielt wird.*

Die Aufgabe, die wir als Kritiker haben, besteht oft darin, den Präsentierenden einige Ideen wegzunehmen, und sie zugleich dazu zu ermuntern, einer Idee umso entschiedener zu folgen. Die Projekte werden zumeist sehr redlich präsentiert, und es gibt weiterführende Nebenideen oder sich in der Architektur verzettelnde Funktionsnachweise. Dann liest man den Text der Ideen gegen und ermutigt: Vergiss diese und jene Nebenwege, verfolge den einen Hauptstrang, triff diese Entscheidung, und zwar konzeptuell klar und entschieden.

Es ist in der Kunst so, dass es diese Nebenwege gibt, die dann noch nicht wirklich zu Ende gedacht sind bzw. wenn es noch Nebenentscheidungen gibt, dann hat man sich selbst noch nicht überzeugen können. Es ist eine grosse Aufgabe, die Möglichkeiten zu reflektieren und zu selektieren. Denn wenn es an die Realisierung eines Konzepts geht, vervielfältigen sich die Möglichkeiten, die alle zu durchdenken sind, aber die Zeit ist oft zu kurz oder der Druck zu hoch. Entscheidungen brauchen Zeit. Wenn sie dann gefallen sind, wird eine unglaubliche Kraft freigesetzt. Das heisst Studieren, eben mit diesen vielen Möglichkeiten jonglieren zu lernen, ohne einen Ball fallen zu lassen oder ins Aus zu spielen, eine ständige Selektion von Strategien zu betreiben. Eine intellektuelle Auseinandersetzung und eine ständige Selbstreflexion bis zu dem Punkt, an dem du weisst, du hast alles richtig gemacht.

In der Architektur droht immer die Forderung, dass ein Gebäude nicht nur die Umsetzung einer Idee sein kann, sondern dass es auch viele Funktionen abdecken muss. Architektur muss was können. Je länger ich bei den Architekten mitdenken durfte, desto weniger habe ich das als Widerspruch erlebt. Das beschreibt auch meine eigene Entwicklung während der vielen Jahre in Zürich. Mittlerweile kann ich mich bestens auf die konzeptuell entschiedenen Architekturpositionen einlassen, ohne mich zu sorgen, dass die Funktionen nicht ihren Platz finden. *Wenn etwas wirklich richtig durchdacht ist oder wenn eine extreme Position nah ist, dann fügt sich alles andere ganz konsequent ein. Weil klare Hierarchien entstehen.* Genau. Die Denkrichtung ist klar, alles andere kann davon ausgehend gelöst und meistens auch sehr spielerisch integriert werden. *An den Problemen kann abgearbeitet werden, was die ganze Geschichte dann nochmal mehr zu einer Konsequenz führt.*

Rückblickend frage ich mich, ob ich die Seminare nicht auch wie eine Kritik gestaltet habe. Sinngemäss sagtest du vorhin: Man stellt sich an die Platte und wartet gespannt, was da kommt. Ich habe dem Dozieren immer das Moderieren vorgezogen. Und gleichzeitig quält einen der Zweifel, oder besser: die Selbstkritik, ob das Format noch stimmt. Weisst du, was ich meine? *Ja, wenn der Ball ins Netz geht oder nicht sauber auf die Platte trifft. Es ist zu schade, wenn etwas misslingt und ich danach genau weiss, warum.* Trifft das auch auf die Erfahrungen an der ETH zu, die unterschiedlichen Lehrformate und Strategien, die du bisher mit deinem Team entwickelt hast? *Genauso! Dort wie auch in meiner künstlerischen Arbeit bin ich ständig dran, und manchmal raubt es mir den Schlaf.*

Die zehn Jahre, die du jetzt an der ETH bist, hat dich das auch in deinem künstlerischen Arbeiten verändert? Du hast zuletzt Kunstausstellungen gemacht, bei denen du massiv in die Architektur eingegriffen hast. In Linz hast du einen Kunst-am-Bau-Wettbewerb gewonnen, bei dem du ausschliesslich mit den Mitteln der Architektur arbeitest. Gibt es für dich diesen Zusammenhang? Für mich kann ich zumindest sagen, dass ich mich sehr zur Architektur hingezogen fühle und dass das Arbeiten mit Massstäben eine grosse Anziehung ausübt. *Ja, das Arbeiten mit Massstäben, vor allem 1:1, passt auch zu unserem Tischkritik-Thema, denn Massstäbe = Spielregeln.* Das überrascht mich, dass du 1:1-Massstab sagst. Vielleicht ist es eher so, dass wir in der Kunst ohne Massstab arbeiten und auch das konzeptuelle Denken weitestgehend ohne Massstab auskommt. Und in der Architektur dreht sich ja alles um den Massstab. *Aber der Massstab war für mich auch schon immer von Bedeutung, also zum Beispiel in den Figuren 1:10, 1:5, also wenn die Dinge verkleinert oder vergrössert werden. Oder du fragst dich, wenn du ein Foto von etwas machst, wie verkleinert oder vergrössert ist das im Verhältnis zur Wirklichkeit? Das war für mich im künstlerischen Tun immer im Hintergrund. Deshalb fällt es mir vielleicht auch in der Architektur so besonders auf.*

Selbst bei den Kritiken gibt es die unterschiedlichen Massstäbe. Es gibt die Tischkritik, es gibt die Zwischenkritik und zu guter Letzt auch die Schlusskritik. Und man denkt jedes Mal, dass es ein etwas grösserer Massstab ist. Also vom privaten zum halböffentlichen Gespräch der Zwischenkritik hin zum institutionellen Sprechen vor Publikum bei der Schlusskritik. Gerade habe ich einen kleinen Text geschrieben über diese drei Kritikformen und resümiert, dass mich die Schlusskritik am wenigsten interessiert hat über die Jahre und dass mir die Tischkritik als das Zentrum der Architekturausbildung erscheint. Weil eben der Druck – oder der Code des institutionellen Sprechens – da noch nicht greift. *Es wird eben komplizierter, wenn viele Personen ins ‹Spiel› kommen.*

Willst du eigentlich nochmal eine Vorhand lernen? *Das kommt auf mein Gegenüber an, bisher schien es nicht unbedingt notwendig, sie zu können. Ich habe immer experimentiert, dabei unterschiedliche Techniken, Module und Abläufe ausprobiert. Im kommenden Semester werden wir anstatt montags jetzt mittwochs unseren Hauptunterrichtstag für die künstlerische Ausbildung haben. Wir sind damit in der Mitte der Woche angekommen. Das ist jetzt der neue Aufschlag, die Angabe, um die wir lange gekämpft haben. Das Spiel kann erneut beginnen.*

Tischkritik

Nikolai von Rosen als Gastkritiker bei der Schlusskritik des Entwurfsstudios ‹Primitive Future› von Christian Kerez und Sou Fujimoto, 2017. Fotografie: Dorothee Hahn.

Karin Sander und Adolf Krischanitz schwebend über dem Dach bei der Höhenermittlungsfahrt für den Transzendenzaufzug, Kunst am Bau, Kunstuniversität Linz, 2016. Fotografie: Archiv Karin Sander.

Nikolai von Rosen und Karin Sander im Gespräch mit den Studierenden. Wahlfach «Künstlerisches Denken und Arbeiten», Frühjahrssemester 2011. Fotografie: Nikolai von Rosen.

«What about critical thought within the design studio, Mr. Lütjens, *Mr. Padmanabhan?*»

«I find it very interesting that you mention the idea of critical thought in relation to architecture and architectural education. Every citizen should train his or her critical thinking. However, when you are an architect or when you train to be one, critical thought can be developed inside the architectural work rather than as an attitude supplied from outside. As designers, our personal experience was that our critical thinking was formed or challenged the most when we were confronted with certain realities that we would not accept.»

«Before being able to be critical, I think that you should be able to truly and without restraints, love something. We show buildings that we love to students, we talk about them, use them as references. Through our work we try to aspire to them, to push the students to engage with them. Of course, this does not mean that they will necessarily love the same thing, as we doubt that they will figure out what they like. You can only be critical about something, including the things you like, if you know what they are.»

«Our cultural situation as a civilization is very confusing. There are no canonic rules anymore in architecture. They have been lost. We do not believe in the reconstruction of a set of rules. We believe in their critical contemplation, case by case. What can you and what can you not do with them? Where are your limits? For us, criticality means understanding the logic of the architectural production, to partially accept it, and partially go against it.»

«How does this take place in your teaching?»

«Even though we are quite young and do not have much experience, I think that we have confidence in what we do and in the way we do it. We put a lot of thought and discussion into it. In the end, we stand in front of the students as the persons that we are, with little distance and a lot of enthusiasm of what architecture could be today. We believe that our teaching is highly optimistic and motivating for the students. We are almost the students' accomplices when we teach. We are not very critical; we do not sit back and say: ‹You should really have to look at that façade because it's not really working›. We try to engage in a precise way to help the students to make a better project. Thus, when the critiques are over they know what to do next. We do not give them tasks as we would do in the office, but we are feeding them with ideas. We believe that the students should come as far as possible so that there is, in the end, an artifact that they can contemplate and really learn from. We believe that they should make five steps rather than one within the short amount of time of a semester.»

«The architectural culture that surrounds us is not always strong enough to support a critical discourse. In other words, we like to feed our students with great examples of architecture so that they look at them, speak about them and make friends with them. If they stare at them long enough they will get a feeling of how great, how dense architecture can be in terms of its expression, sensuality, and ideas. We like to surround our students with what is for us the best buildings. Sometimes they are not from this place and sometimes they are not even from this time. After they have befriended these examples they can try to work with them. Because we do not give them directions on how to do it, their critical mind has to be super active. They have to make lots of tiny decisions in a very short time, they have to ask themselves: ‹What makes it good? Is it the construction, is it the form, is it the way it casts a shadow, is it the proportion, the texture or the figure?› We think that the immersion into the material is a precondition for any critical discourse or discussion.»

«We had this student who was always questioning everything. In the end, I had this feeling that he did not have a clue but that he was very good at questioning things. That also does not lead anywhere. There are a lot of briefs in competitions that you have to fulfill. Of course, you have to look for the possibilities, for the potential to produce something amazing. But if you do a ‹Genossenschaft› housing, they really know what they want, and it's not so boring. You can fulfill it and find out that something in this brief makes a possibility for amazing architecture.»

«We do not think that competition briefs should be changed. Rather we know that the brief does not ask for what we call architecture. It does not require the urbanity that is essential to our profession. We know that we have to fulfill it in the best possible way, better than anybody else. At the same time, we feel obliged to do architecture as we understand it. It's like another burden, another brief that's always there. If you do not do it your life is much easier. You can just glue things that function together and end up with a product to which you give a façade. For us saying: ‹no, it's not enough› is a profoundly critical operation. We feel that it's always an obligation to think of a possibility of the city in every single project.»

This text is taken from the interview with Oliver Lütjens and Thomas Padmanabhan led at their office in Zurich the 13th of June 2017 by Vincent Bianchi and Yann Salzmann.

Projected Monsters
Philip Dörge, Emanuel Falk, Pierre Marmy and Christian Ott

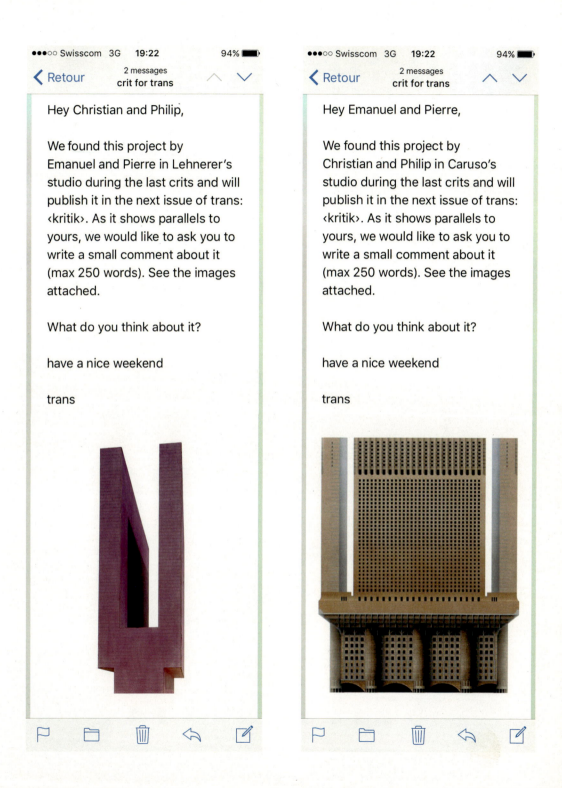

The project is conceived of three parts. The base supports the middle part that is a plateau for the four towers. The facade of the base appears heavier with fewer but larger windows. The character of the facade of the base is given by the apparent structure. Dungeon-like towers surround the base. Big arches suggest multiple entries on the ground floor. Little arches mark the link between the base and the middle part. The middle part looks like a mirrored pyramid. The structure is visible and becomes ornament. The middle part has no windows. The middle part is structural. The towers are all the same. The structure disappears from the facade. The body is defined by a repetition of windows of different sizes. The top of the towers is detailed and the structure of the slabs reappears. It is impossible to distinguish elements that come from structural or compositional considerations. The project is mythical. History evaporates to serve the myth. The myth embodied in the project can be enjoyed without knowing where it comes from. Myth doesn't need history. Historical fragments are here emptied of their meanings and recombined in a new constellation. The project strives to achieve an ahistorical representation. The building wants to be progressive. The progressive ideas are acceptable only if they express past values. The project binds fiction and similitude. The project re-interprets figures belonging to other tradition and culture. The building is eclectic. The style serves to link the new and the old. The style allows to introduce something new but still looking familiar. The aim of the facades' aesthetic is to make the project acceptable. The project quotes stylistic references. The project refers to elements that were parts of a certain culture. To be meaningful the project recombines elements that are already invested with meanings. The building embodies several signifying aspects. One signifier is the architectural code in play here. Another signifier is the object. There is a dichotomy between the signification of the facade and the one of the architectural object. The function of the building doesn't give meaning to its form. The project adopts codes whose meanings are already given by culture and history. The original meanings of the element used on the facade are now diffuse and vague. The project creates a split between the technological and structural aspect and the need for meaning. The result is a "kitsch object" where meanings are relegated to empty metaphors.

‹Clichés›

In der Peripherie der vier einwohnerreichsten Städte der Schweiz entsteht je ein gleichnamiges Bürohaus: das ZurichBuilding, das GenevaBuilding, das BaselBuilding und das LuganoBuilding. Ein jedes als starker Solitär in der freien Landschaft, ein Satellit seiner Stadt.

Im Umgang der Autoren mit der Bauaufgabe des modernen Bürohauses als Beziehung von Form zu Inhalt lassen sich Parallelen zu Hans Kollhoffs Architekturlehre der 90er Jahre ableiten:

«Heutige Programme scheinen nicht mehr die Kraft zu haben, Ausdrucksformen hervorzubringen, die dem Vergleich mit Beispielen des 19. und frühen 20. Jahrhunderts standhalten könnten. […] Ganz anders als im Zeitalter der Mechanisierung entziehen sich die neuen Technologien einer direkten formalen Festlegung. Aber selbst hinter dem banalsten Programm verbergen sich Spuren von Phänomenen, die implizit Formkraft haben. Man muß sie nur suchen.» (Hans Kollhoff, im Gespräch mit Nikolaus Kuhnert, ‹Architektur contra Städtebau›, in: Archplus 106, Oktober 1990)

Dort, wo die Nutzung unmittelbar ablesbar ist, verbildlicht das Konzept auf radikale Art den Übersetzungsprozess vom toten Programm des Bürohauses hin zu einem lebendigen Ausdruck.

Überspitzt zielt der Entwurf gar auf eine Konzeptualisierung im Sinne Oswald Mathias Ungers ab – alle Existenz ist, hypertrophierte Materie – am Beispiel des GenevaBuildings als einem zentralen, überdimensionierten und von der restlichen Baumasse gerahmten FlughafenTower. Bleibt dem Betrachter jedoch dieses Innenleben verborgen, droht sich die Form vom Inhalt zu lösen und in Symbolhaftigkeit umzuschwenken – in ‹Clichés› abzudriften.

Erst wenn ein jedes dieser Konzepte auf dieser Grundlage so klar wie möglich entwickelt ist, kommt es zur Konfrontation mit dem Kontext.

Im Inneren sind die Häuser in allem was über die Erschliessung hinausgeht Rohlinge – anonyme ‹Systeme›. Ähnlich der italienischen radikalen Neoavantgarde der 60er Jahre, die scheinbar alle Möglichkeiten offen hielt, jedoch von jedem Identifikationswert befreit war. Jedweder individuellen Gestalt und Präsenz entledigt, bestimmt die Regel dem Bürohaus entsprechend das innere Bild. Auch wenn die programmatische Auslegung der Gebäude teils vage bleibt, repräsentiert das Projekt dennoch eine verdichtete, funktionale Architektur der Grossform als in der Landschaft stehende, kommunizierende Artefakte.

1967–2017

Conference
"Founding Myths"
28 September 2017

Debate
"End of Theory?"
28 September 2017

Exhibition
"Phantom Theory"
28 September to
20 December 2017

Round-Table
"Perspectives"
29 September 2017

www.gta.arch.ethz.ch

Cornelia Escher
Zukunft entwerfen
Architektonische Konzepte des GEAM (Groupe d'Études d'Architecture Mobile) 1958–1963
2017. 16,5 x 24,5 cm, Klappenbroschur, 428 Seiten, 179 Abbildungen
60.00 CHF   ISBN 978-3-85676-365-7

Moritz Gleich, Laurent Stalder (Hg.)
Architecture / Machine
gta papers 1
Englisch
2017. 21 x 29,7 cm, Broschur, 180 Seiten, 102 Abbildungen
25.00 CHF   ISBN 978-3-85676-363-3

www.verlag.gta.arch.ethz.ch

gta Verlag

Gabriela Güntert, Bruno Maurer, Arthur Rüegg (Hg.)
Trix + Robert Haussmann
Kultur der Formgebung
2017. 25 x 30,5 cm, Leinen, 380 Seiten, 973 Abbildungen
130.00 CHF   ISBN 978-3-85676-360-2

Philip Ursprung
Der Wert der Oberfläche
Essays zu Architektur, Kunst und Ökonomie
2017. 15,1 x 22,7 cm, Broschur, 232 Seiten, 28 Abbildungen sw
29.00 CHF   ISBN 978-3-85676-366-4
Auch als E-Book erhältlich

DARCH
    Kritik

We don't know who you are,

we don't know your studio,

we don't know your studios output,

we don't know what your studio stands for,

we don't know your studios students,

we don't know your studios dogma,

we don't know your studios reputation.

Now - what is it you want to tell us?

Productivity can start before the deadline - with student-based participation.

call for initiative - **studioenact@arch.ethz.ch**

S AM SCHWEIZERISCHES ARCHITEKTURMUSEUM STEINENBERG 7 CH - 4051 BASEL
WWW . SAM - BASEL . ORG

ÖFFNUNGSZEITEN:
DI: MI: FR: 11–18 H
DO: 11–20:30 H
SA: SO: 11–17 H

AKTUELL :
NOCH BIS
12.11.2017

IN AUS

SWISS ARCHITECTS ABROAD

LAND LAND

DEMNÄCHST :
2.12.2017–
6.05.2018
VERNISSAGE :
1.12.2017 19 UHR

DIE VIBRIERENDE ARCHITEKTURSZENE IN BANGLADESCH

BENGAL STREAM

S AM

ETH zürich

Freies Thema
Masterarbeit

D-ARCH

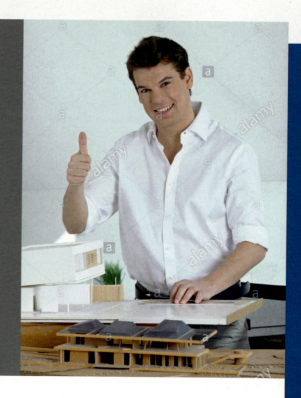

Interessierte Studierende haben die Möglichkeit, eine Ideenskizze als Vorschlag für ein freies, selbstgewähltes Thema einzureichen. Wird der Vorschlag gutgeheissen, wird unter der Leitung des Master-Professors während eines Semesters ein Arbeitsprogramm erarbeitet. Der Master-Professor entscheidet, ob das Arbeitsprogramm im Rahmen einer Lerneinheit "Entwurf V-IX" angerechnet werden kann. Wird das Arbeitsprogramm akzeptiert, kann es im folgenden Semester als freie Master-Arbeit bearbeitet werden. Die Durchführung der Master-Arbeit als Gruppenarbeit (max. drei Studierende) kann bewilligt werden, wenn dies nach Inhalt, Umfang und Bearbeitungsweise gerechtfertigt erscheint. Ebenfalls zu beachten ist der zeitliche Ablauf einer freien Master-Arbeit.

Freie Master-Arbeit im HS

Spätestens zu Beginn des vorhergeheden FS

Kontaktnahme mit gewünschtem Masterprofessor (DP) und Koexaminator (KE)

Freie Master-Arbeit im FS

Spätestens zu Beginn des vorhergeheden HS

Kontaktnahme mit gewünschtem Masterprofessor (DP) und Koexaminator (KE)

Bri-Collagen
Erscheint am 1. September 2017

Ruinen
Erscheint am 1. Dezember 2017

Swiss Performance 18
Erscheint am 1. März 2018

Normen vs. Deregulation
Erscheint am 1. Juni 2018

Junges Bayern
Erscheint am 1. September 2018

Studierende profitieren

archithese
Über die Zukunft der Architektur

Vier Ausgaben für CHF 64.– statt CHF 128.– inklusive E-Paper
Bestellungen an info@archithese.ch oder über archithese.ch

Vorlage einer gültigen Studienbescheinigung erforderlich, senden Sie die Bescheinigung bitte via Email an den Verlag.

Das Abonnement beginnt mit der nächsten erscheinenden Ausgabe.

All das gibt es mit dem Hochparterre-Abo ...

... und Studierende zahlen nur 89.50 Franken.

www.hochparterre.ch / abonnieren

Zeitschrift für Architektur, Planung und Design

Für Studenten zum Spezialpreis.

www.reportagen.com/studentenabo

Reportagen schickt die besten Autorinnen und Autoren rund um den Globus. Für Geschichten, die bleiben.

Eidgenössische Technische Hochschule Zürich
Swiss Federal Institute of Technology Zurich

Departement Architektur
Architektur und Kunst

ETH Zürich
Prof. Karin Sander
HIL F 48
Stefano-Franscini-Platz 5
CH – 8093 Zürich Hönggerberg

Telefon +41 (0) 44 633 28 42
Telefax +41 (0) 44 633 15 86
sander@arch.ethz.ch
www.sander.ethz.ch

Arbeitszeugnis

San Keller, geboren 19.01.1971, wohnhaft in Zürich, arbeitete vom 1.8.2008 bis 30.8.2017 als künstlerischer Mitarbeiter und Dozent an meinem Lehrstuhl. Mein Team von 15 künstlerischen und wissenschaftlichen Mitarbeiter/innen vermittelt den Studierenden künstlerisches Denken und Arbeiten innerhalb ihrer Architekturausbildung an der ETH. San Kellers Aufgabe bestand in der Planung und Durchführung des Seminars „Performance und Intervention". Konkret ging es dabei um den Unterricht und die Betreuung einer Koje mit ca. 30 Studierenden, die Vermittlung von Kunst sowie die Unterstützung der Studierenden bei der Entwicklung und adäquaten Umsetzung eigener Projekte. Die Schulung des Wahrnehmungs-, Vorstellungs- und Ausdrucksvermögens waren dabei integraler Bestandteil des Unterrichts.

Der Unterricht fand während des Semesters jeweils montags von 10 bis 17 Uhr statt. Insgesamt nahmen ca. 30 Studierende aus dem ersten Studienjahr erfolgreich am Unterricht von San Keller teil, den sie selbst entwickelten und innovativ durchführten. Es gelang ihm dabei, auf die unterschiedlichen Begabungen und Interessen der Studierenden einzugehen und sie in das künstlerische Denken einzuführen. Durch seine Kreativität und Empathie wurde sein Unterricht für jede/n Einzelne/n zu einem wichtigen Bestandteil der Ausbildung. Es gelang ihm, die Studierenden zu motivieren und mit ihren unterschiedlichen Voraussetzungen individuell zu fördern. Die Präsenz von San Keller in der konkreten Lehrsituation und sein persönlicher Umgang mit den Studierenden führten zu sehr guten Ergebnissen, die in Schlusspräsentationen öffentlich ausgestellt oder einzeln vorgestellt wurden.

Vorbildlich und für alle Beteiligten inspirierend waren darüber hinaus auch seine Lehrtätigkeit im Wahlfachbereich, wo er den Kurs „Künstlerisches Denken und Arbeiten" leitete, sowie seine hingebungsvolle und kenntnisreiche Betreuung zahlreicher Diplomarbeiten, deren Bestandteil das Fach „Architektur und Kunst" als integrierte Disziplin war. Neben seiner organisatorischen und didaktischen Begabung war es das grosse Vertrauen, das San Keller allenthalben in seinem beruflichen Umfeld geniesst, das mich dazu bewog, ihm am Lehrstuhl die Oberassistenz für Leitungs- und Planungsaufgaben zu übertragen. Auch hier bewies er sich zu meiner vollsten Zufriedenheit.

San Keller hat sich zu jeder Zeit kompetent und vorbildlich verhalten, als Lehrender im ersten Studienjahr und in der Masterbegleitung wie als künstlerisch Handelnder. Er lud beispielsweise Studierende morgens zu sich ins Schlafzimmer ein, um ihnen (im Schlafanzug) aus dem Bett heraus eine Vorlesung zu halten oder er bat sie während der Unterrichtszeit in der Hochschule zu schlafen. Sein „Long Way Home" - das gemeinschaftliche nach Hause bringen aller Studierenden – wurde zu einer Zürcher Kultwanderung.

Nun verlässt San Keller die ETH auf eigenen Wunsch und ich wünsche ihm einen auch weiterhin erfolgreichen Long Way. San Keller war eine Bereicherung für meinen Lehrstuhl, die Kommunikation verlief reibungslos und sehr angenehm. Er nahm seine Aufgaben als künstlerischer Mitarbeiter an meinem Lehrstuhl zu meiner vollsten Zufriedenheit wahr. Ich danke ihm für seine zuverlässige und innovative Mitarbeit und wünsche ihm für seinen weiteren Berufs- und Lebensweg alles Gute.

Prof. Karin Sander

We Believe that World Change Starts with Educated Children.®

We envision a world in which all children can pursue a quality education that enables them to reach their full potential and contribute to their community and the world.

www.roomtoread.org

Célestine from l'Atelier Magazine also wonders "where does the pool go?"
Call for Papers — September 30th http://www.latelier.epfl.ch

Mineralfarben digitalisieren?

Echte Mineralfarben wollen erlebt sein.

KEIM – die Mineralfarbe seit 1878.

Das ganze Spektrum der Mineralfarben

KEIMFARBEN AG
Wiesgasse 1
CH-9444 Diepoldsau
Telefon: 071 737 70 10
info@keim.ch
www.keim.ch

Biografien

Armen Avanessian
geb. 1973, ist Autor und Herausgeber zahlreicher Bücher, zuletzt ‹Miamification› (Merve, 2017). Er ist editor-at-large beim Merve Verlag und leitet das Theorieprogramm der Volksbühne in Berlin. Er lehrte unter anderem an der Freien Universität Berlin, war Gastprofessor an der Columbia University sowie an der Yale University. Seine Arbeiten rund um den ‹spekulativen Realismus› und dem ‹Akzelerationismus› haben ihm in den letzten Jahren zu einiger Aufmerksamkeit verholfen.

Vincent Bianchi
born in 1992, obtained a bachelor's degree in architecture at EPFL Lausanne in 2017.

Saida Brückner
geb. 1993, ist seit Februar 2017 Co-Redaktorin des trans Magazins. Sie studiert seit 2012 Architektur an der ETH Zürich.

Axel Chevroulet
born in 1991, currently working at Bovenbouw Architectuur in Antwerp. After the completion of his bachelor of Architecture in between EPFL Lausanne and the Royal Danish Academy of Fine Arts in Copenhagen in 2013, Axel worked for one year at Herzog & de Meuron. He completed his studies at the ETH Zürich in 2016.

Paola De Martin
geb. 1965, studierte Textilgestaltung an der SfG Zürich. Sie gründete 1996 mit Studienkolleginnen das Label Beige. 2011 schloss sie an der Universität Zürich das Lizentiat in Allgemeiner Geschichte, Kunstgeschichte und Wirtschaftsgeschichte ab und war von 2012-2016 wissenschaftliche Assistentin am Lehrstuhl von Prof. Dr. Philip Ursprung, wo ihre laufende Dissertation «Give us a break! Lebenslauf, Lebensstil und Werkbiografie von Gestaltern mit bildungsferner Herkunft in Zürich (1970-2010)» angesiedelt ist. Paola De Martin lehrt Designgeschichte im Departement Design und Interkulturalität im Departement Art Education der ZHdK.

Dieter Dietz
Arch. Dipl. EPFZ, Associate Professor, Head of ALICE: Educated at the Swiss Federal Institute of Technology in Zurich (Architecture Degree 1991), Dieter Dietz also studied at the Cooper Union in New York with Diller/Scofidio. In 1997, after working with Diane Lewis Architects, New York, and Herzog & de Meuron in Basel, he founded, with partner architect Urs Egg, UNDEND Architecture, a Zurich based architectural practice with award winning entries in national and international competitions. Currently he is building up dieterdietz.org, a firm engaged in projects in urban design, media and architecture. From 1996 to 1999, he taught as Junior Faculty with Prof. Marc Angélil at ETH Zurich. Since 2006 he is Associate Professor for Architectural Design at EPFL, Lausanne, and director of the ALICE laboratory in the ENAC faculty. He collaborates with the ALICE team on research projects at diverse scales with labs inside and outside EPFL. His teaching activities include the direction of the first year architectural design course as well as projects at master and thesis level.

Philip Dörge
geb. 1991, lebt in Zürich. Absolvierte sein Bachelorstudium an der TU Dortmund. Seit 2014 studiert er Architektur im Master an der ETH Zürich.

Tom Emerson
is professor for Architecture and Construction at ETH Zurich in the third year. He founded 6a architects with Stephanie Macdonald in London in 2001. Recent projects include two contemporary art galleries in London: Raven Row in Spitalfields and the South London Gallery in Peckham. He studied at the University of Bath, the Royal College of Art in London and the University of Cambridge. Before joining the ETH, he taught in Cambridge (2004–10), the Architectural Association (2000–04) and in the Department of Fine Art at Chelsea School of Art.

Jan Engelke und Lukas Fink
haben beide an der ETH Zürich Architektur studiert. 2016 haben sie gemeinsam den Katasterplan verschoben und dabei seine «Schönheit» entdeckt. Die dabei entstandene freie Masterarbeit am Lehrstuhl von Alex Lehnerer wurde mit der ETH-Medaille und dem Heinrich Hatt-Bucher-Preis ausgezeichnet.

Emanuel Falk
geb. 30.05.1990, BTU Cottbus Architektur Bachelor 2010 bis 2014, Praktikum POOL Architekten 2014 bis 2015, ETH Architektur Master 2015 bis 2017. Verheiratet.

GruppoTorto
founded in 2016, is a research collective of young architects who graduated at Politecnico di Milano and work now in different international studios across Europe. The main research topics revolve around architecture and urbanism whereby the focus is directed on the analysis of dysfunctional conditions of our cities.

Dorothee Hahn
geb. 1990, ist Co-Redakteurin des trans Magazins. Sie studiert Architektur an der ETH Zürich.

Martin Hartung
has been a doctoral fellow at the Chair of Prof. Dr. Philip Ursprung since 2014, where he conducts

the first critical assessment of the Max Protetch Gallery Archive (New York and Santa Fe). Previously, Hartung served as a Curatorial Assistant in the Department of Media and Performance Art at MoMA, New York (2011–13). He was a visiting scholar at Columbia University in 2016 and a scientific assistant at ZKM | Museum of Contemporary Art in Karlsruhe, Germany. Martin is a member of the editorial board for the ‹Art Market Dictionary› (De Gruyter).

Jonathan Hill
is Professor of Architecture and Visual Theory at the Bartlett School of Architecture, UCL, where he directs the MPhil/PhD Architectural Design programme. Jonathan is the author of The Illegal Architect (1998), Actions of Architecture (2003), Immaterial Architecture (2006), Weather Architecture (2012), and A Landscape of Architecture, History and Fiction (2016); editor of Occupying Architecture (1998) and Architecture—the Subject is Matter (2001); and co-editor of Critical Architecture (2007).

Roman Hollenstein
Roman Hollenstein promovierte in Kunst- und Architekturgeschichte an der Universität Bern. Danach arbeitete er für die Sammlungen des Fürsten von Liechtenstein in Vaduz und Wien. Von 1987 bis 1990 leitete er die Sparte Kunstgeschichte am Schweizerischen Institut für Kunstwissenschaft in Zürich. Anschliessen war er bis 2017 Redaktor für Architektur und Design im Feuilleton der Neuen Zürcher Zeitung.

Sophie Keel
geb. 1996, ist Studentin des ersten Jahres am Architekturdepartement der ETH Zürich.

Rabea Kalbermatten
geb. 1989, hat an der ETHZ studiert und arbeitet heute als Architektin in Zürich. ‹Das Grandhotel in Brig› ist das erste Projekt der Gruppe ‹Das Blaue Becken›. Unter diesem Namen schloss sich vor zwei Jahren eine Gruppe junger Oberwalliser Architekten zusammen. Durch Wettbewerbsbeiträge und Ausstellungen will die Gruppe eine Plattform bieten, um über das Architekturgeschehen im Wallis zu diskutieren. Zusammen mit Simon Zemp (1989) hat sie das Projekt ‹Das Grandhotel in Brig› entwickelt. Er hat an der ETHZ und an der Harvard Graduate School of Design studiert und arbeitet heute als Architekt in London.

Christian Kerez
wurde 1962 in Maracaibo, Venezuela geboren und studierte an der Eidgenössischen Technischen Hochschule in Zürich. Nach einer Grosszahl von Veröffentlichungen auf dem Gebiet der Architekturfotografie, eröffnete er 1993 sein eigenes Architekturbüro in Zürich, Schweiz. Seit 2001 ist Christian Kerez als Gastprofessor an der ETH Zürich tätig und wurde 2003 zum Assistenzprofessor und 2009 zum Professor berufen. 2012–13 führte er den Kenzo Tange Chair an der Harvard University, Cambridge. 2016 bespielte er den Schweizer Pavillon an der Architekturbiennale in Venedig.

Torsten Lange
is Visiting Lecturer for the Theory of Architecture at the Institute gta, ETH Zurich. He is one of three Parity Delegates of the AAA in the Department's Conference. He studied architecture at the Bauhaus University Weimar and earned a Master's in Architectural History from the Bartlett/UCL, where he also completed his PhD. He is co-editor of the three-volume publication ‹East West Central: Re-Building Europe, 1950–1990› (Birkhäuser, 2016). His work has been published in edited volumes and journals including, among others, archimaera, Arch+, The Journal of Architecture, Field, and trans. Together with Sophie Hochhäusl, he is coordinator of the EAHN special interest group ‹Architecture and Environment›.

Alex Lehnerer
is an architect and urban designer. He currently holds a position as assistant professor at ETH Zurich in Switzerland. Prior to that he was based in Chicago, where he was a professor at the University of Illinois, School of Architecture. He received his PhD from ETH Zurich, his MArch from the University of California in Los Angeles (UCLA), is partner of the firm Kaisersrot in Zurich, and founded the Department of Urban Speculation (DeptUS) in Chicago. His Zurich based architectural practice CIRIACIDISLEHNERER ARCHITEKTEN tries to understand architecture as cultural practice by relentlessly exploring urban and architectural conditions—their forms, ingredients, and rules.

Sebastian Linsin
geb. 1988, hat Architektur an der ETH Zürich und der Accademia di Architettura in Mendrisio studiert. Gegenwärtig arbeitet er am Future Cities Laboratory in Singapur und schreibt an seiner Dissertation zu gegenkulturellen Architekturexperimenten im amerikanischen Südwesten.

Biografien

Oliver Lütjens
geboren 1972, studierte Architektur an der ETH Zürich und der EPF Lausanne. Nach seinem Diplom 2002 arbeitete er für Diener & Diener, Meili Peter und OMA/Rem Koolhaas. Er unterrichtete von 2007 bis 2014 als Assistent an der Gastdozentur von Adam Caruso und Peter St John und als Oberassistent an der Professur von Adam Caruso an der ETH Zürich. Seit 2007 führt er mit Thomas Padmanabhan das gemeinsame Architekturbüro Lütjens Padmanabhan Architekten in Zürich. Er hat 2015 zusammen mit Thomas Padmanabhan als Gastdozent an der TU München unterrichtet und war 2016 bis 2017 Gastprofessor an der EPF Lausanne.

Niklas Maak
geb. 1972, studierte Kunstgeschichte, Philosophie und Architektur an der Universität Hamburg und an der École des Hautes Études in Paris. Nach seiner Promotion 1998 zu Fragen der Entwurfstheorie bei Le Corbusier und Paul Valéry war er als Redakteur im Feuilleton der Süddeutschen Zeitung tätig, bevor er die Leitung des Kunst- und Architekturresorts der Frankfurter Allgemeinen Zeitung übernahm. Parallel unterrichtete er unter anderem als Gastprofessor für Architekturgeschichte an der Frankfurter Städelschule. Im Hanser Verlag erschienen unter anderem seine Bücher «Der Architekt am Strand», der Roman «Fahrtenbuch» sowie der Essay «Wohnkomplex». Für seine Essays und Bücher erhielt Maak unter anderem den George F. Kennan Award, den Henri-Nannenpreis und den BDA Preis 2015. Zur Zeit lehrt er Architekturtheorie in Harvard.

Anna MacIver-Ek
born in 1991, currently working at Architecten DeVylder Vinck Taillieu in Ghent. After graduating from Copenhagen Business School in 2013, Anna started studying architecture at the Accademia di Architettura di Mendrisio. She will continue her studies at the ETH Zurich in September.

Charlotte Malterre-Barthes
is an architect and urban designer. Program Director of the Master of Advanced Studies in Urban Design (Architecture Department, ETHZ), she is completing her dissertation on ‹Food Territories, case study Egypt.› Charlotte studied at the ENSA Marseille, TU Vienna and ETHZ, and co-funded the urban research office OMNIBUS. She lectured at the AA, the Storefront for Art and Architecture, at Hong-Kong University, among others. Various magazines (San Rocco, AD, Tracés, etc.) published her works and she edited with Marc Angélil ‹Housing Cairo: The Informal Response.› Part of Syndicat Culotté, a collective focusing on gender and spatial practices, Charlotte is a funding member of the Parity Group.

Marija Marić
is an architect and a researcher based in Zurich. Currently, she works as a teaching assistant at the Chair for Architecture and Design with Prof. Arno Brandlhuber, and is a PhD candidate at the Institute for the History and Theory of Architecture (gta) working with Prof. Philip Ursprung, both at ETH Zurich. Her interests evolve around the questions of labor and property in architecture and urban planning.

Metaxia Markaki
is an architect, urban researcher and curious about various other themes. She studied Architecture at NTU-Athens and ENSAPLV-Paris and received a Master of Advanced Studies in Urban Design at ETH Zurich. Since 2013, she has been engaged in teaching and research at ETH Studio Basel and Harvard GSD with Jacques Herzog and Pierre de Meuron. In 2015, she joined Architecture of Territory ETH, where she is currently developing her research on Greek rural landscapes. Metaxia's work spans theory, writing and architecture. She has published various essays, short stories and participated in several exhibitions and architectural publications.

Pierre Marmy
1993, 1000 Vers-chez-les-Blanc, a d'abord étudié à l'EPFL pour ensuite réaliser son master à l'ETHZ. Intérêt pour la photographie et les chats.

Adrien Meuwly
born 1993, studied architecture at EPF Lausanne. He is now pursuing his master degree at ETH Zurich. He is Co-Editor of trans magazine since September 2016.

Johanna Muther
geb. 1985, studierte Fotografie in Wien und Zürich. Seit 2007 arbeitet sie als freischaffende Fotografin und gründete 2016 mit Claudia Breitschmid ‹jmcb – Kollektiv für visuelle Feldforschung›. Ihr Interesse an kollaborativer Arbeit lebt sie zudem im ‹Impact Hub Zürich› und dem dream tank ‹BEAM› aus.

Philippe Nathan
born 1982, collaborated with Brussels-based architecture office ‹51N4E› for 3 years and returned in 2010 to Luxembourg to found the office ‹2001›. ‹2001› is a studio—atelier—lab, which is developing territories, buildings, spaces, ideas and strategies. Beside 2001's practice in architecture, urbanism and territorial development, Philippe Nathan is continuously engaging in juries, lectures and the writing of essays within the local cultural context. He taught at the

University of Brussels in 2015 and at the summer school of the University of Luxembourg on the theme of ‹architecture and migration› in 2016. In August 2016 he joined Studio Swinnen (ETH Zurich) as teaching assistant.

Luca Ortelli
is a Professor at the EPFL, ENAC School of Architecture, where he is the head of the Construction and Conservation laboratory. He is the author of numerous articles on domestic architecture, with emphasis on Nordic examples. Ortelli chairs the 3rd year Bachelor Design Studio on Housing, as well as the Master-level courses on History of Housing and Architecture and Renovation.

Christian Ott
geb. 1989, lebt in Zürich. Nach seiner Lehre zum Hochbauzeichner absolvierte er sein Bachelor-studium an der FHNW Muttenz. Seit 2015 studiert er Architektur im Master an der ETH Zürich.

Thomas Padmanabhan
geb. 1970, studierte Architektur an der RWTH Aachen, Università di Roma ‹La Sapienza› und der Cornell University Ithaca. Nach seiner Master Thesis arbeitete er für Skidmore Owings and Merrill, Meili Peter und Diener & Diener. Er unterrichtete von 1998 bis 2000 als Assistent bei Arthur Ovaska und David Lewis an der Cornell University und von 2007 bis 2013 als Assistent an der Professur von Peter Märkli und Markus Peter an der ETH Zürich. Seit 2007 führt er mit Oliver Lütjens das gemeinsame Architekturbüro Lütjens Padmanabhan Architekten in Zürich. Er hat 2015 zusammen mit Oliver Lütjens als Gastdozent an der TU München unterrichtet und war 2016 bis 2017 Gastprofessor an der EPF Lausanne.

Elena Pibernik
geb. 1994, studiert seit 2013 Architektur an der ETH Zürich.

Jane Rendell
teaches and writes across architecture, art, feminism, history and psychoanalysis. She has introduced ‹critical spatial practice› and ‹site-writing› through her authored books: The Architecture of Psychoanalysis (2016), Site-Writing (2010), Art and Architecture (2006), and The Pursuit of Pleasure (2002). With James O'Leary, Jane teaches experimental and spatialized forms of architectural writing on the new MA Situated Practices. Jane is Professor of Architecture and Art at the Bartlett School of Architecture, UCL, where she is Director of History & Theory and leads the Bartlett's Ethics Commission.
www.janerendell.co.uk

Nikolai von Rosen
geb. 1967, lebt als Künstler in Berlin und Fergitz. Von 2007 bis 2016 lehrte er Architektur und Kunst an der ETH Zürich.

Yann Salzmann
born in 1994, obtained a bachelor's degree in architecture at EPF Lausanne in 2017, during which he made an exchange year at ETH Zurich.

Karin Sander
geb. 1957, lebt als Künstlerin in Berlin und Zürich. Seit 2007 ist sie Professorin an der ETH Zürich für Architektur und Kunst.

Claudio Schneider
geb. 1981, studierte Architektur an der ETH Zürich. Nach seinem Abschluss 2010 arbeitete er bei Valentin Löwensberg Architekt und Caruso St John Architects. 2013 gründete er mit Michaela Türtscher das Büro ‹Schneider Türtscher› in Zürich. Seit 2015 ist er Entwurfsassistent bei der Professur für Architektur und Konstruktion Adam Caruso an der ETH Zürich.

Jack Self
born in 1987, is an architect based in London. He is Director of the REAL foundation and Editor-in-Chief of the contemporary culture magazine Real Review. In 2016, Jack curated the British Pavilion at the Venice Architecture Biennale with the show ‹Home Economics›. Jack's architectural design focuses on alternative models of ownership, contemporary forms of labour, and the formation of socio-economic power relationships in space. Jack's first book ‹Real Estates: Life Without Debt› (2014: Bedford Press) is now in its second printing. He is a Contributing Editor to the Architectural Review and Editor-at-Large for 032c.

Selina Sigg
geb. 1991, studiert seit 2012 an der ETH Zürich Architektur.

Benjamin Thomas Summers
born in 1992, studied Architecture at the University of Liverpool. In 2016, after two years at Mole Architects in Cambridge, he began his MSc in Architecture at TU Delft. Starting in autumn 2017, he will be undertaking a year-long design thesis on collective housing and alternative methods of housing procurement, as part of the ‹Explore Lab Graduation Studio›.

Biografien

Peter Swinnen
is guest lecturer at ETH Zurich since autumn 2016. He currently practices architecture at his Brussels based office CRIT. and conducts PhD research at the KUL University on the political praxis of architecture. Between 2010 and 2015, Swinnen enrolled as state architect for the Flemish Region, a public mandate for which he developed strategic pilot instruments allowing architecture to become—again—a leading policy making discipline. The pilot programs focused on collective housing, health care infrastructure, blackfields and energy landscapes. In 2013 he co-curated ‹The Ambition of the Territory› at the Architecture Biennale Venice. From 1998 till 2014 Swinnen founded and spearheaded the architectural office of 51N4E, with key projects such as C-MINE, TID Tower, Skanderbeg Square, ISTANBUL 2050, BUDA Arts Centre and the walled Arteconomy residence. In 2011 he edited the publications ‹Reasons For Walling a House› and ‹Double or Nothing›.

Mélissa Vrolixs
born in 1990, studied at the EPF Lausanne, ETH Zurich and Harvard University. In parallel with her studies, she collaborated with Made in Sàrl (Geneva – Zurich) and the Chair for the Theory of Architecture of Laurent Stalder (ETH Zurich). After graduating with Professor Tom Emerson, she joined Studio Sito Architekten (Zurich) for the development of a large single-family house project in Switzerland. In August 2016 she joined Studio Swinnen (ETH Zürich) as teaching assistant and founded in January 2017 the office ‹Marginalia› in La Chaux-de-Fonds.

Erik Wegerhoff
geb. 1974, studierte Architektur in Berlin und London und unternahm 2005 eine ‹Grand Tour› per Vespa. 2006–2009 als Doktorand an der Bibliotheca Hertziana in Rom, Promotion über die nach-antiken Aneignungen des Kolosseums an der ETH Zürich bei Andreas Tönnesmann («Das Kolosseum. Bewundert, bewohnt, ramponiert», 2012). 2010–2016 wissenschaftlicher Mitarbeiter bei Dietrich Erben an der TU München, seit 2017 Oberassistent an der Professur für Geschichte und Theorie der Architektur, Maarten Delbeke. Arbeitet derzeit an einem Forschungsprojekt über das Automobil im Architekturdiskurs des 20. Jahrhunderts.

«Before being able to be critical, I think that you should be able to truly and without restraints, love something.»*

*Oliver Lütjens, page 142

Escalier d'amour

Let's love
trans 32